HEROIN

HUMBERTO FERNANDEZ

With a Foreword by
DAVID E. SMITH, M.D.,
and RICHARD B. SEYMOUR

 HAZELDEN®

Hazelden
Center City, Minnesota 55012-0176
1-800-328-0094 (U.S., Canada, Virgin Islands)
1-612-257-4010 (outside U.S. and Canada)
1-612-257-1331 (Fax)
http://www.hazelden.org

04 03 02 01 00 99 98   7 6 5 4 3 2 1

Library of Congress Cataloging-in-Publication Data
Fernandez, Humberto, 1950–
    Heroin / Humberto Fernandez.
        p.   cm.
    Includes bibliographical references and index.
    ISBN 1-56838-153-0
    1. Heroin—History.   2. Heroin habit.   3. Heroin habit—
Treatment.   4. Methadone maintenance.   I. Title.
HV5822.H4F47   1998
362.29'3—dc21   98-9564
                                                        CIP

Book design by Will H. Powers
Typesetting by Stanton Publication Services, Inc.
Cover design by David Spohn

Editor's note

Hazelden offers a variety of information on chemical dependency and related areas. Our publications do not necessarily represent Hazelden's programs, nor do they officially speak for any Twelve Step organization.

The Twelve Steps are reprinted with permission of Alcoholics Anonymous World Services, Inc. Permission to reprint the Twelve Steps does not mean that AA has reviewed or approved the contents of this publication, nor that AA agrees with the views expressed herein. AA is a program of recovery from alcoholism *only*—use of the Twelve Steps in connection with programs and activities which are patterned after AA, but which address other problems, or in any other non-AA context, does not imply otherwise.

All the stories in this book are based on actual experiences. The names and details have been changed to protect the privacy of the people involved.

FOR

James,

Carlos,

Vanessa,

and Julian

CONTENTS

FOREWORD

The Drug That Never Went Away

Celebrity drug overdose deaths involving heroin, such as the death of comedian Chris Farley from a heart attack induced by using a speedball (cocaine and heroin), have raised the visibility of heroin as though the current wave of addiction were something new. Actually, heroin addiction never went away. Until recently, however, it's been eclipsed in the media by the phenomena of runaway crack cocaine and methamphetamine abuse. In reality, even though America has experienced a period of intensified stimulant abuse, unfortunately with methamphetamine abuse still rising and yet to reach its peak, the need for treatment of heroin addiction has continued to be a prominent feature of the American drug scene. Every stimulant abuser is a potential heroin addict, because of the well-known upper-downer cycle, a drug pattern observed at the Haight Ashbury Free Clinics every decade for the past four decades. Viewed from a statistical, public health standpoint, the focus on specific drugs of abuse is a matter of degree, not totality.

An increase in heroin abuse has been expected and can be seen as one phase of an ongoing oscillation between stimulant and depressant drugs that has been identified and followed over the past thirty years by Dr. John Newmeyer, of the Haight Ashbury Free Clinics, and other epidemiologists working in the addiction field. Just as individuals may become entangled in an upper-downer cycle, our drug-using society has experienced approximately ten-year cycles of predominant upper or downer abuse throughout the century. This is how it works. Following each stimulant epidemic, whether it involves amphetamine or cocaine, significant numbers of addicts turn to heroin to calm the side effects of long-term stimulant abuse, such as anxiety, insomnia, or paranoia. Heroin, or diacetylmorphine, works through the opioid receptors in the brain and initially provides relief from these side effects, along with euphoria and relaxation. In its turn, however, heroin can rapidly produce physical dependence with severe withdrawal when the user tries to stop using.

Even though the current rise in heroin use was predictable, this rise, like its predecessor in the late 1960s, has its idiosyncratically alarming aspects, primarily due to the appearance of heroin abuse in new populations, particularly in younger populations with no previous history of narcotic abuse or addiction.

The highly publicized death from a heroin overdose of a nineteen-year-old rock musician in San Francisco in the fall of 1997 brought the growing problem of heroin addiction among youth to general public attention. Behind the headlines, those of us in the drug treatment field have become increasingly aware of dramatically expanded heroin use by young people.

One aspect of the rise in heroin use among young people is the appearance of "heroin chic." For some inexplicable reason, perhaps even a growing use of the drug by individuals within the fashion and entertainment industries, heroin use has come to be glamorized in films and in ads appearing in fashion magazines. Heroin abuse has become fashionable.

Tolerance (needing more and more of the drug to achieve the desired effect) builds rapidly to heroin, so that while the addict is actively using, he or she may progress to a dose that would be potentially lethal to a person who has not developed tolerance. It should be noted that tolerance decreases rapidly when a heroin user enters treatment and engages in abstinence and recovery. Fatal overdoses may occur when recovering heroin addicts slip and inject a dose comparable to the amount of the drug they were taking at the height of their active use.

In addition, the purity of heroin varies greatly in the drug culture. Variations in tolerance to and purity of the drug contribute to the potentially fatal overdose.

Heroin overdoses need not be fatal. The toxic effects of heroin can be reversed with a short-acting opioid receptor antagonist known as Narcan. The antagonist literally kicks the heroin molecules out of their binding sites in the brain. Naltrexone, a longer-acting opioid receptor antagonist, is used for relapse prevention by recovering heroin addicts.

Longer-term treatment of heroin addiction ranges from drug-free recovery through Narcotics Anonymous (NA) to methadone maintenance. Although there are a variety of treatment approaches for heroin addiction, the best is not to start using in the first place. As one young heroin addict said a number of years ago, "It's so good, don't even try it once."

We have also seen a rise in young people experimenting with heroin by smoking it, with the mistaken belief that you can't be an addict unless you stick a needle in your arm. Unfortunately, once they acquire a taste for heroin, the needle, disability, and death may soon follow.

In *Heroin*, Humberto Fernandez has provided a detailed historical background to the present situation, showing the why of heroin chic. If ever a comprehensive book on heroin were needed, it is now, and Fernandez has filled that need by providing a fully developed history, psychology, physiology, and pharmacology of heroin addiction. Moving on from those basics, *Heroin* explores the variety of treatment approaches, presents case histories of addicts, and places the drug within a detailed social context that includes public health, organized crime, the criminal justice system, popular culture, and the media.

DAVID E. SMITH, M.D.
Founder, President, and Medical Director
Haight Ashbury Free Clinics, Inc.

RICHARD B. SEYMOUR, M.A.
Managing Editor
Journal of Psychoactive Drugs and International Addictions Infoline

ACKNOWLEDGMENTS

There were many people who helped make this book a reality. To the hundreds of substance abuse professionals who gave so freely of their time to answer questions about their experience with heroin users during 1995 and 1996, I remain grateful.

Special thanks to the crew at Hazelden, particularly Joe Fittipaldi, Dan Odegard, Bill Hammond, Don Gargaro, and Kevin Frazzini, the copyeditor who made sense out of the many facts and statistics. I am also indebted to Cathy Broberg, senior manuscript editor, for her critical eye and creative contributions. Thanks to Gordon Thomas for his marketing prowess. A chance lunchtime meeting with Steve Lehman, acquisitions editor, planted the seed, and over this time I have gained a friend in him. His ideas, inspirations, and sharp pencil kept me on track during the fifteen months of writing. I am indebted to David Spohn for his artwork and design of a striking cover, and I will always treasure the many friends and experiences with the sales and marketing staff I have shared over the past three years. Special thanks to literary agent Elaine Markson for her professional advice and generosity.

Heartfelt thanks to Dr. Michael Rehmar and his lovely wife, Miriam Pollock, in New York. This book would not have been possible without the help of Dr. David Smith and Rick Seymour of the Haight Ashbury Free Clinics in San Francisco, who provided invaluable support and wisdom, along with many others, including Dr. George Kolodner of the Kolmac

Clinic in Washington, D.C., Mark Parrino in New York, Dr. Roy Spungin, Bruce Bracco, Howard Lotsof, and Edna Covington of Hampton Hospital in New Jersey.

While researching this project I had the task of being on both sides of the law, hanging out with the lawbreakers, the users and addicts, as well as with the folks whose job it is to stop them, the law enforcers. To all the heroin users who so willingly gave of themselves for this book, I will always be touched by your humanity. Frank S. turned on a light in my life. I look to him for inspiration when the gray days seem to cloud my own resolve. To the brave people of the Drug Enforcement Administration (DEA) and New York City Police, I remain grateful and respectful for the kindness you showed and your willingness to help make this a reality. Their job is impossible, but their spirit and resolve to make a difference, to make the world a better place, remain undaunted. Special thanks to the New York DEA, particularly special agent Robin Waugh, associate special agent in charge William Mochler, special agent Angel Calderon, and especially special agent in charge of the New York DEA Field Office, Lewis Rice Jr. Without the assistance of Mari Maloney, former New York assistant district attorney, none of this would have been possible. To special narcotics prosecutor for the City of New York Robert Silbering, thank you and good luck in your future endeavors.

A very special debt of gratitude is owed to all the folks at the Partnership for a Drug-Free America, particularly Carrol Goerke, who religiously sent me weekly updates on news from around the country pertaining to heroin. A word of thanks to Sally Marshall and Sean Clarkin for their availability in answering whatever questions I had. A special thanks to Bernard Gross, a vice president of the Partnership, for putting me in touch with this important organization and for being my mentor and idol.

The many months of effort it took to bring this project to fruition could not have been possible without the love, support, and encouragement I received from Bernard Gross and his beautiful wife, Dr. Rita Charon, whom I consider it an honor to call family.

To the rest of my family who suffered through this seemingly unending project, thank you. Without the love of my mother, Mercedes, and the hero who is my father, Humberto, I would not be here. And finally, words cannot express the gratitude and love I feel in my heart for my wife, Lonnie, who put her own writing career on hold to have a baby this past year and to be my in-house editor. As always, she is my partner in life, and I will always be in debt to her for dialing 911 and saving my life.

PART

one

THE DRUG

CHAPTER

1

The History of Heroin:
The Discovery of Opium and the China Trade

For the drunkard and the glutton shall come to poverty;
and drowsiness shall clothe a man with rags.

Proverbs 23:21

Her eyes closed in spite of herself, and she forgot where
she was and fell among the poppies, fast asleep.
"What shall we do?" asked the Tin Woodman.
"If we leave her here she will die," said the Lion. "The
smell of the flowers is killing us all, I myself can scarcely
keep my eyes open and the dog is asleep already."
L. FRANK BAUM, *The Wonderful Wizard of Oz*

The poppy is a flower of exquisite beauty. A blossom of deli-
cate rounded petals of vibrant scarlet color encases a black
heart perched atop a tall wavy stalk. Golden-green seed bulbs
stand or droop alongside the blooms, and disheveled, feathery
leaf clusters are stationed randomly along the stem. Not surprisingly, the poppy has long been a favorite subject of still-life
and landscape painters, particularly the Impressionists. Claude
Monet's *Les Coquelicots* depicts the flowers as tiny explosions
of orange-red tumbling down a small hill, appearing to flow
onto the feet of a small girl and young woman with an um-
brella strolling in a field of yellow-green grasses. In his paint-
ing *Field of Poppies*, however, the brilliant, silky flowers are

thickly bunched to form an oncoming scarlet wave that fills the bottom third of the picture and seems to be rushing directly toward the viewer, about to crest over the lower edge of the frame. It is a scene like this that must have inspired the oceanic poppy field in the 1939 MGM film *The Wizard of Oz*. In *The Wonderful Wizard of Oz*, the book on which the movie was based, L. Frank Baum described the scene as follows:

> They walked along listening to the singing of the bright-colored birds and looking at the lovely flowers which now became so thick that the ground was carpeted with them. There were big yellow and white and blue and purple blossoms, beside great clusters of scarlet poppies, which were so brilliant in color that they almost dazzled Dorothy's eyes.
>
> "Aren't they beautiful?" the girl asked, as she breathed in the spicy scent of the flowers.
>
> "I suppose so," answered the scarecrow. "When I have brains I shall probably like them better."
>
> "If only I had a heart I should love them," added the Tin Woodman.
>
> "I always did like flowers," said the Lion, "they seem so helpless and frail. But there are none in the forest so bright as these."
>
> They now came upon more and more of the big scarlet poppies, and fewer and fewer of the other flowers; and soon they found themselves in the midst of a great meadow of poppies.

Even in Baum's fairy tale, however, there exists another aspect of this beautiful flower besides its vibrant color and delicious scent, an ominous side to its nature that is foreshadowed in the chapter titled "The Deadly Poppy Field." The narrative continues:

> Now it is well known that when there are many of these flowers together their odor is so powerful that anyone who breathes it falls asleep, and if the sleeper is not carried away from the scent of the flower he sleeps on and on for-ever. But Dorothy did not know this, nor could she get

away from the bright red flowers that were everywhere about; so presently her eyes grew heavy and she felt she must sit down to rest and to sleep.

This is, of course, allegory, and read as such we know it was not the beauty of that field of red flowers that put the Oz seekers to sleep, nor was it the power of the flowers' collective fragrance. Baum's reference in the story was to opium, the powerful analgesic that is derived from the seed bulbs of the poppy plant. And the opium found in the poppy has its own story, a larger human tale of euphoria and the individual's search for transcendence. It is a story that encompasses a vast historical landscape: addiction, war, the rending of the fabric of whole societies, death on a mass scale. It is a story that begins thousands of years ago.

Men and women have been using psychotropic substances throughout history for a number of reasons: to attain euphoric physical states, for recreational pleasure, to escape the travails of earthly suffering, and to seek spiritual transcendence and enlightenment through altered states of consciousness. The earliest written history of humanity's romance with the opium poppy is found in the writings of the Sumerians dating back to approximately 3300 B.C.

Opium as Medicine, Recreation, and Commodity

The Sumerians, a dark-skinned, short-of-stature, heavy-boned tribe, are believed to have migrated from Persia (now Iran) by navigating the estuaries of the Tigris and Euphrates rivers; they settled into the region of land between the southern ends of the two rivers, just north of the Persian Gulf. There they flourished and traded with their neighbors, Persia and Elam to the east, Akkad and Assyria to the north. They built their homes, initially mud huts, along the marshes of the lower Euphrates, and through sheer determination and imagination survived the occasional floods of the twin rivers.[1] Using sophisticated irrigation techniques to hydrate their crops with the ever-flowing waters of the rivers, they avoided reliance on rain, effectively eliminating one of early man's greatest fears: drought.

Farmers to the north, who prayed for rain, produced only 10 percent of what Sumerian farmers regularly harvested. The Sumerians' waterways strategically irrigated their crops and enabled them to harvest abundantly as often as three times a year.

Living within an agrarian society, the Sumerians grew barley, dates, and grain as their primary crops. They also grew the opium poppy, *Papaver somniferum.* The cereal crops came in the spring and were used to feed sheep and cattle during the hot summer months. The dates came in the fall. They traded their surplus with the Persians, and it is in these exchanges that we can begin to trace the spread of the opium poppy.

The Sumerian civilization comprised twelve cities, each a territory unto itself, with infighting a common practice over such issues as irrigation rights. Each city had a monarch who

A poppy field
in Southeast Asia

Photo courtesy of the
Drug Enforcement Administration,
U.S. Department of Justice

Papaver somniferum,
the opium poppy

Photo courtesy of the
Drug Enforcement Administration,
U.S. Department of Justice

ruled and served as a keeper of justice. From Sumerian writings we can trace the development of legal concepts, such as those concerning private property and civil liberties, that protected the rights of the less affluent. The monarch of a city, for example, had to pay for land if he desired to own it; he could not just take it. It was decreed that powerful men should not oppress widows and orphans, nor should a man of limited means be taken advantage of by one with more riches.

The first city the Sumerians settled is believed to have been Eridu, located at the southernmost end of Sumer, on the north shores of the Persian Gulf. The settlers eventually learned to use bitumen to hold mud bricks in place, enabling them to build stronger homes than the mud huts they initially inhabited, and to erect temples to their gods that reached high into the heavens. They received precious gems in trade for their surplus crops and used them to decorate their temples, which they surrounded with thick walls. The walls served two purposes. They kept out larcenous intruders, and they formed the last refuge if the people came under attack. Mention of these multistoried temples appears in the Bible, as in the story of the Tower of Babel. Sumerian temples were predecessors of the cathedrals that would be built throughout Europe thousands of years later.

The Sumerians are known to have used sailboats, chariots, and plows drawn by animals. They also are credited with inventing the potter's wheel. They built a sophisticated society by early standards, as witnessed by recovered artifacts including many copper and bronze tools and objects found in graves from the city of Ur, dating to about 2800 B.C.

The Sumerians' most significant contribution to the advancement of civilization was the invention of writing, around 3300 B.C. Archaeologists have unearthed more than four hundred thousand clay tablets on which are recorded Sumerian times and achievements. The Sumerians used the soft clay from the banks of the Tigris and Euphrates rivers to form the sun-dried tablets, on which they inscribed wedge-shaped markings with the ends of reeds, also abundant along the rivers. Although the images they inscribed were pictorial and told stories of their daily life, the primary initial function of the recordings was financial; they were used as a means of recording transactions and documenting food supplies stored in the temples. This writing came to be known as cuneiform, from the Latin word *cuneus,* which means "wedge."[2]

It was in this form that the Sumerians recorded the earliest information about the cultivation of opium. How the opiate content of the poppy and its psychotropic qualities were discovered is not known. We do know that the Sumerians used it for both medicinal and recreational purposes. They referred to it as *hul gil,* or "plant of joy."

Opium was not the only crop they used for pleasure. Historians believe that as much as 40 percent of the Sumerians' barley crop went to the production of beer. So whether by chance or design, the Sumerians placed themselves in a position to trade with their neighbors these substances that intoxicated and relaxed.

At some time between 700 and 140 B.C. the secret of opium poppy cultivation was shared with the Akkadians, Sumer's neighbors to the north. The Akkadians in turn passed it along to the Assyrians who, through trade with the Syrians and Egyptians, eventually spread the secret of the poppy to the west and north, as far away as Greece.

There is little historical documentation of the spread of the opium poppy to the west during this time, but there is mention of opium in Greek pharmacopoeia as early as the fifth century B.C. As was the case in later times, its spread has been attributed to Arab merchant traders who carried opium, recognized for its medicinal and recreational values, and other commodities.

Opium's healing powers are described in the writings of the Greek physician Hippocrates, who in about 400 B.C. prescribed it to patients suffering from insomnia. A Greek physician, Galen (A.D. 129–199), recorded the first opium overdose. Galen was the appointed physician to the Roman emperor Marcus Aurelius Antoninus. Galen acquired much of his knowledge about opium's healing properties from the Egyptians, and he became such an advocate of the practice of eating opium, and of other vegetable therapies, that for centuries these preparations were known as "Galenicals."[3] In the first century A.D., the Greek physician Dioscorides wrote what became the leading medical text of the day, *De Materia Medica*, in which he described opium and its medical value. He wrote that, mixed in liquid, opium was a powerful cure for insomnia, diarrhea, and nausea and that it had aphrodisiac qualities.[4] Dioscorides detailed how the pod of the poppy plant should be crushed and mixed with a liquid for maximum benefit.

The most common method of opium ingestion was as a liquid elixir. The sappy white milk, raw opium, that is found in the poppy seed bulb was usually mixed with wine or water and produced a dreamy, euphoric effect when ingested.

We even find an indirect mention of opium in the Bible. Matthew 27:34 reads, "They gave him vinegar to drink mingled with gall: and when he had tasted thereof, he would not drink."[5] Matthew was speaking of the Crucifixion, when Jesus was offered a sponge soaked in bitter wine. Biblical scholars theorize that the "gall" mixture may have been opium and wine, offered to dull his pain. Opium, when mixed with wine, has a bitter taste, hence the meaning of the word *gall* as "something bitter."[6]

What little recorded history survives traces the spread of the opium poppy from the Middle East westward to Greece and eastward to the Far East—India and China. Gradually making its way along overland trade routes, carried as one of many commodities by Arab merchants, the addictive fruit of the poppy reached China in approximately the seventh century A.D.[7] In A.D. 973, Chinese scholars recorded in the *Herbalist's Treasury* that "the poppy's seeds have healing powers."[8] They recommended mixing the seeds of the poppy with bamboo juice boiled into gruel.

The All-Sea Trade Route to the Far East

In 1271, the Venetian traveler Marco Polo set off for China with his father and uncle. They reached Shang-tu, China, four years later, the first Europeans to travel so far east. Polo and his father stayed in China until 1292 and arrived back in their hometown of Venice in 1295. Three years later, serving as the captain of a Venetian galley, Polo was captured in a battle between Genoa and Venice and imprisoned until 1299. It was during his imprisonment that he dictated to a fellow prisoner *The Travels of Marco Polo*.[9] It was perhaps one of the most important books in history because it gave medieval Europe its first detailed knowledge of China and other Asian countries. Polo wrote of Thailand, Japan, Java, Cochin China (now part of Vietnam), Sri Lanka, Tibet, India, and Burma (now called Myanmar). His book was used to record the first accurate maps of the Far East in Europe, and it helped inspire navigators like Christopher Columbus to sail due west from Europe in search of the all-sea route to India. This route was discovered not by Columbus sailing west, of course, but by the Portuguese navigator Vasco da Gama in 1497–98, when he journeyed south and east around the tip of Africa to reach India.

With the ability to sail around the world, Europe established a model for the global opium trade that exists to this day. Although their primary objective was to obtain the silks, spices, and porcelain that were to be found in the Far East, the Portuguese soon discovered the value that opium had in the international trade market.

The Portuguese reached Canton, China, by 1513 and spent the next fifty years establishing control of seaports stretching from Calcutta, India, to the island of Macao and as far east as the Spice Islands of Indonesia. They faced competition from rival sea merchants and were known to pirate and plunder as they went, confiscating cargoes.

While the spices, silks, and goods the Portuguese carried back to Europe in their wooden galleys commanded a high price, there was little Europe produced that the Far East needed or would pay for. The Europeans suffered a trade imbalance but learned from the experience of Arab and Indian merchants who had been selling opium grown in India to the Chinese for hundreds of years. The Chinese were known to cultivate opium by this time, but it was a minimal crop, and Indian opium was of a higher quality and potency.

With the advent of the sailing ship, the Europeans were able to expand their distribution network and secure more and more ports, delivering high-quality opium at faster speeds than before. Prior to this, opium had been distributed along overland trading routes, a much slower delivery process. The introduction of the sailing ship gave rise to a quickly growing addict population in the Far East during the period between 1500 and 1700.

The Portuguese are credited with introducing the smoking pipe to the Chinese. Spanish sailors brought the practice of smoking tobacco in pipes to Europe after their explorations of the New World. Smoking a pipe filled with tobacco soon became fashionable in Europe. Portuguese sailors carried tobacco grown in Brazil, by now a Portuguese colony, to the Chinese, who smoked it with Indian opium in wooden pipes made in Spain. The technology of the pipe accelerated the use of opium in the Far East. Opium dens began to spring up everywhere, spreading from coastal ports to inland villages and towns. The stronger effect of smoking opium, rather than drinking it, resulted in more severe addiction, or physical dependence, and the numbers of habitual users in China swelled.

The Dutch followed the Portuguese and began trading in opium by the beginning of the seventeenth century. The French were also involved in the opium trade. It seemed virtually impossible for any of these countries to trade with China without dealing in opium. Britain, though one of the last sea powers to enter this market, became a dominant force in the politics of India, and played a significant role in the rapid growth of the opium trade to China.

None of this would have been possible were it not for the formation of the East India Companies, the most notable of which was the British East India Company, chartered on December 31, 1600, by Queen Elizabeth I. The agents of the company, merchant adventurers, were authorized to acquire territories wherever they could and to exercise in those territories the various functions of government, including legislation, the issuance of currency, the negotiation of treaties, the waging of war, and the administration of justice. It was, in effect, a charter for colonization. They were also free to move opium from India to the Far East. The company established a monopoly on trade to Asia, Africa, and the America colonies,[10] and controlled the Asian opium trade from the 1770s until 1833, when trade was opened to all foreign merchants, enabling American sailing captains to now compete openly in the increasingly profitable opium business. This socially debilitating trade went on despite the banning of all opium importation by the Chinese emperor in the 1790s.

An indication of how addiction in China was spreading can be measured by the steadily increasing weight of East India Company opium cargoes. In 1660 the Dutch East India Company reported shipping approximately 1,350 pounds from India to China. By 1720, the British were shipping to China 15 metric tons a year, increasing the amount to 75 metric tons by 1773. Importation continued to grow, stabilizing at about 250 metric tons annually in 1800. By 1833, when the British East India Company gave up its monopoly on Asian trade, the numbers were on their way to new, dizzying heights. Chinese importation of Indian opium in 1820 was 270 metric tons per year. By 1840, the annual cargo reached a high of 2,555 metric tons. The human cost of this dramatic increase: three million Chinese opium addicts.[11]

China was faced with the problem of how to react to a hungry addict population being fed by greedy foreign merchants (similar to the problem with which the United States is now struggling). The Chinese government had banned opium smoking in 1796, making it a capital offense, but found that this did little to curb the spread of the drug throughout the country. By 1838, the issue was the most pressing concern to the imperial court and one that involved nothing less than China's economic and spiritual survival. Feeling that a crisis point had been reached, the emperor appointed a mandarin named Lin Tse-hsu as a special commissioner to Canton and charged him with a twofold task: assess the problem and determine a solution, then act decisively on that determination.

Lin Tse-hsu arrived in Canton and summarily demanded the surrender of all opium cargoes from the foreign ships in port. The British merchants delayed, and after what appeared to be a standoff, surrendered 95 metric tons of opium to the Chinese. It took the Chinese several days, working day and night, to burn the seized cargo.

Great Britain, in response to the seizure, dispatched 7,000 troops and a fleet of six warships to retaliate. This was the beginning of the first of two Opium Wars China fought with Britain. The British military forces captured Canton in May 1839 and spent the next two years marching north, seizing China's major coastal cities. Whether Chinese government officials underestimated Britain's response to the opium seizure is open to conjecture, but the result was a crushing military defeat, which the Chinese accepted in 1842, when they were forced to sign the Treaty of Nanking. The treaty forced China to cede Hong Kong to the British and open five new ports to foreign trade. The Chinese also agreed to pay the equivalent of $21 million as reparations for the 95 metric tons of opium they had seized and destroyed. In addition, they ceded the right to try British citizens in Chinese courts.[12] In spite of this, China still refused to legalize opium.[13]

China's refusal to legalize opium, even under enormous diplomatic and military pressure from Britain, ultimately led to the second of the Opium Wars, also known as the "Arrow War." This war pitted the Chinese against the combined forces of France and Great Britain.

As is the case in many wars throughout history, a single incident sparked a declaration of war. In October 1856, Cantonese police boarded the British ship *The Arrow*. They lowered the British flag and seized the ship and its cargo, charging its crew with smuggling opium. Historians believe the British were looking for an excuse to renew hostilities, so as to expand their trading rights, and used the incident to once again wage war. The French, also looking to capitalize on the lucrative trade market in China, decided to join forces with Britain. They used the killing of a French missionary in the interior of China as their excuse for military retaliation, but their primary motive for engaging in the war was monetary greed.[14]

The British and French forces proved to be an overwhelming enemy and methodically defeated Chinese forces in battle after battle. The Europeans occupied Canton by late 1857, and in 1858 brought the Chinese to the treaty table again, this time forcing them to sign the Treaty of Tianjian. The treaty negotiations temporarily halted the fighting. Britain and France proposed an agreement that called for opening new trading ports, allowed residence in Peking for foreign emissaries, gave freedom of movement to Christian missionaries, and permitted travel by foreigners in the Chinese interior. The Chinese refused to sign the treaty, prompting an Anglo-French attack on Peking itself and the burning of the summer palace of the emperor. Finally, in 1860, the Chinese admitted defeat and signed the Treaty of Peking, promising to observe the terms of the earlier Tianjian treaty.[15]

Perhaps the most significant result of the Chinese defeat was the legalization of opium importation by China in 1858.

The aftermath of legalization was an unprecedented explosion in the number of addicts. By 1900, China had 13.5 million addicts consuming 39,000 metric tons of opium per year.[16] In 1906 the imperial government reported that 27 percent of adult Chinese males were opium smokers.[17]

In contrast, during 1995 there were only 4,000 metric tons of opium cultivated globally. America's demand was about 13 metric tons, consumed by an estimated 2.8 million users.[18] By imagining the United States with four to five times its current number of hard-core addicts, consuming ten times more opium derivatives, one can get an idea of what social conditions in China had become by the beginning of the twentieth century.

Opium in the West

As China was being devastated by opium smoking, England and the United States were slowly cultivating their own addicted consumer base for the fruit of the poppy.

While the opium trade was exploding in the Far East during the 1800s, the scientific minds of Europe were busy discovering various medical uses for opium derivatives. Morphine, derived from processed opium, was discovered by the German pharmacist Friedrich Wilhelm Adam Seturner in 1803. He devised a process to isolate morphine (described in chapter 3) and named it for the Greek god of dreams, Morpheus.

Another German pharmacist, Heinrich Emanuel Merck, began commercial production of morphine twenty-three years later, in 1827.[19] The Merck family had produced a line of chemists that dated back to 1668, when Friedrich Jacob Merck took over a pharmacy in Darmstadt, Germany, called Engelapotheke, meaning "at the sign of the angel." Today, the company is known as E. Merck and Company.

E. Merck and Company dates its U.S. beginnings to the Philadelphia firm Zeitler and Rosengarten, founded in 1822 by German-American chemist George David Rosengarten, who arrived in America in 1818. Rosengarten worked for four years after his arrival as a pharmacist, and when he had saved enough money, he bought a half interest in Zeitler and Seitler, a company that by 1822 had been making quinine sulfate for almost a year. Zeitler and Rosengarten later manufactured morphine and strychnine, among other chemical products, for legal, commercial distribution in the United States and Europe.[20] The company was renamed Powers-Weightman-Rosengarten in 1905, and became known as E. Merck and Company in 1927.

Heinrich Merck began commercial production of the anodyne codeine in 1836, ten years after morphine had been introduced. He would begin commercial production of cocaine in 1862.[21]

In Europe and the United States the preferred way of using opium was in its liquid form. Laudanum, or "black drop" as it was also known, was introduced by the Swiss-born alchemist Paracelsus in 1541. This liquid preparation of opium was what many women and men used to experience the effects of the opium high. In the early 1800s it was not socially acceptable for women to frequent bars or saloons, so laudanum conveniently became the drug of choice for many women. Easily available at the local apothecary, it was also a suitable substitute for alcohol for men who did not wish to appear to be drunkards. Laudanum is odorless. A gentlemen could take a swig of it in place of alcohol and go about his business with no one the wiser.

Gradually, the use of opium in laudanum and in patent medicine remedies reached epidemic proportions in England and the United States. The remedies were marketed in magazine and newspaper advertising. If there wasn't a drugstore nearby, you could place your order through a mail-order distributor. Many of the remedies, with such brand names as Mother Bailey's Quieting Syrup, were spoon-fed to children. Mothers used opium-based remedies to suppress coughs, cure diarrhea, and to quiet the occasionally cranky child. They inadvertently addicted their children and themselves to drugs like Mrs. Winslow's Soothing Syrup. Use of the opium-laced remedies was so widespread that it became a national problem. The German philosopher Friedrich Engels reported on England's opium problem in *The Condition of the Working Class in England* in 1844. Engels described how children who were given ever-increasing doses of liquid opium by their mothers became "pale, stunted and weak" and generally died before they were two years old."[22]

Many in the world of the arts succumbed to laudanum dependence. The English writer Samuel Taylor Coleridge was addicted to laudanum, and it is believed that his poem "Kubla Khan" was inspired by a vision he experienced while using the drug. Coleridge wound up physically and intellectually debilitated by his addiction. Thomas De Quincey extolled the virtues of opium in his book *Confessions of an Opium Eater* in 1822. He described how opium enhanced the creative powers of the intellect, and he is thought to have been the first to use the term *tranquilizer* in describing opium's effect.

The use of laudanum and patent medicine remedies enabled Europeans and Americans to become legally addicted to products they could purchase over the counter, order through the mail, or obtain by a doctor's prescription at a drugstore. While the chemists' intentions may have been to ease pain and cure physical ailments, the age-old human desire for intoxication created a problem with which we still struggle: narcotic addiction.

The result for Chinese and European addicts was basically the same, though their methods of ingestion were different. The Chinese smoked opium and became dreamily euphoric, lost in a world of lessened stress and relaxation, while Americans and Europeans drank or injected liquids filled with what the patent medicine companies called "secret remedy ingredients" to achieve a similar state of euphoria, the "nod." Regardless of the method of ingestion, the user must, as every opiate addict eventually finds out, return to a reality where the overriding edict is: use more or suffer physical and emotional pain. This is the fundamental nature of addiction.

A pharmacy receipt for the purchase of laudanum, 1843

Hazelden-Pittman Archives

A tin of No-to-bac, a nineteenth-century smoking cessation aid that contained opium. The label on the Watkins Cough Remedy bottle states that it contains 11 percent alcohol and ⅛ grain of heroin per ounce of elixir. The laudanum bottle label boldly proclaims "POISON" and bears the skull and crossbones warning symbol, yet its instructions read, "Dose—for a child two to four years old, two to three drops; six to ten years old, five to eight drops; fifteen to twenty years old, ten to twelve drops; adults, fifteen to twenty drops."

Photo: Dennis Becker

CHAPTER

2

The History of Heroin:
Heroin in America and the World Trade

A frightful endemic demoralization betrays itself in the frequency with which the haggard features and drooping shoulders of the opium drunkards are met with in the street.

OLIVER WENDELL HOLMES SR.

In the United States the character of addiction to opium and its derivatives was entirely different from the character of the Chinese experience. It was the introduction of the smoking pipe that allowed opium to be consumed in a more powerful, effective way in China. But it was the development of the hypodermic syringe in 1853 by Alexander Wood that pushed addiction to new levels of destruction in America.

An ad for Mrs. Winslow's Soothing Syrup, an opium-based product to be given to infants suffering teething pain.

Hazelden-Pittman Archives

The decade before the Civil War found the United States armed with the most powerful painkiller known to man, morphine, and the technology with which to easily inject it into the body. At this time, the opium-addicted population in the United States consisted mainly of Caucasian women who legally purchased opium-laced cough syrups and elixirs, such as Mrs. Winslow's Soothing Syrup, at their local pharmacies, or who obtained laudanum, a tincture of opium, by mail. It was a quiet addiction, almost invisible, because the women stayed at home. This was due in part to male dominance in the social sphere and the perception that it was not right for a decent woman to frequent bars or saloons, let alone an opium den. Eugene O'Neill characterized this phenomenon in his play Long Day's Journey into Night. In the play, the mother of a family, Mary Tyrone, is portrayed as a frail individual whose hands shake often. The implication is that she is in a state of withdrawal. The family members do not speak openly of her "problem" but allude to it often. She, like many during the late nineteenth and early twentieth centuries, supposedly developed her addiction as a result of seeking relief from rheumatoid arthritis. Many women took laudanum to alleviate pain or settle coughs and became dependent on the opium-based mixtures.

Opium Dens

Surveys between 1878 and 1885 indicated that 56 percent to 71 percent of opiate addicts in the United States were middle- to upper-class white women who purchased the drug legally. The rate of addiction was 4.59 addicts per 1,000 Americans compared with today's rate of 2.04 per 1,000.[1]

After the U.S. Civil War, large numbers of men who had been wounded and treated with morphine became physically addicted to the drug. Upon their return home, they found it easy to soothe their war wounds with patent medicine remedies available legally or with opium, available in dens that began springing up in major metropolitan areas such as San

Francisco and New York. It seemed that in any city with a significant Chinese population, or that had a "Chinatown," opium dens could be found.

Between the years 1852 and 1870, more than 70,000 Chinese came to the United States to work on the railroads and in the gold mines of the West Coast. Some brought opium habits

FINELY-FITTED "OPIUM JOINT"

Mr. and Mrs. Bailey Had an Elaborate
"Lay-out"—Pipes Embossed with
Gold and Silver.

Edgar Bailey and his wife, who occupy a flat at 227 West Fifteenth Street, were taken before Justice Simms in the Jefferson Market Court yesterday on a charge of keeping an "opium joint." A policeman went into the place Saturday night shortly after 11 o'clock. He was let in by the woman, who told him that there was no one in the flat but her husband and herself.

The policeman pushed his way into the bedroom and found the husband lying on the bed smoking opium. He arrested both the man and woman and took charge of all the articles about the place.

There were three heavily embossed opium pipes—one with copper, one with gold, and one with silver—half a dozen lamps of great beauty, three ivory "sticks," a pair of scales for weighing the opium, made of ivory inlaid with gold; four empty cans that had contained prepared opium, about one pound of crude opium, a dozen lichee nut shells full of opium, a jimmy, a pair of iron knuckles, a sweatboard cloth, a roulette cloth, and a revolver.

The man and woman were well dressed, and were indignant at what they termed the outrage of their arrest. Justice Simms held them in $500 each for trial.

Among the complaints against policy shops which were received at Police Headquarters last week was one against a shop which, it was alleged, was being run at 539 Canal Street. The communication was not signed, and was turned over to Policeman Cohen, of Inspector McAvoy's staff. After telling of the evils wrought by the place, the letter went on to give instructions as to getting into the place. It read: "First floor, windows covered with wall paper; entrance west side of hall, rear door. Knock once and scratch three times."

Cohen went to the place Saturday afternoon. He knocked once, scratched three times, got into the place, and arrested John D. Barr. In the Jefferson Market Court yesterday Barr was held for trial.

Report of an opium den raid from the February 18, 1895, The New York Times

with them; others developed them here. Opium smoking occurred primarily on the West Coast, because it was the closest
port of entry for opium from the Far East. The opium trade in
America, however, was relatively light and paled in comparison to the Chinese opium trade controlled by Europeans.

Americans were known to frequent traditional opium
smoking dens. This has been characterized by Hollywood in
movies like *Once Upon a Time in America*, starring Robert De
Niro, and the more recent *Wild Bill* starring Ellen Barkin as
Calamity Jane and Jeff Bridges as Bill Hickok. In *Wild Bill*,
Hickok struggles with his failing eyesight and turns to the
comfort of the opium pipe. The opium den is depicted as an ex-
otic, mysterious place, with subdued colors, where one can re-
treat to the privacy of one's own dreams. In the den, Hickok is

*A graphic example of the "yellow journalism" prominent
in late nineteenth-century newspapers that portrayed
Chinese immigrants using opium to seduce white women.*

cared for by an attentive Chinese woman who fills his pipe every so often; he smokes and drifts off to a dreamworld where he can escape his fears.

Opium dens, however, were predominantly the domain of Chinese immigrants, whom many viewed as undesirables in the 1870s when the American economy stalled and went into a depression. Newspaper stories described "horrifying opium dens where *yellow fiends* forced unsuspecting white women to become enslaved to the mischievous drug."[2]

This powerful racist propaganda was fueled, in part, by feelings that the depression was caused by the country's surplus of Chinese workers. It was feared that Chinese immigrants were taking jobs from European Americans. Many European Americans on the West Coast believed that the Chinese, with their alien culture and mysterious ways, would undermine American society. The opium dens of San Francisco were publicly condemned for stealing the mythic virtue of white women, in much the same way that black men were seen by white men in the southern United States as a threat to white women following emancipation. David Musto highlights this period in his book *The American Disease*. "The fear of the cocainized black coincided with the peak of lynchings, legal segregation, and voting laws all designed to remove political and social power from him," he writes.[3] Here again, the racist and sexist perception of white women as being frail and unable to withstand the temptations of drugs, and the fear of them falling into the clutches of foreigners and black men, drove the proponents for reform to lobby with particular passion.

The Advent of Heroin

The year 1874 was a turning point in the history of opiate addiction due to the discovery of heroin by British chemist C. R. Alder Wright. He found that boiling morphine with acetic anhydride produced diacetylmorphine, or heroin. Soon heroin found its way into patent medicine remedies to complement the morphine and codeine mixtures already available.

Heroin powder proved to be more potent and addictive than the opium-based laudanum most women drank. It was easily dissolved in liquid and was initially thought to be non-addictive. More important, heroin powders became available at local pharmacies, and the practice of self-injection began to claim lives as a result of overdoses. The practice of selling patent medicines containing morphine, opium, and heroin had no legal regulation in this country until 1906 when the Pure Food and Drug Act was passed.[4]

During the last twenty-five years of the 1800s, a backlash against the increasing use of drugs, both legal and illegal, began to occur. It had become apparent that drug use was a grave social problem in America. Between 1875 and 1877 the country's first opium laws were passed in San Francisco, California; Virginia City, Nevada; and Portland, Oregon.[5] The laws were primarily aimed at outlawing the opium dens that had proliferated with Chinese immigration. It was not until 1887 that Congress passed a bill prohibiting the importation of opium by both U.S. and Chinese citizens. The law created a black market for opium in its crude, smokable form and ignored the opium derivatives morphine and later heroin, which were claiming the souls of thousands of men and women.

A serious problem faced by reformers and prohibitionists was the economic power that the chemical companies had achieved. The companies were among the largest advertisers in newspapers of the day. Newspapers were reluctant to point out the addictive qualities of some of the patent medicines because the companies had escape clauses built into their advertising contracts allowing them to pull their business if their products were banned from sale. Thus, consumers continued to drink patent medicine remedies with innocent-sounding names, unaware of the addictive contents, until the Pure Food and Drug Act required labeling and disclosure of all ingredients.

Heroin was introduced under its own brand name as a cough suppressant by the forty-eight-year-old German chemical-pharmaceutical company Farbenfabriken Vorm. Friedrich Bayer and Company in 1898.[6] It was available as a powder, diluted in liquids, and also available in powder capsules. Users could swallow or inject the powerful new drug. Heroin was indicated as a medicine for chest pain, pneumonia, and tuberculosis, among other maladies. It was widely advertised as a general cure for common ailments of the day, and its use was unrestrained. The year following its introduction, Bayer and Company introduced a less harmful analgesic, acetylsalicylic acid, or aspirin as it is known commercially, and marketed it under the brand name Bayer Aspirin. Ironically, this new analgesic was available only by prescription when it was introduced.

A reform and prohibitionist movement, determined to eliminate the use of opium and its derivatives in patent medicines, sprang up in the last quarter of the nineteenth century. The movement was led by Protestant men such as Samuel Hopkins Adams, the Right Reverend Charles Brent, and Dr. Harvey Washington Wiley. Adams was known for his series published in *Collier's* magazine detailing the crimes committed against unsuspecting citizens who became addicted to patent medicines.

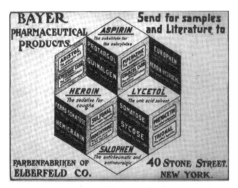

A Bayer ad for the Heroin and Aspirin brands. Heroin, which was introduced on the market as a "cough sedative" in 1898, could be purchased over the counter; Aspirin, which appeared a year later, was initially available only with a prescription.

Between 1905 and 1907, he campaigned vociferously against the manufacturers of such medicines. Rt. Rev. Brent attacked the practice of using drugs, focusing on individual behavior and proposed federal legislation outlawing its use in any form. Like Adams, Dr. Wiley went after the manufacturers, taking on none other than the Coca-Cola Company for its use of caffeine in its soft drink. (It was not until 1903 that Coca-Cola began substituting caffeine for the cocaine with which it previously infused its beverage.) In an amusing anecdote in *The American Disease*, Musto reports that Wiley, who was perceived to be too radical in his demands, irritated Theodore Roosevelt when he criticized the president's cherished habit of using the sugar substitute saccharin.[7] The reform movement went up against an industry that by 1900 grossed $250 million a year.[8] The reformers' measurement of success was the number of antidrug laws enacted, and as more laws were passed, the patent medicine trade braced itself for a backlash.

It wasn't until the late 1890s that the medical community began to understand the seriousness of the country's opiate-addiction problem. By the turn of the century the estimated number of addicts in the United States was 250,000. In 1900, Dr. John Witherspoon delivered a speech to the American Medical Association, which had been founded in 1847, warning his colleagues of the perils of opiate addiction. Clearly, by this time, Americans were beginning to realize the extent of the problems caused by the production, sale, and consumption of opium-based products.

In 1903 the federal government established the U.S. Opium Commission for the purpose of studying ways to regulate opium and its derivatives. Dr. Hamilton Wright, a prominent doctor from Washington, D.C., who had traveled throughout the Far East and was knowledgeable about the scientific aspects of opium use, was appointed head of the commission by President Roosevelt in 1908. Wright estimated that in 1907, 160,000 pounds of opium were imported into the United States for smoking and eating. The alarming numbers led to a congressional act in 1909 prohibiting the importation of opium for all but medicinal purposes.

The Prohibition of Opium

What would sound the death knell for the legal opium business, the Harrison Narcotic Act of 1914, was initially debated and killed in Congress in the 1910–11 session. That first round of debates took place in 1910 and struck down what was called the Foster Bill, named after David Foster, the congressional representative from Vermont who introduced the legislation. Although Foster introduced the bill, Wright was the driving force behind the legislation and was the one who drafted it. Wright had become a visible force in the anti-opium debate, again appealing to the racist fears of the dominant white culture in arguing that "one of the most unfortunate phases of the habit of smoking opium in this country are the large number of women who have become involved and are living as common-law wives or cohabiting with Chinese in the Chinatowns of our various cities."[9]

The Foster Bill was the direct predecessor to the Harrison Act and focused on detailed record keeping as it related to any importation of opium, cocaine, or marijuana. It did not outlaw prescription or medicinal products but was designed to make the record keeping so cumbersome that it might discourage the importation of those drugs.

On December 17, 1914, President Woodrow Wilson signed the Harrison Act, also known as the Federal Narcotics-Internal Revenue Regulations, to become effective March 1, 1915. The legislation was introduced in Congress by Francis Burton Harrison, a representative from New York, who had been enlisted in Wright's quest for narcotics prohibition. Harrison believed, as did Wright, that legislation should be enacted that eliminated all narcotics use except for medical purposes. The act divided drugs into four categories: Class A (highly addictive), Class B (moderately addictive), Class X (exempt), and Class M (especially exempt). Although the bill was intended to license and tax the importation, manufacture, and sale of opium and cocaine, it was unclear how much police power the federal government would be able to exert in its effort to prosecute addicts. The government went on to use the bill to police and prosecute drug addicts, distributors, and doctors who prescribed to addicts.

Wright envisioned the law doing what the states had not been able to do: stop the use of narcotics. Several challenges to the law occurred between 1915 and 1919. In Memphis a district court judge ruled in favor of a defendant who had been prescribed one pound of opium, stating that there was nothing in the law that prohibited a doctor from prescribing such quantities. It seemed there were problems in the wording of the law, and the court felt that the law as written could not be enforced to prohibit doctors from writing prescriptions to addicts for maintenance. This will be discussed at greater length in chapter 7 as it relates to early maintenance efforts, the predecessors of methadone clinics.

In 1919, two U.S. Supreme Court decisions bolstered the strength and constitutionality of the Harrison Act. In *United States v. Doremus,* the Court decided that a doctor from San Antonio, Texas, Charles T. Doremus, was in violation of the law for prescribing morphine to an addict. The court stated that the law was meant to control the way drugs were prescribed "in the course of professional practice only." This struck at the issue of maintaining addicts by prescription, for purposes other than curing the addiction. The other major case was *Webb et al. v. United States*. In this case both a druggist and a physician, Dr. Webb, were indicted for maintaining an addict. The Court concluded "that to call such an order for the use of morphine a physician's prescription would be so plain a perversion of meaning that no discussion of the subject is required."[10] Finally, then, the Harrison Act became what Wright had originally envisioned it to be: a means to prohibit, among other things, the dispensing of drugs by doctors to addicts for the purpose of maintaining their addiction. The government was now free to zealously pursue enforcement and began to lock up addicts and the doctors who prescribed drugs to them. The underlying logic was that addiction was not a disease, and as such had no need for prescription. The Harrison Act was the one law the newly created Treasury Department's Narcotics Division (1923) used to successfully prosecute drug addicts and their suppliers.

This did not, of course, end heroin or opium addiction. It did, however, change the social makeup of the typical addict from that of the middle-class white woman to the lower-class white man, along with proportionate numbers of minority men. These addicts needed heroin to continue functioning, so they turned to illegal suppliers. The criminalization of heroin use and incarceration of heroin addicts created a new product from which organized crime syndicates could profit. Already adept at smuggling liquor during prohibition, they were proficient at setting up distribution networks for heroin and opium as well. The difference between alcohol and heroin was that alcohol was made legal again, after thirteen years of prohibition, in 1933. Heroin, on the other hand, would never again be legal, creating an extremely profitable long-term substitution for liquor as a black-market commodity.

The Narcotics Division of the Treasury Department was initially judged ineffective in combating the heroin problem, and was crippled by scandal in 1929 when a New York City grand jury uncovered corruption. Field agents were accused of protecting certain drug dealers from arrest, and the son of the division's chief was found to be working as an accountant for Arnold Rothstein, a notorious crime syndicate member of the time.[11] In response, Congress created the Federal Bureau of

Narcotics in 1930, and President Herbert Hoover appointed Harry Anslinger as its first director.

Anslinger would run the agency for more than thirty years until his retirement in 1962. He was a former prohibition officer who concentrated on domestic enforcement until after World War II, leaving international attention to the problem of heroin trafficking in the hands of the League of Nations.

Harry Anslinger, appointed in 1930 by Herbert Hoover to be the first director of the Federal Bureau of Narcotics, stands alongside several crates of Turkish opium, the only strategic war material in good supply for the United States and Allies at the beginning of World War II.

*Internal Revenue Service special tax stamp
from 1946 for the legal dispensing of opium*
Hazelden-Pittman Archives

The result of Anslinger's domestic enforcement effort was a reduction in the U.S. addict population from an estimated 200,000 in 1924 to 20,000 by 1945.[12] His agents, using rough, perhaps legally marginal street tactics, proved effective in arresting criminals. In addition, the extra security mounted during the war years to prevent sabotage resulted in the seizure of many shipments of heroin as they arrived at the shipyards in the major ports of the country.

Treatment for heroin addiction during this period was rudimentary and unsophisticated, and heroin addicts were perceived and treated as criminals. The result or, perhaps, cause of this perception was that there were only two places a heroin addict could obtain treatment in the United States. A law passed in 1929 authorized the U.S. Public Health Service to "confine and treat" heroin addicts in either Lexington, Kentucky, where a federal hospital was completed in 1935, or in Fort Worth, Texas. This was the case until 1944, when the Public Health Service Act authorized the treatment of addicts at any of the Public Health Hospitals.[13]

The Resurgence of Heroin in America

Why then did the situation with heroin become worse, not better, after World War II? As stated above, enforcement efforts and the restriction of high-seas smuggling during the war years, when major ports were under close scrutiny for sabotage, reduced the supply of heroin to a point where complete elimination of heroin addiction was thought possible. How did it come to pass that by 1997 more than 250,000 Americans were serving time in prison for drug law violations, and drug use that year caused 500,000 emergency room visits? In 1996 there were 1.6 million Americans arrested for drug abuse violations.[14] Of these, almost 40 percent were for heroin and cocaine—nearly 600,000 individuals arrested for possession with intent to sell or for simple possession. What happened? There are no simple answers to this question. Many factors contributed to the resurgence of heroin use in postwar America, but one can look to the start of the cold war era as a turning point.

In order to gain a better understanding of the postwar upswing in heroin use, we need to look at postwar American society's perceptions of both heroin addicts and communists, perceptions that drove both foreign and domestic policy. After the end of World War II in 1945, American foreign policy and public sentiment was fervently anticommunist, as witnessed by the Joseph McCarthy–led House Committee on Un-American Activities in the 1950s and its witch-hunting attempt to ferret out anyone with left-wing ideas. It was a time in which, for example, it was dangerous to have spoken out against fascism for fear of being branded a communist sympathizer.

After the war, the Central Intelligence Agency was created under the Truman administration. Its primary responsibilities were investigation of international espionage and covert actions. In essence, this agency was America's number-one anticommunist weapon.[15] By aligning itself with anticommunists worldwide, however, the CIA often found itself helping underworld figures establish global heroin distribution networks.

The two major threats to America's anticommunist foreign policy were the former Soviet Union and mainland China. In its effort to halt the spread of communism throughout Western Europe, the CIA formed alliances with almost any group, no matter how unsavory its other activities, as long as it could help the CIA stop the communists. As a result of alliances with Corsican underworld figures in its fight against the French Communist Party, the CIA inadvertently—or with callous disregard for consequences beyond its own narrow anticommunist agenda—ceded control of the seaport at Marseilles, France. For more than twenty-five years, this port played a significant role in global heroin trafficking, serving as a major processing center well into the 1970s. Morphine and heroin were refined there from opium grown in Turkey and Lebanon. Marseilles was made famous in 1971 by Hollywood in the film *The French Connection*, starring Gene Hackman as "Popeye" Doyle. Doyle was a tough, streetwise New York City detective who helped bring down the largest heroin smuggling ring of his time. The movie is based on a true story and much of the real Detective Doyle's personal story is depicted.

CIA involvement with foreign armed forces sympathetic to opium growers and heroin traffickers spanned the decades of the fifties, sixties, and seventies. In the early fifties, for example, the CIA backed Nationalist Chinese forces in a failed attempt to invade mainland southwestern China. Afterward, the CIA helped set up the Nationalists in Myanmar, then called Burma, along the border of China. The Nationalist Chinese forces served the purposes of American foreign policy there, acting as a barrier to a Chinese invasion of Southeast Asia. By the early sixties, however, the Nationalists had made Myanmar's Shan state the largest opium producer in the world.[16]

It is perhaps ironic to note that during World War II, Federal Bureau of Narcotics Director Harry Anslinger helped the OSS (Office of Strategic Services) by lending the agency personnel from the Narcotics Bureau. The OSS, predecessor of the CIA, was restructured in 1947 under President Truman to become the Central Intelligence Agency.

In a 1956 report on a narcotics bill before the U.S. Senate Judiciary Committee, the number of American addicts was said to have reached 60,000, triple the number reported in 1945.[17] The report also stated that addicts were responsible for a majority of all crime, particularly burglary, theft, and prostitution. The primary sources of heroin at the time were reported to be China, Thailand, Turkey, Lebanon, and Mexico.

The government's response was to pass the Boggs-Daniel Bill (House Resolution 11619). The bill was named after its two sponsors, Hale Boggs, representative from Louisiana, and Price Daniel, senator from Texas. It passed into law on July 18, 1956, and provided for harsher penalties for narcotics law violators. One of the provisions in the law called for the death penalty for anyone convicted of selling heroin to minors.

During hearings before the House Ways and Means Committee, it was decided that it was unrealistic to implement government clinics for the purpose of providing heroin addicts with "legal" heroin in order to take the profit out of trafficking and to curb addiction. The Boggs-Daniel Bill officially outlawed heroin importation and manufacturing for any purpose. But there were still small supplies at hospitals and in the hands of druggists, and the bill called for the surrender of all heroin within 120 days of the law's passage for fair compensation. "The heroin was to be destroyed except for small amounts which the treasury might distribute for approved scientific research."[18] Interestingly, more study was recommended, but no action was taken on proposals for antinarcotic teaching in schools.

By 1960 the CIA was involved in Laos, which borders Myanmar. Over the next fifteen years they helped create a secret army of 30,000 Hmong tribesmen to battle Laotian Communists near the border with North Vietnam. The Hmong were highlanders whose main cash crop was opium, and because the CIA needed their help during the Vietnam War, the agency helped transport opium from the rough terrain of the hilly villages to processing labs in the Golden Triangle (the geographic area where Laos, Myanmar, and Thailand have common borders). The CIA's "Air America" planes were reportedly used in the illegal trafficking.

It was from the Golden Triangle laboratories that high-quality number-four heroin (90 percent to 99 percent pure) made its way to South Vietnam for use by American and Australian soldiers.[19] After the complete withdrawal of U.S. troops in 1975, these labs started to export directly to the United States and accounted for about one-third of the American heroin market.

The Golden Triangle, a major source of the world's opium supply

Perhaps the most detailed and comprehensive look at CIA involvement in the heroin trade is the book *The Politics of Heroin: CIA Complicity in the Global Drug Trade*, by Alfred W. McCoy. McCoy makes a strong case for the theory that CIA involvement actually enabled the heroin trade to expand to its current levels. He states that "at two critical junctures, the late 1940s and late 1970s, when America's heroin supply and addict population seemed to ebb, the CIA's covert action alliances generated a sudden surge of heroin that soon revived the U.S. drug trade."[20]

McCoy also stated that the successor to the Federal Bureau of Narcotics, the Bureau of Narcotics and Dangerous Drugs, failed to stem the flow of heroin from Southeast Asia. He credits the Drug Enforcement Administration (DEA), which was set up in the early 1970s, for being "a more professional agency with a global network of agents," but he says that the DEA was "unwilling to challenge the CIA when any of the CIA's covert operations become involved in the drug trade."[21]

The use of heroin by American soldiers in Vietnam during the late sixties and early seventies had reached proportions that caused great concern to military leaders, as witnessed by a crackdown on July 28, 1971, when it was announced that almost all U.S. personnel were to be tested by the Army specifically for heroin use.[22] Some believe that it was the return of the soldiers that changed the American public's perception of the heroin addict. During that time, these observers say, treatment facilities sprang up across the country, and Veteran's Administration hospitals began to treat heroin addicts in greater numbers. New treatment methods were being explored, and one of the more prevalent models was methadone maintenance.

Ebb and Flow in the Heroin Trade

Methadone is a synthetic opiate that was first experimented with during World War II by German scientists. The war had caused a shortage of morphine with which to treat the wounded, and in response the Germans invented Dolphine, which was renamed methadone in America after the war. Methadone is a highly addictive analgesic like heroin but does not produce a euphoric effect or distorted behavior once tolerance to the drug has been established.

Congress unanimously approved passage of House Resolution 9323 on November 1, 1971, permitting the use of methadone in narcotic addiction treatment programs. The Senate passed it on September 5, 1972.[23]

Methadone served two purposes: It curbed criminal behavior in addicts, and the methadone programs helped identify at least some of the country's heroin addicts because they had to register for treatment. Opinion is divided on the subject of methadone use with heroin addicts, but the drug is still being used to treat heroin addiction and is seen by many to be a viable option for many addicts. More on the history of methadone and its use as a treatment modality appears in chapter 7.

Because of treatment and law enforcement efforts by the DEA, the number of heroin addicts in America dropped from an estimated 500,000 in the late 1960s to 200,000 by the mid-1970s. Again, the United States reached a point where the tide was going in the right direction, and again international foreign policy got in the way. In 1979 the CIA supported Afghan rebels fighting the Soviet army's occupation of Afghanistan. The rebels' most valuable commodity to use in raising cash to buy arms was opium. Since the rebels' military interests coincided with American cold-war foreign policy interests—that is, stopping the spread of communism at all costs—the CIA was willing to look the other way as Afghans captured more than 60 percent of the American heroin market within one year.[24] The number of addicts swelled to its previous number of a half million by 1980.

The cocaine trade that exploded on the American and worldwide scenes during the 1980s also changed the course of the heroin trade. The major exporter of cocaine for the world is South America, specifically Colombia, which has become a major player in the heroin trade. During the 1980s Colombia did not cultivate the opium poppy; by 1997, the DEA reported that 62 percent of its heroin seizures were of Colombian heroin. In May 1996, Barry McCaffrey, head of the Office of National Drug Control Policy, estimated that Colombia cultivated 65 metric tons of opium in 1995. This is still a small percentage of the total 4,000 metric tons that were cultivated globally that year, but in light of Colombia's expertise and success in marketing cocaine, fears of increasing Colombian heroin production in years to come are not unjustified.

During the 1980s, Colombian drug cartels (notably the Cali and Medellín cartels) established sophisticated cocaine distribution networks throughout the United States. They used bribery, murder, and the lure of incredible sums of money to entice legitimate businesspeople to help them launder the billions of dollars they accumulated.

In 1990, Colombia did not have an opium crop. Colombians shied away from opium cultivation, preferring to grow coca plants, as they had for centuries. In a very short time, however, they have become a force to contend with in the heroin trade. With their U.S. cocaine distribution networks already in place, it wasn't a long stretch for them to branch off into heroin smuggling. The profits are often even greater with heroin than with cocaine. Heroin is more expensive than cocaine—a pound of pure heroin can cost ten times more than a pound of cocaine—and as a result, shipping one hundred pounds of heroin will yield a much higher profit than will shipping a hundred pounds of cocaine. In addition, heroin addicts keep coming back for more as they become increasingly dependent, because heroin is more physically addictive than cocaine. Thus, the Colombians diversified into heroin, now selling it in addition to their mainstay, cocaine.

There are many other countries producing heroin, and over

the last seven years we have seen the flow of heroin increase at alarming levels. If we look at the 1980's crack cocaine epidemic in the United States, we can appreciate what might happen now that Colombia is involved in the heroin trade. There have been reports of ever increasing purity levels of "street" heroin, and of greater numbers of people becoming addicted. Because of the higher purity it is now possible for individuals to become addicted without using a needle; the drug can be used by "sniffing" it through the nose, or by smoking it, called "chasing the dragon" in street vernacular.

No longer carrying the same stigma, perhaps because now it can be divorced from needle use, which has been one of the most reliable ways to contract the AIDS virus, heroin is attracting more middle-class American users, many of whom are becoming addicted. According to many clinicians working in the field of addiction, there seems to be a strain of denial or ignorance at work that leads these middle-class users to believe that they will not become addicted to the drug if they don't inject it.

One can look to daily news reports from around the world and conclude that we are in the midst of a resurgence of heroin use. A recent *Newsweek* article quotes Barry McCaffrey: "The bad news is heroin is back." The article states that the "Partnership for a Drug-Free America now worries that heroin will be *the* drug of the '90s."[25] It seems impossible, on close analysis, to deny that political factors continue to cause the global surges of heroin production, distribution, and use.

On one hand, American law enforcement has become heavily invested in interdiction and eradication programs with opium-producing countries, while on the other hand, the CIA may be continuing to covertly support rebel guerrillas who control the territories where the opium is cultivated. The United States has paid farmers to stop growing opium and coca, reimbursing them for lost revenues. It has helped governments, like that in Colombia, purchase helicopters and weapons to wage war with drug lords in remote jungle locations. Although current U.S. policies and actions may well be a case of the right hand not knowing what the left hand is doing, the result is a global heroin resurgence.[26]

Heroin around the World

Recent examples of foreign policy contradicting the goals of the drug war include the following:

In Afghanistan, where the Taliban fundamentalists recently overthrew the Kabul regime installed by the Soviets on their departure, farmers are starving. Desperate to make a living, they are again growing opium poppies. Coincidentally, the Taliban rebels have controlled the Helmand province in the south and the Nangahar province in the east, which together account for 80 percent of all poppy cultivation in Afghanistan. The rebels have been using the cash derived from sale of opium poppies to purchase weapons. In the face of this, the Taliban send a mixed message, asking the international community for help in fighting narcotics. "Educating people against drugs is a basic need of our people," Taliban-controlled Kabul Radio declared.[27]

No one knows how the political situation will unfold in Afghanistan, but an indicator of things to come is a report stating that half the villages in poppy-growing areas that are not already cultivating the plant were willing to start doing so in 1998. This will probably result in more heroin being available in European and American markets during 1998.

In Colombia, on October 9, 1996, the biggest heroin processing plant ever found in the country was destroyed by the government's elite antidrug police. The plant, located in the southwest part of the country in a remote mountain region, was controlled by leftist rebels of the FARC, or the Revolutionary Armed Forces of Colombia. According to a report from Reuters, "The Colombian government, and more recently U.S. anti-drug officials, have highlighted the close links between drug traffickers and leftist guerrilla movements. They say the FARC, the country's largest and oldest guerrilla force, specializes in protecting illicit drug plantations and clandestine laboratories, a charge its spokesmen deny."[28]

In Brussels, according to the European Monitoring Center for Drugs and Drug Addiction, it was reported that between 500,000 and 1,000,000 European Union citizens take heroin regularly.

In Russia, Interior Ministry officials reported that as much as 15 percent of the country's 150 million people have had contact with narcotic substances. About 80,000 crimes linked to drugs were committed in 1995, up from 16,000 in 1990. Russians are switching from drugs like hashish to heroin in increasing numbers. Much of the heroin making its way to Russia is from the Golden Triangle. Alexander Sergeyev, of the ministry's antidrug department, said that "Russian authorities were firmly against the decriminalization of any drug. The experience of countries like the Netherlands that have taken a more liberal stance showed that legalizing certain substances did not eliminate the problems of addiction."[29]

In Vietnam, Joern Kristensen of the United Nations Drug Control Programme reported that number-four heroin is being marketed near schools and colleges by food hawkers and others, often immediately outside school gates. Although it is consumed primarily by smoking, it is also mixed into cakes and drinks, or it's sold in 20-milligram packages for other forms of administration. "Vietnam has produced its own opium for many years and continues to do so in some areas despite official attempts to stamp the practice out," Kristensen states. "But drug experts say the communist country is increasingly being used as both a market and conduit for narcotics heading to Australia and the United States from the notorious Golden Triangle producing area. We don't know if all the figures are true, but in one case they took samples at a school and found a third of all the children had heroin in their urine."[30]

In Beijing, China, while Colombia's national police chief, General Rosso Jose Serrano, was visiting, the possibility of co-operation between the Chinese Mafia and Colombian drug cartels was investigated. Serrano said intelligence reports indicated that Colombian drug lords were cutting deals with members of the Chinese criminal underworld in Vancouver, British Columbia, and shipping the drug through distribution channels in North America.[31]

In Naples, Italy, a man died and two others needed emergency medical attention after overdosing on heroin while they were patients in the AIDS unit of a hospital. "The death of AIDS sufferer Giovanni Manzo, 35, at Cotugno Hospital followed a protest by another patient in the unit who set fire to sheets and a mattress to draw attention to what he alleged was open access to patients for drug pushers."[32]

The U.S. government has accused Colombian President Ernesto Samper of using drug cartel money to help finance his election campaign, sending relations between the United States and Colombia into a tailspin. Meanwhile, Brazilian and Colombian officials met in the hope of signing a cooperative agreement to combat drug smuggling along their shared border. Brazilian officials reported that Washington's offer of $710,000 in aid to fight drug smuggling was "laughable." Colombia's vice minister for justice, Carlos Alberto Malagon, said, "It's necessary that before starting talks with Washington, Latin America agrees on a unified criteria for the battle against narcotics trade."[33] Colombia was to receive $40.5 million in U.S. aid to help finance the drug war in 1996. The money was part of $112 million earmarked by Washington to be spread among Colombia, Mexico, Venezuela, Peru, and eastern Caribbean countries.

The money Colombia was to receive was to go primarily toward the purchase of river patrol boats, airplanes, all-terrain vehicles, thirty-two UH-1H helicopters ("Hueys"), and other military equipment. Approximately $30 million was to go to the military, with the rest going to the National Police. The equipment was also to be used in the fight against insurgents, since both the United States and Colombia assert that guerrillas are in control of the remote regions where drugs are cultivated and processed. This is, of course, a political issue. Is the United States in fact supporting the ruling government in its struggle against guerrillas who have been fighting in the jungles for more than thirty years, or is it helping the country's antidrug effort?

Here in the United States the White House Office on Drug Control Policy cites the National Household Survey on Drug Abuse to report that in 1994 there were 191,000 "admitted" users of heroin, an astonishing leap up from 80,000 in 1993. One can question the validity of such a survey, however, because it is hard to imagine that heroin addicts would take the time to answer such a survey in any comprehensive number. The key word here is *admitted*. The DEA estimates that more than 2.3 million people age twelve and older have used heroin.[34]

After the death in July 1996 of the rock band Smashing Pumpkins' keyboard player, Jonathan Melvoin, by heroin overdose, addicts on Manhattan's Lower East Side were desperately scrambling for the strain of heroin that killed the musician, "Red Rum"—*murder* spelled backwards—according to New York City police.[35]

"Heroin is the pot of the '90s," says Caroline Lettieri, *Sassy* magazine fashion editor. She claims to have heard fourteen-year-old Los Angeles–area high school students say offhandedly, "Everyone at school is smoking black tar, a low-grade Mexican heroin."[36] In Los Angeles, U.S. Congresswoman Maxine Waters accused the CIA of helping to sell crack cocaine in black neighborhoods to fund right-wing Contra rebels in Nicaragua in 1986. The CIA has denied any involvement and there has been no hard evidence to support the claim, but the Justice Department began an investigation and the CIA began an internal inquiry into the matter.[37] Not surprisingly, the mainstream media were quick to discredit the claims and nothing has come of the amazing accusations.

All around the world, government officials are meeting and trying to devise strategies to combat the resurgence of heroin production and use. Meanwhile, the news media chronicle the epidemic as if it were a new phenomenon. The fact is, heroin never left and never goes away totally. Its use merely ebbs and flows, and when the drug begins to strike at the majority white culture, it becomes newsworthy—while for decades people of color living in poverty have been caught, from generation to generation, in the heroin scourge.

One thing is certain: because of the various geographic locations where heroin starts on its journey into the bloodstreams of addicts, it would be highly problematic to assume that interdiction and eradication programs are the only or even the best course of intervention. Addicts will always find a way to procure drugs. It is not enough to limit the supply without also decreasing the demand for the drug with prevention, education, and treatment programs, and addressing the underlying social problems that create subcultures of poverty and drugs.

CHAPTER

3

The Pharmacology
and Physiology
of Heroin Use

I spent a lot of time being sick. . . . It got so bad I was
afraid I *wasn't* gonna die.

A HEROIN ADDICT DESCRIBING WITHDRAWAL

Approximately thirty to sixty seconds after injecting heroin
intravenously, the user feels a surge of warmth, emanating
from the low spinal area, as a "rush" of sensation glides
through the central nervous system. An overriding sense of
well-being quickly envelops the user. This sense of well-being
is the user's grail, the reason the user engages repeatedly in
what objectively may appear to be the utterly bizarre seeking,
acquiring, and self-administering behaviors involved with
heroin use—behaviors that risk imprisonment, interpersonal
violence, social condemnation, physical disfigurement, disease, and death. Although many of these risks result from the
laws concerning heroin rather than anything inherent in the
drug's effects on the user's body and mind, per se, that the feeling induced by heroin could draw a person to repeatedly run
so severe a gauntlet does speak to the potency of that "sense of
well-being" and to the substance's addictive power. What is
this sensation really all about? Where does this chemical diacetylmorphine—heroin—come from, and what does it do
when it is introduced into the bloodstream?

The Chemical Manufacture of Heroin

The trail leading to this climactic rush of drug-induced euphoria begins with the planting and harvesting of the opium poppy plant, *Papaver somniferum*, on remote mountain hillsides in Colombia, Myanmar, Mexico, Thailand, Laos, Afghanistan, and Pakistan, among other locales around the globe. When the poppy flower petals fall it is time for harvest (usually two crops are yielded per year). The harvester makes several incisions on the seed bulb that is left standing, using a short, crescent-shaped knife. A milky white sap oozes from these incisions. This sap is left to dry in the hot sun; when it has turned brown, it is harvested by scraping it from the bulbs into burlap bags. The bags are secured with rope by field hands who transport the harvest, usually on the backs of mules, to clandestine chemical processing plants or refineries, where the dried brown poppy sap undergoes the transformation from raw opium to pure morphine under the supervision of an experienced chemist.

The chemist first heats the raw opium in a large oil drum filled with water, stirring with a wooden stick or paddle until it dissolves. He then adds ordinary lime fertilizer, which adheres to any organic waste, leaving a milky substance floating near the surface. The liquid is then poured through a flannel filtering cloth into another drum. While this liquid is heated and stirred again, the chemist adds concentrated ammonia, causing the morphine to solidify and drop to the bottom of the drum. The drum is again drained and filtered, leaving behind chunks of white morphine to be dried. The ratio of raw opium to pure morphine is usually 10 percent; that is, one hundred pounds of raw opium yield ten pounds of pure morphine.

After drying, the morphine is ready to be processed into diacetylmorphine, or heroin. A four-stage chemical process is used to refine the morphine into number-four heroin, the purest form of illegal high-grade heroin.

*A worker scoring
poppy bulbs to harvest opium
in the Arghandab valley
in southern Afghanistan*

Reuters/Stringer/Archive Photos

*Collecting raw opium
in a poppy field in
southern Afghanistan*

Reuters/Stringer/Archive Photos

*Raw opium oozing from
incisions on a poppy bulb.
The opium is ready to be harvested.*

Photo courtesy of the
Drug Enforcement Administration,
U.S. Department of Justice

*An antidrug agent holds
confiscated opium in a
drug lab in Osh, Kyrgyzstan.*

Reuters/Shamil Zhumatov/
Archive Photos

First, equal amounts of acetic anhydride and morphine are mixed in a glass flask and heated for six hours at exactly 185 degrees Fahrenheit. The acid and morphine bond together, leaving an impure form of heroin.

In the second stage, the solution is treated with water and chloroform until the impurities solidify and drop to the bottom, leaving a somewhat higher grade of heroin. This is then drained off into another container and sodium carbonate is added until the crude heroin particles begin to solidify and drop.

After the heroin particles are filtered out of the sodium carbonate solution under pressure by a small suction pump, they are purified in a solution of alcohol and activated charcoal. The new mixture is heated until the alcohol begins to evaporate, leaving relatively pure granules of heroin at the bottom of the flask. This is stage three of the process and produces what is known as number-three heroin.

In the fourth stage, the heroin is placed in a large flask and dissolved in alcohol. As ether and hydrochloric acid are added to the solution, tiny white flakes begin to form. The flakes are filtered out under pressure and dried, resulting in a white powder that is 80 percent to 99 percent pure heroin, depending on the chemist and lab facilities. This is known as number-four heroin.[1]

Street Heroin

Until recently it was unusual to find number-four heroin at the street or retail level. As the drug wends its way through the distribution network it is "cut," or adulterated, with any number of additives in order to increase the quantity, thereby increasing profit. Cutting agents such as quinine, milk sugar, starch, powdered milk, and even talcum powder have been discovered in samples confiscated from retail buyers. One of the many dangers that heroin users face comes from the adulterants added by the person selling the drug. For example, talcum powder does not dissolve when injected into the bloodstream, but forms little particles that can cause vein blockage. In the summer of 1995, New York City recorded fourteen heroin overdoses in one weekend as a result of heroin laced with fentanyl, a synthetic opioid.

Because heroin is a black-market commodity, it is difficult for users to determine the relative quality of the products they buy. In the competitive heroin street market, however, as in commercial markets for legal products, retailers seek to gain an advantage by developing "brand names." New York City police recently discovered, for example, that a deadly heroin street brand called "Tango & Cash," which had resulted in the deaths of several users, had originated from a lone retailer on the Lower East Side of Manhattan. They were able to determine this because heroin dealers routinely stamp the glassine envelopes in which the drug is packaged with their own brand names—names such as "DOA," as in "dead on arrival," or the equally candid and evocative "Body Bag." Authorities in Baltimore, Maryland, faced an emergency situation in 1996 with a rash of overdoses resulting from a brand of heroin called "Red Rum"—*murder* spelled backwards. The results in both cities were numerous deaths and emergency room interventions.[2]

Contrary to what one might expect, overdoses are not bad for a particular brand name's business. A common practice among heroin users looking to make a retail purchase is to ask other users who has the "good product" on the street. They may hear, for example, that "Poison" is good tonight, but stay away from "Over the Top." Invariably, the prospective buyer is being told to avoid a particular brand not because the heroin will cause an overdose, but because it has been adulterated too much, resulting in a weak "high." Reported overdoses from a particular brand mean a purer product to the street addict; thus, that brand usually becomes more desirable on the black market, not less.

As in the world of legal commerce, brand names provide a

mechanism for dealers to develop return customers. An effective marketing technique used by street dealers is to put a brand on the street with a higher-than-average level of purity for two or three days. The word that a dealer's heroin is especially potent rapidly spreads among the users, so that by the fourth day many users will be looking for that brand. The dealers will then slowly decrease the purity of the heroin they sell over the next few days, maximizing their profits, until

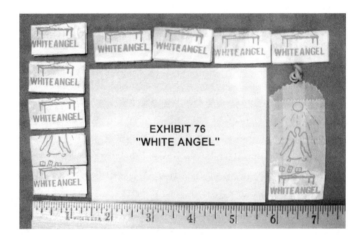

Seized glassine envelopes of heroin stamped with brand names

Photo courtesy of the Drug Enforcement Administration,
U.S. Department of Justice

word gets out that a particular brand has become unacceptably adulterated, at which point the users will drift away to try to find whoever is retailing the purer heroin. Competing dealers will often be forced to increase their purity levels to regain customers or to capture the market for short periods of time.

In 1980, according to figures released by the Drug Enforcement Administration, the average bag of street heroin was less than 4 percent pure; today, the average purity can be as high as 71 percent. New York City and Newark, New Jersey, have reported heroin purity levels as high as 79 percent, and in isolated cases in Manhattan during 1995, the DEA made undercover purchases of $10 bags that were 94 percent heroin. Baltimore, Maryland, and Philadelphia, Pennsylvania, have also been deluged with abnormally pure heroin.[3]

The increase in purity can be attributed largely to greater availability, more sophisticated processing labs, and the marketing techniques used by street-level retailers of the drug. Certainly, the involvement of Colombian drug cartels in the heroin business since 1991 has been a major factor in the presence of number-four heroin at the retail level. According to the DEA, informants report that because of the first processes used by Colombian chemists, their number-four heroin was initially hard to adulterate. Early attempts at cutting the pure heroin resulted in ruined product. Retail distributors decided to just put the heroin on the street as it was delivered, causing an increase in hospital emergency room visits for the users unaccustomed to such pure heroin. The smuggling and distribution of heroin will be discussed further in later chapters.

Using Heroin

Administered intravenously, "sniffed" through the nose, or smoked, heroin is distributed through the body by the bloodstream. When insufflated through the nose in powder form or through the mouth by smoking, the heroin enters the bloodstream by absorption into the capillaries of the lungs. Heroin can also be injected via a hypodermic syringe into a muscle, subcutaneously (just below the skin; called "skin popping"), or directly into a vein.

The most potent form of ingestion is intravenous injection, also called "mainlining." The effect of the drug is almost immediate using this method, whereas the effects of smoking or sniffing heroin usually occur within several minutes of inhalation and are milder. With the trend toward higher purity levels, however, sniffing has risen steadily in popularity over the past five years, partly due to the fear of HIV infection from needle sharing and a general stigma attached to needle use. Drug treatment facilities across the country, particularly on the East Coast from Maine to Florida, report a dramatic increase in the number of individuals they are seeing addicted to heroin as their primary drug. They report greater numbers of both heroin inhalers and heroin injectors. The Pulse Check Report for the summer of 1997 concluded that the increases could

A woman injecting heroin
Popperfoto

"Works" for administering heroin intravenously
Photo: Dennis Becker

have been due to addicts graduating from sniffing to injecting, further proof of the highly addictive nature of high-quality heroin. Interestingly, many hospitals report seeing rising numbers of cocaine addicts who use heroin as a secondary drug, possibly in an effort to counter the sleeplessness and anxiety that typically result after several days of bingeing on cocaine.

Almost invariably, heroin users start by inhaling the drug, via sniffing or smoking, and eventually graduate to needle use. This can be largely attributed to increased tolerance, because regular heroin use demands that increasing quantities be consumed for the same effect, and to the user knowing that injection will provide a greater euphoria. Another reason for graduation to needle use is that exposure to drug culture can reduce the stigma of mainlining and present the opportunity to use a sterile needle. Using unsterile needles, or needle sharing, occurs out of desperation and limited availability of clean syringes; it can result in HIV infection, as well as septicemia (blood poisoning), hepatitis, endocarditis (inflammation of the heart lining), skin abscesses, or tetanus.[4]

Once an addict buys heroin, the next stop is to the person who usually stands up the block, not far from the heroin dealer, advertising his wares with an almost mantralike pitch— "Sealed works. . . . I got sealed works." To the uninitiated it is an unintelligible solicitation, but to the addict with a jumpy stomach, it is a call that brings him or her a step closer to home. "Sealed works," an unopened syringe package, is what the addict looks for, and it becomes important to know who are the reputable retailers of syringes and who is selling used, repackaged syringes. The problem is that the user will not know until he or she opens the wrapper and feels the sharpness of the needle against his or her skin. An unused needle should pierce the skin easily, but if it doesn't, the addict has to live with the next decision—to finish the shot or put everything away and go back out to buy another syringe.

Once the user decides to inject the drug, he or she performs a ritual that may come to provide comfort, gratifying in and of itself, as the familiar steps leading to the high. In field interviews conducted with heroin addicts during 1996, many reported that they experienced nausea and gastrointestinal reactions immediately before they injected themselves. To a nonuser this doesn't sound appealing, but to a preconditioned mind, the psychosomatic nausea signals anticipation of a strong dose and is welcomed.

"Shooting" heroin is a relatively complex process. First, the powdered heroin is poured from the glassine envelope into a spoon, metal lid, or bottle cap. Water is then drawn into a syringe and squirted into the powder. Heat must be applied to the bottom of the spoon with a match or cigarette lighter in order for the powder to fully dissolve and for any adulterants to burn away. (It should be noted that the higher the purity level, the quicker the powder dissolves; some addicts report that high-quality heroin has a distinct odor when heated.) Once the heroin is fully liquefied, a piece of cotton, or the white fibrous filter tip torn from a cigarette, is used to filter the liquid into the syringe. Impurities are left behind in the form of a milky liquid. The next step is to apply a tourniquet to the upper arm if injecting into the crook of the arm (the antecubital fossa), or to the lower forearm if the point of injection is the back of the hand. When the veins engorge, the needle is slowly inserted directly into a vein at a forty-five-degree angle. This is arguably the trickiest point in the process, because "missing," or improperly injecting away from the vein, results in a painful, hot, swollen blister and minimal euphoria. Commonly referred to by addicts as "blowing the shot," it is considered a waste of heroin after what can sometimes be a long and dangerous effort to purchase the drug.[5]

Once the needle pierces the skin and a vein is located, the user slowly pulls back on the syringe plunger; if he or she is in the vein, a trickle of blood will come up into the syringe, signaling a successful attempt. The tourniquet is loosened, and the dose can then be administered by pushing down on the plunger of the syringe. Some users reportedly "boot" several times after all of the liquid is injected; that is, they draw back on the plunger, drawing out blood and reinjecting it. There is no medical proof that this practice increases the effect of the heroin; it has become a part, nonetheless, of drug-culture ritual and myth.

The Physiological Effects of Heroin

All of the effects that result from a heroin injection occur very rapidly, usually within thirty to sixty seconds after the heroin enters the bloodstream. Affected are the central nervous, cardiovascular, respiratory, gastrointestinal, genitourinary, and endocrine systems, and the skin.[6] What was described earlier as an initial warm rush of sensation is the reaction of the central nervous system. An instant euphoria combined with sedation

A heroin addict experiencing "the nod" following injection.
Photo courtesy of the Drug Enforcement Administration,
U.S. Department of Justice

results in what is known as "the nod," or sleepiness, most users exhibit. Stress and anxiety are immediately reduced, and physical pain is greatly diminished. The pupils of the eyes become constricted, or "pinned" in street vernacular. Medically, this constriction of the pupils is known as miosis, and it occurs almost immediately after injection. The "pinning" is a measure of how strong or pure the heroin is—the smaller the pupil becomes, the purer the heroin.

Also within seconds, both the rate and depth of respiration sharply decrease. Although heroin causes minimal effect on the cardiovascular system, with only a slight reduction in blood pressure and heart rate noted in a supine position, in a heads-up or sitting position, hypotension, or lowered blood pressure, often results. Many users report fainting when they attempt to stand up after injecting heroin. This is caused by orthostatic hypotension, a condition occurring when the blood in the veins and arteries in the lower parts of the body is not returned to the heart, lungs, and brain quickly enough.[7]

In the gastrointestinal tract there is decreased propulsive movement of the intestines after a dose of heroin, and increased tone or tightening of the anal sphincter.[8] Thus, a strong dose of heroin usually results in constipation. Nausea and vomiting may also occur. Urination often becomes difficult and sometimes painful due to increased tone of the bladder sphincter and ureter. A dribble instead of a steady stream of urine often results.

Following heroin ingestion, the endocrine system increases the release of ACTH (adrenocorticotropic hormone), which places strain on the adrenal glands. Increased production of the female hormone prolactin occurs along with a decreased release of luteinizing hormone. Prolactin is the hormone associated with lactation. Luteinizing hormone affects ovary function and sperm production. In the male, sperm production is decreased; in the female, menstrual cycles can be altered.[9]

Heroin use causes the skin to feel flush and warm and can

cause sweating and a general itchiness. Many addicts gauge the purity of the drug by how quickly they begin to sweat and how itchy they feel, although quinine, sometimes present as a cutting agent, can also produce itchiness.

Again, all of these effects occur almost immediately, giving the user instant gratification. To an addict, ill effects such as constipation, lowered blood pressure, and inability to urinate are a small price to pay for the analgesia, or elimination of physical and emotional pain, that a dose of heroin provides. The warm, glowing feeling has been equated metaphorically by some with a return to the womb. It is no wonder that this euphoria is found to be so compelling psychologically and physically; after all, pain and pleasure are our most primal motivators. Thus, the compulsion to use despite adverse consequences is fueled by very basic brain functions, perhaps the most important element to consider when trying to understand why someone would use such a dangerous, addictive substance.

Heroin and the Brain

The psychoactive ingredient in heroin is morphine; it is the agent that causes the euphoric effect, analgesia, and sedation associated with the heroin high. Morphine is a relatively simple molecule produced in the body when its organs metabolize heroin. The heroin high occurs as the morphine molecules attach themselves to opiate receptors located in the central nervous system.

Once the liver rapidly metabolizes heroin into morphine molecules, the morphine works its way to the brain. It was discovered in 1973 that opioid compounds such as morphine exert their effects on the body through a system of receptors located throughout the central nervous system. One of the pioneers in this field was Stanford University pharmacologist Avram Goldstein, who was researching neurons in the brain.[10] He theorized that the body had a chain of receptors that produced pleasure when flooded with an opiate. In 1974, Solomon Snyder and Candace Pert, working at Johns Hopkins University, discovered that there were indeed opiate receptors located in the brain that fit, or bonded with, morphine molecules. They determined this by injecting into test subjects radio-labeled naloxone (an antagonist that reverses the effects of an opiate) that was later identified with a radiation counter. They found that the naloxone bonded specifically to several regions of the brain.[11]

Why would humans and all other vertebrates have receptors that respond to the derivatives of the opium poppy plant? Heroin is a synthetic substance. Why would we be designed biologically to accommodate the morphine molecules it produces in the body? These were the questions on the minds of scientists as they considered the discoveries of Goldstein, Snyder, and Pert. They theorized that the body must produce a naturally occurring opioid for which these receptors were intended. With this theory in mind, John Hughes and Hans Kosterlitz, working at the University of Aberdeen in Scotland, were the first to isolate, in 1975, a substance from the brains of pigs that had the same activity as morphine. They called the substance enkephalin, meaning "in the head."[12] They discovered that enkephalins are peptides, or small chains of amino acids, that the body produces naturally in response to internal and external stimuli. For example, the body produces this natural opioid in order to relieve the stress of danger or pain of a wound, preventing shock. So, the receptors are not really opiate receptors at all but enkephalin receptors, although they have come to be commonly known by the former term.

The enkephalins are similar in architecture to the morphine molecules produced when heroin is metabolized, though the morphine molecules are not peptides and have a different chemical makeup. The key is the architectural similarity. Because morphine is "built" similarly it locks into the receptors designated for enkephalins, and the body responds with pleasure and euphoria. A good comparison would be two interlocking pieces of a jigsaw puzzle or a key fitting into a lock. When the morphine binds to an enkephalin receptor, pain is reduced and pleasure or euphoria results.

Subsequent research has proved that the body produces endogenous morphines, or natural morphines, also known as endorphins. Endorphins are well known among long-distance runners as the biochemical that produces the "runner's high." After running thirty to forty minutes or longer, many runners experience a joyful, euphoric state. The body releases the endorphins to relieve the stress and pain the runner is experiencing. But endorphins aren't just for runners. Tests have shown that when a woman is in labor and suffering contractions, endorphins are released into the blood at a rate as high as ten times the normal level. This is the body's natural effort to survive the stress and pain of childbirth and to preserve the life of the mother and unborn child.

The brain is an amazing computerlike organ that is programmed for survival. When it receives stimuli warning of impending danger, it responds with the chemical necessary to weather the crisis. Studies have shown that stress causes endorphins to be released from the pituitary gland, located at the base of the brain; it is the body's way of protecting itself from pain.[13]

Just as heroin is highly addictive, the body's endogenous morphines also are addictive. It seems that any agent that binds to the opiate receptors proves to be addictive, a result of the brain's perception that it needs these substances in order to survive. Once a heroin-dependent state is achieved, the brain will send signals to the rest of the body, summoning it to feed more morphine into the bloodstream. A quick tolerance is developed, however, and the body will require increasingly larger doses to achieve a state of euphoria, until it reaches a point where heroin needs to be taken every four to six hours just to stave off withdrawal syndrome. A heroin-dependent state can be achieved after a relatively short time, depending

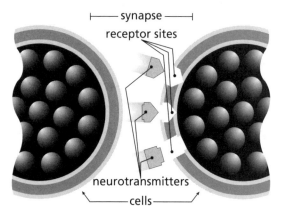

There are several types of neurotransmitters, including enkephalins, endorphins, dopamine, epinephrine (adrenaline), and norepinephrine. Each type is shaped to fit into its corresponding receptor site in the nerve cell.

Medical Aspects of Chemical Dependency Workbook, Hazelden Publishing

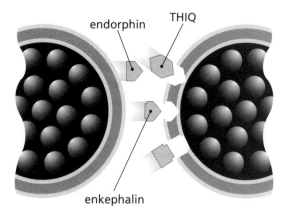

A chemical called THIQ is produced when the brain breaks down narcotics. THIQ, which is shaped almost like an endorphin or enkephalin, fits directly into those receptor sites.

Medical Aspects of Chemical Dependency Workbook, Hazelden Publishing

on the purity of the drug, how often it is taken, and the person's rate of metabolism. For example, a person injecting heroin every day for five to ten days will likely wake up on the eleventh day experiencing withdrawal syndrome.

— Heroin withdrawal signs and symptoms may include sleeplessness, lacrimation (excessive tearing of the eyes), yawning, muscular aches and spasms, piloerection (goose pimples), stomach cramps, hyperventilation, hypothermia, mydriasis (excessive dilation of the pupils) and inability to focus one's vision, joint pain, vomiting, diarrhea, alternating hot and cold flashes, anxiety, and hostile behavior. The expression "cold turkey" is derived from the way the skin looks with goose pimples. The onset of withdrawal usually occurs within twelve hours after the last dose of heroin and can last as long as seventy-two to ninety-six hours, peaking at about thirty-six to forty-eight hours. The severity of heroin withdrawal depends on the severity of dependence and the amount to which the user is accustomed. A person with a slight habit can generally go to bed with what appear to be flu-like symptoms and feel well enough to return to work after a day or two, whereas a person who is using large quantities each day will feel like screaming for relief from the torture of withdrawal.[14]

Much study has been conducted in the area of physical effects of withdrawal, but less is known about the psychological and emotional effects of the syndrome. Field interviews with heroin addicts reveal that the level of despair one feels can be excruciating. Hopelessness, regret, and guilt pervade the addict's consciousness. The combination of physical and emotional symptoms serves to place the addict in an extremely vulnerable position. Consequently, this is one of the best times in addiction treatment to confront the addict's denial of addiction.

Once the initial stage of withdrawal is past, usually within five days, a secondary phase of protracted symptoms can last for several months. The secondary phase is characterized by low blood pressure, dilated pupils, and a general listlessness. The user experiences strong cravings for the drug and usually winds up repeating the cycle of use, leading to tolerance and dependence all over again, unless he or she receives proper medical and pharmacological treatment, psychosocial counseling, and peer support.

Withdrawal from heroin is not life threatening, but it is, as we have seen, very uncomfortable. In a supervised medical detoxification setting, prescribed drugs can be given to alleviate some of the symptoms. For example, clonidine is commonly used to counteract increased blood pressure. Methadone eliminates the body's physical craving for opiates. For detoxification purposes, a therapeutic dose is given periodically, usually twice a day, and the patient is gradually weaned off the methadone over a period of two to three days, depending on the severity of withdrawal and pain. This will be discussed at greater length in chapter 7.

Overdose

What happens when too much heroin is ingested? Heroin toxicity, or overdose, causes the user to become stuporous or comatose, and if the amount consumed is large enough, death can result.[15] As noted earlier, heroin suppresses the respiratory rate and depth, and with large doses, the rate of breathing can fall to as low as two to four breaths per minute. As respiratory rate declines, blood pressure begins to drop. Body temperature plummets, and the skin becomes cold and clammy, eventually turning blue-gray in color. Seizures may occur and, eventually, respiratory failure occurs. The portion of the brain (brain stem) that controls breathing becomes flooded with the drug, and the message to the diaphragm and lungs to breathe is disrupted. The body just stops breathing.

It is possible to reverse these effects with timely medical intervention. An injection of a narcotic antagonist like naltrexone or naloxone will counteract the effects of the heroin. The antagonist molecules will bind to the opiate receptors, displacing the morphine that was flooding the site. The result is an instant state of withdrawal, and the patient is resuscitated.[16] Oxygen is administered to help the patient resume breathing, since the initial breaths taken after an overdose are extremely painful, and leave a burning sensation with each attempt to draw air into the lungs.

If a heroin user overdoses and there is no one to summon medical help, however, he or she will slip into a comatose state, stop breathing within twenty to thirty minutes, and die.

It is common in the culture of heroin for an addict to discover an overdose victim, check for a pulse to see if he or she is alive, and then go through the victim's pockets for money or drugs. An addict often will check the empty bags of heroin lying around a victim for a brand name, then seek to buy that brand because he or she knows it must be potent. Again, this is a powerful indication of the insidious nature of heroin addiction.

two

THE ADDICT

CHAPTER

4

The Psychology and Culture of the Heroin Addict

You don't need a Ph.D. to figure this out. I got high
'cause it was good to me. . . .

JOHN M., recovering heroin addict

John M.'s Story

John M. drives up to the Holland Tunnel tollbooth in his ten-year-old car, hands the attendant a $20 bill, and waits for his change. As he waits, his stomach flutters, reminding him it's been two days since his last shot of heroin. *Why does he have to count the money three times?* John thinks. *Come on already.* He takes his change and steps on the gas. The car responds with the low rumble of a muffler in need of repair. He makes a mental note to get it fixed and hopes it's not loud enough to cause him to be pulled over. It's not like he needs another reason to stand out. The old car, the long hair, the New Jersey plates in a drug neighborhood. But these concerns are all secondary to the mission at hand. He is on his way to cop.

His stomach started acting funny that afternoon after lunch break. That morning, his boss called him into the office, and he thought he was in trouble; he knew he shouldn't have taken off last Monday, but he just couldn't help it. If he had come to work in the shape he was in he would've been fired on the spot. But it wasn't trouble after all, just his boss giving him an

envelope for Christmas, three days away. A hundred and fifty bucks cash. Found money. His wife didn't know about it so there would be no questions about what he did with it. It was then he started to feel queasy. He hadn't been feeling so great to begin with, but that was nothing new. He was learning how to get through the weekly withdrawals. This was something else—it was that feeling he always got when he knew he was going to get high. His hands got sweaty, his stomach churned, and the clock didn't seem to move fast enough. It was usually on paydays that he got this way. Every Thursday, except those paydays when his wife told him not to come home if he didn't have all the money. There were bills to pay, the rent was overdue by three weeks, and Christmas was just three days away. He thought for a moment of buying that Fisher-Price toy for the baby, maybe that necklace his wife had admired in the jewelry store window. But it lasted only a moment.

He asked to leave work forty-five minutes early to beat the holiday rush-hour traffic. And now here he was. He waits at the light on Canal Street, makes the left onto West Broadway, and heads north toward Houston wondering who is going to be out on the street tonight and hoping his purchase will be quick, and good. He pulls the car over two blocks past Clinton into a rare open parking spot. This is a good sign, the god of parking spaces is with him—definitely a good omen. He starts to feel good as the cold December air seeps through his thin coat, his lucky coat—he hasn't ever been busted wearing this one. The smell of pine as he walks past a stand selling Christmas trees reminds him of past years, believing in Santa Claus, the way his mother's house smelled on Christmas morning. His mother.

There seems to be a looseness in the neighborhood tonight. Even here in the ghetto, where cool and wary is a way of life, the hard edges feel softer tonight. He watches an overweight lady struggling with two oversized shopping bags, one in each hand, a roll of wrapping paper standing at attention in one of the bags. She wishes a merry Christmas to two men who wave and smile at her through the window of the barbershop. Their smiles fade when he catches their eyes.

At the end of the block he spots a cluster of people leaning against the familiar building. He recognizes a couple of the men, their ragtag appearance evidence of their heroin habits. *That's good*, he thinks. The men and one young woman are standing in line waiting for a man to come out of the building with a bundle. Two lookouts sit across the street on a stoop, eyeing the group and the other pedestrians on the street. Another lookout is stationed on the roof opposite from where the people are standing in line.

John takes his place in the line. A beefy, round-faced man who appears comfortable in his role as bouncer keeps order. If he doesn't know you, you can't get in line. His job is to keep undercovers from making buys. "Ho, ho, ho, you all, just sit tight. Be another couple of minutes," he says.

No one speaks to the others in line. This is the hardest part, these few minutes of vulnerability, exposed for all to see, not knowing when the man is going to come out. Sometimes, if the man is spooked they make you walk around the block a few times; other times, they aren't open for business at all. But tonight they are open. A teenage boy rides up on a jazzy bicycle. As if synchronized, the man emerges from the building, grabs a small brown paper bag from the boy, and approaches the line of waiting addicts.

John can see the glassine bundles in the man's hand. He stands fifth in line and hopes that they won't run out before he gets his turn. That would mean a walk around the block a few times, or he would have to search out his plan-B spot. By this time his stomach is really dancing. He can't stop his jaw from shivering, though it isn't that cold. The bouncer barks orders. "Have your money ready, no singles."

Finally, he is at the head of the line. "Six, gimme six." The man counts out six glassines marked in red ink with a rubber stamp: "Poison." He gives the man three crisp $20 bills. For some reason he wishes the dealer a merry Christmas, then feels funny about it when the dealer gives him a quizzical look and says, "Yeah, merry Christmas to you too. Next."

He pockets the heroin and rounds the corner heading to Stanton Street. In the middle of the block he takes two dollar bills out and gives them to an old woman missing her top two front teeth. She dances from one foot to the other trying to keep warm and greets him with, "Sealed works, fresh works." He takes the plastic-wrapped syringe from her hand and hides it in his coat lining through the hole in the pocket. He knows her to be reputable, not like the guys on 2nd and Avenue B who sell used needles resealed in their original wrappers. He notices his stomach has calmed down. He continues walking and takes the steps leading up to the doorway of the building where he will buy his cocaine.

Taking the stairs two at a time, he makes his way to the third floor, catches his breath, and knocks out the code on the door. He sees the peephole darken, then hears the metallic snap of the deadbolt unlocking as the door opens for him.

"Yo, merry Christmas," he greets the doorman.

"Yeah, merry Christmas," the man says, smiling.

He walks into the kitchen just to the right of the entrance where a young man with shiny, walnut-colored skin sits behind a folding card table. A balance scale, tablespoon, strainer, and pocketknife are on the table; a single kitchen chair sits facing him. Chinese food containers and a couple of paper plates crowd a small counter next to the sink. A cheap radio blares out a fast-paced merengue, its dizzy, frantic rhythm distorted by the tiny speaker. He can't understand how they can listen to it without going crazy, yet it always seems to be playing when he comes here. Seems like it's always the same song, too, or maybe they all just sound the same to him.

He slaps and shakes the young man's hand.

"What can I do for you today?" the young man asks. It was always the same, right down to business.

"Half a gram." He takes out a twenty and places it on the table, watching as the cocaine is weighed out. The young man's hands are deft and his sharp eye is probably just as accurate as the O'Haus scale he uses to measure the half gram. As the glistening little rocks are scraped into a piece of foil, he experiences an antiseptic, hospital taste in his mouth. Addicts describe this as tasting the way a hospital smells. This is the moment he has anticipated for hours.

"Can I use the bathroom?" he asks as he takes the foil package.

He walks down a dark narrow hallway, lit only by the warm light spilling from an open bedroom door. As he passes the bedroom, he is startled to see the figure of a young woman stretched across the bed on her stomach, sipping from a can of Pepsi. She smiles a dreamy, sad smile at him and brushes the hair away from her eyes. As she moves, her bathrobe opens just enough for him to see she isn't wearing a bra. He smiles back and keeps walking.

The bathroom is at the end of the long hallway. A nearly spent, dark gray lightbulb angles precariously, half screwed into the wall socket above the small clouded mirror and sink. He screws the bulb in so that it lights the room; then he closes and latches the door. He works his arms out of his coat, takes out the packaged syringe, and places two of the heroin glassines on the edge of the sink. Next, he removes from his front left pants pocket the lid from a jar of Hellmann's mayonnaise. It seems warm in the room; he feels the wetness under his arms. He empties the heroin into the lid and then opens the syringe. He turns on the faucet to draw some water into the Hellmann's lid but nothing comes out. He bends down to check the main water valve under the sink and tries again. Nothing. No water. *The water must have been turned off,* he thinks. The building super is probably working on a stubborn furnace in the basement. He tries the other faucet. Again, nothing, no hot or cold water. His stomach rises up to meet his throat; it is all he

can do to keep it down. He curses to himself. *Now what?* he
thinks. He can't go into the kitchen and ask for water because
there's probably none in there either, and he knows they don't
want anybody getting off in the bathroom. He was warned
about this once before but gets away with it if he is quick and
careful not to leave any blood or empty bags behind.

The toilet. Looking into the seatless toilet he notices there
is a pool of water about four inches deep in the bowl. Lifting
the heavy enamel top from the toilet's water tank, he gingerly
places it on the floor so as to not make any noise. The tank
is full.

The hell with it, he thinks, as he draws up a syringe full of
water from the tank. He holds the syringe up to the light, in-
spects the water, and decides it looks okay.

He pushes the plunger on the syringe, squirting water into
the heroin powder, then strikes a match and waves it just under the metal lid. The liquid bubbles and the heroin quickly
dissolves with very little heat required. *That's good*, he thinks.
Sometimes the dope is so good it needs hardly any fire to dissolve it. Next, he shakes in a couple of small rocks of cocaine
from the foil wrapper and is impressed that they vanish immediately in the solution. He swirls the liquid around, rips open
the filter from one of his Marlboros, and uses the white fibers
as a strainer through which to draw the liquid speedball into
the syringe. He carefully places the loaded syringe between his
teeth. He rolls up his sleeve, removes his belt with one hand,
and takes a seat on the edge of the toilet. He wraps the belt
tight around his right arm and hopes he can get a clean hit on
one of the veins he watches come up. *There, I'll go there.*

The needle point feels sharp going in, which is good; it
means he's got an unused needle. When he pulls back on the
plunger a little stream of blood slithers up into the syringe, dis-
coloring the slightly yellow liquid. He loosens the belt, careful
not to dislodge the needle from the vein, takes a breath, and
slowly pushes the liquid into his arm. He doesn't bother draw-

ing back once all of the solution is injected; he just pulls the needle out and dabs with his finger at the drop of blood left behind on his arm. As he does this he feels the freeze in his arm from the cocaine. His arm feels numb. Then it reaches his stomach and mouth. His heart races. He tastes the medicinal flavor just as the first wave of rushes is reaching his brain. His stomach heaves. His scalp tingles and he gets a little scared at first—the wave of sensation is stronger than usual. As he fights the urge to vomit, the heroin kicks in and the nausea retreats as the warm, heroin heat replaces the heart-thumping freeze caused by the cocaine. His heart starts to slow down, or so it seems. A quiet, hollow siren rages in his head. The familiar beads of perspiration crowd each other on his forehead, and one drops onto his arm when he bends over to begin cleaning everything up. He puts away his paraphernalia, threads his belt into his pants, and sits down again. *Good stuff, very good*, he thinks as he nods for a second.

Loud pounding on the door. "You all right?"

He flushes the toilet, undoes the latch, and walks past the scowling doorman, who growls, "I ain't going to tell you again, man."

"That's okay, man, I'm all right."

On the way out he wishes them a merry Christmas.

"Yeah, you too. See you next week."

Making his way back to his car he is filled with the warm glow of heroin, Christmas, and memories of his mother. He wonders if she can see him from wherever it is you go to in the next life. He hopes not.

Back on Houston Street now, he decides to have a cup of espresso in a little coffee shop he comes upon. Sitting back at a table with a view of the street, he savors the thick hot coffee, lights a cigarette, and blows the smoke to the ceiling. *Nothing hurts,* he thinks. The lousy job that he needs to hold onto, the flak he catches from his wife, the fact that he is turning forty and doesn't have anything to show for his life—none of it fazes him, but he still thinks about it. A spotty work history, no college, and rent that is three weeks late don't matter right now. He feels warm, loose, and sexy. Was the waitress's smile a flirt or was she smiling because she caught him nodding? *Doesn't matter.* He smiles back anyway, and thinks maybe he can buy his wife a gold-plated necklace instead of the real one. It will look just like the one she pointed out anyway.

And that was what he did.

The Psychology of Addiction

The preceding narrative was reconstructed from seven interviews with John M., a New York City heroin addict in early recovery, during January 1997. The more I listened to John recalling one of his last heroin episodes, the more aware I became of how much his story revealed. I had him tell it to me over and over again. His faithful recollection of how he felt at the time and what was going on both internally and all around him allows us to clearly identify his pain, and to see how important ritual was to him. He used heroin to offset his boredom and frustration with his economic station in life. He used heroin to connect, to establish relationships, to meet unfulfilled sexual fantasies, and to feel like an important man.

None of this, of course, was based in reality. In truth, John did everything he could to sabotage the real relationships he had, such as his primary ones with his wife and child. He performed poorly at work due to his drug use and was in danger of losing yet another job.

Where did this all start for him? Was he genetically predisposed to addiction or was his social environment one that brought him into contact with other addicts and drugs? Oddly, John didn't have a family history of alcoholism or addiction. He grew up in a suburban town no different from many and was not exposed to hard drugs until he was in his mid-thirties. Yet something drew him to the heroin culture. Something inherent in the culture met needs he chose not to satisfy anywhere else.

Dr. Lawrence Kolb, the first medical director of the Public Health Service Narcotic Hospital in Lexington, Kentucky, wrote in the 1920s that addicts were thrill seekers. He believed them to be people of modest capabilities who used drugs to overcome feelings of inferiority. Drugs allowed them to feel grandiose, larger than life. John certainly fit this description. He often spent paychecks that should have gone toward paying bills and complained that he never got anywhere because he didn't have any college education. Yet, he never took responsibility or positive action to change his circumstances.

John wouldn't talk about his mother. He claimed it was too painful to talk about. He did say that she died just after he began his slide into heroin addiction. Shame and guilt filled his thoughts of her, and he was only able to cope by using more heroin.

Manhattan therapist Dr. Roy Spungin did his doctoral dissertation on the effects of knowledge, attitude, lifestyle, and social network on the AIDS risk behaviors of intravenous and intranasal heroin users. Spungin believes that there is validity to the theories of addiction to which the traditionalist school of psychologists adhere.

The traditionalists, and Spungin, believe that all forms of addiction stem from the first year of life and the quality of care given to a new baby. Spungin believes babies take on the mother's feelings, that they become the feelings the mother gives off. According to Spungin, "The qualitative nuances of a mother's nurturing or lack of nurturing determine much of the child's future. Insofar as the *good enough mother* is one who feeds when the child is hungry, anxious, or needy, and is there most of the time, *on time*, enables the child to receive the nurturing he or she so desperately needs. The mother whose voice is usually soft and tender, whose skin quality is smooth, and who smells pleasant is a comfort to the child. The good mother is gentle and slow in movement and holds and nurtures the child." He gives as an example a child born in a war zone. If the mother is constantly stressed and in fear for her life, the baby picks up on that. The child's world is full of fear and the struggle for survival. Spungin takes it one step further and points out how many of our inner cities are like war zones in that they are physically blighted, disaffected environments where danger is a daily constant. The mother who is worried about the rent, having enough to eat, and struggling to get by as a single parent is sometimes hard-pressed to give the nurturing care an infant needs.

Spungin compares the euphoria of the heroin high to breast-feeding. He points out that a baby looks euphoric at his mother's breast and will assume the same drowsy nature that characterizes heroin addicts. He implies that what the heroin addict is really looking for is the mother's breast, the nurturing moments when he can be held in her arms and made to feel that the world is a safe and warm place. Many addicts describe the heroin high as "warm" all over, or as a rush of warmth, lending credence to this theory.

On the other hand, a lot of babies during the 1950s and 1960s were not breast-fed. Does everyone who missed the proper nurturing as an infant wind up addicted to heroin? The traditionalists say no, but a person who lacked a nurturing environment will have some form of addictive behavior. He or she may not wind up a heroin addict but could be a sex addict, a workaholic, a food addict, a gambling addict, or any one of the other assorted addictions known to us today.

For an individual to become a heroin addict there must be other contributing circumstances. Biological, social, cultural, and environmental factors create heroin addiction. A heroin user must live where he or she can access the drug. If the potential addict lives in just about any large city in America, this is not a problem. Most suburbs are within an hour's drive from drug-selling areas, and there are also suburban dealers. Often, a person who received inadequate nurturing as a child may find himself or herself in a social circle where using heroin is not so taboo. If he or she comes from the predominant white culture, heroin use can be seen as a form of rebellion, a way to feel like an outlaw, the credentials for being cool. Driving to the city, braving the dangers of a drug neighborhood, and making it back home to the suburb all validate the person's courage and ability while displaying reckless disregard for the conventions of society. Each drug-seeking episode is another opportunity to outsmart the police, feel the thrill of the hunt, and come back alive to feel the high, which in and of itself is ample justification.

For people of color born into inner-city culture, heroin is right on the corner or just up the street most of the time. Many long-term heroin addicts describe their early heroin experience as a rite of passage, part of becoming an adult. They use it to prove to their peers that they are old enough and tough enough to tackle the hardest drug of them all. The irony is that no one ever wins against heroin—it always beats you, until you leave it alone and stop using. No one can say, "I used heroin my whole life, and I got the better of it." In order to "beat" heroin the addict invariably must admit defeat, learn to put it down, and begin a life in recovery.

The heroin subculture of the inner cities of America has been a contributing factor to the continuation of the welfare state and generational poverty. For decades we have had an underground economy in which addicts can sell stolen property, convert food stamps to cash, and make money illegally in any number of ingenious ways, whether by selling drugs or their bodies. People of color living in inner cities have been excluded from the dominant culture geographically, culturally, and, consequently, in access to social and political power. To a large extent, they have been denied the ability to compete due to poor education and racism in hiring practices, and as a result a few have decided that the only option available to them is to create their own economy. In this context, heroin dollars make life easier to bear.

Heroin can be seen as a social lubricant, connecting people to one another. It provides an opportunity to step outside the isolation imposed by an increasingly complex, technologically driven society. It allows people to take part in the camaraderie of ritual. Why would two people share needles? From desperation and the need to get high, certainly, but also to connect with each other. Sharing a needle says, "I trust you." This may also drive the psyche of the heroin-addicted prostitute who says to a customer, "You don't need to wear a condom." She may be looking for a deep human connection of which she has been deprived, more than likely as a child. Sadly, the connection is often a death pact when it comes to needle sharing or unprotected sex in the age of AIDS. What two such people are really saying is, "I'm willing to take a chance on dying with you, and if we do that's okay. Our souls will be connected in death." Granted, this is false, even delusional romanticism. But the desperate nature and magnitude of the need to connect with another human being—a need so powerful one would risk one's life for it—speaks to the levels of pain and emptiness heroin addicts experience.

The heroin culture provides a social identity for its members. A heroin addict can feel disenfranchised, lonely, inferior, and incapable of competing with the rest of society, but still feel like an equal citizen within the heroin subculture. For example, many methadone patients' only social interactions take place at their clinic. The clinic offers the addict an opportunity to get out of the house every day, see familiar faces, and establish relationships with fellow addicts. Even if the relationships are based on drug-seeking behavior, such as hanging out in the park trying to buy pills to boost their methadone, they are still interacting, making connections. They might have a conversation about the latest headline in the news or they might compare notes about drugs. Given enough time these relationships may progress to an emotional level and be loving and nurturing as bonds deepen.

The dilemma for the heroin addict comes when faced with the decision to stop using. To stop using heroin is to take away the social network, identity, and the one thing that makes life easier to bear. Many addicts refer to heroin as their medication. When they are in withdrawal they "need to get cured." When you take away heroin from an addict, you often have a person who feels insecure, inferior, ashamed, and ill equipped to negotiate his or her way in the world. Poor social skills, lack of education, and the stigma of being branded an addict—a person with an incurable disease—add to the burden. It is not surprising that so few seek treatment when faced with these choices. Still, many do choose treatment and recovery, despite the pessimism of those who are skeptical of the efficacy of treatment, the concept of addiction being a disease, and the belief that it is possible to recover. For those who do seek recovery it is essential to fill the empty holes in their psyches that heroin once occupied. They must learn to establish relationships and make strong connections with other recovering individuals. Some find a spiritual way of life and embrace the comfort this brings. Most successful recovering heroin addicts have strong ties to the self-help fellowships of Narcotics Anonymous or Alcoholics Anonymous. In essence, heroin addicts must restructure their subculture and replace destructive habits and behaviors with healthy ones in order to recover.

Going Home

John looks at the clock on his dashboard and thinks that he made good time on the drive home. He passes the Budweiser plant outside Newark on Route 1 & 9. It is one of the ugliest stretches of highway he has ever seen, but he always feels good when he gets to this part of the ride. It means he has only ten minutes before he reaches his home in Rahway. It also means he's made it past the most dangerous part of the drive. There are never any state troopers from this point on; he knows he's home free.

The Budweiser plant's giant red, white, and blue neon logo sits perched atop the tall building. The colors on the sign change until the eagle appears and majestically flaps its wings, never leaving the circle, then disappears and is replaced by billowing gray clouds of smoke lazily climbing into the night sky.

Pulling into his driveway he sees the string of Christmas lights he had hung last Sunday with his wife. They had drunk hot cocoa and laughed at the baby with tinsel in her hair as they decorated the tree.

He checks himself in the rearview mirror for signs that would tip his wife to where he has been that night. He thinks he can pass the test. As he steps from the car and walks up the drive, he sees his wife through the living-room bay window. She is dancing with the baby in her arms. His daughter's head is thrown back and she laughs as she is spun around. They both look happy. He is home.

John M. put down his heroin habit on January 2, 1997. As of this writing he is clean and sober and has recently celebrated his first anniversary as a recovering heroin addict.[1]

CHAPTER

5

Case History: Heroin Addiction

Running

March 22, 1997, Reggie Lewis Athletic Center,
Boston, Massachusetts

The whistling, foot stomping, and hand clapping of the electrified crowd all blend into one loud roar in his mind. The nervous butterflies in his stomach long gone now, Frank focuses on his teammate taking the last turn on the wooden indoor running track. Frank sways back and forth, his eyes intent on the small pack of runners hitting full stride now as they come into the straightaway. Running slowly, gradually increasing his stride, he readies himself for the baton exchange. As the sound of the racers' shoes pounds louder into the wooden boards, he feels the energy of the track come up through his legs, pitching him forward. He takes the baton in a clean exchange.

He runs shoulder to shoulder with a shorter man who bumps him, almost throwing Frank off his stride, but he quickly recovers and soon takes a short lead. His two teammates have given him a good position. He is running the third leg in the four-man relay race. All he has to do now is hold on, four quick turns around the track, and he will hand off to the anchor man for the final 800 meters. The first two times around the track he has to hold back—his legs want to go, but he knows if he pushes too hard early there'll be nothing left for the last 100 meters. The pace feels comfortable, a result of the hours spent in training, pushing himself to higher thresholds of pain than he ever dreamed he could endure. Now it's all Zen. He hears the noise of the crowd cheering him on and sees the colors in the stands blurring as he steps up his pace a notch. He is heading into the final lap.

Frank feels the runner who had bumped him closing in, trying to take the inside lane. It's a little earlier than he had planned, but it's now or never, he thinks, and goes into his kick, letting it all out. He doesn't dare look back for fear of losing a step, but he instinctively knows the other runner is fading when he can no longer hear the short man's labored breathing alongside him. Rounding the last turn at full speed he heads for the stretch where he sees his anchor man crouched and ready for him.

The last 30 meters were pure joy. This is why he runs, to feel his body cut the air, to become one with the track and the wind and the crowd. His body screaming, he moves with a fluid beauty and grace, his arms pumping his legs forward faster and faster. At that moment, as he often does while running, he feels a spiritual shudder, a wave of contact with something *other*. It is a rare moment of serene pleasure that lasts but a second. He knows his team is going to win the race. He realizes he is about to hand the baton, and the lead, to Byron Dyce, a member of the 1968 and 1972 Jamaican Olympic track team. And he thinks, *I just handed the lead to an Olympic athlete— there's no way we're going to lose now.*

He walks off the track, his legs feeling slightly rubbery in the afterglow of the intense 800 meters, and watches as Dyce tears up the track, winning by a large margin. The four teammates throw their arms around one another and laugh, exhilarated and high, knowing they have just become the Men's National Masters Champions in the 4-by-800-meter relay event. Frank had finished his own 800-meter leg of the race in two minutes and sixteen seconds, a 4:32 mile pace. Not his best time but enough to hold the lead and help win the race.

Frank listens to the loudspeakers as his team, the Central Park Track Club from New York City, is declared the winner in the event. During the awards ceremony shortly after, as their names are announced, a rising flood of emotion fills his chest. He thinks, *I'm not going to get all emotional now, it ain't that big a deal*, yet the tightness of his throat and the wetness building in his eyes want to have their way.

He doesn't cry. But as he dresses he begins to think about what he has just accomplished. He is now undeniably one of the fastest runners in the country, in his age category. He had turned forty-four that year, and has finally become a national-class runner and champion. An All-American. No one can take that away from him.

The path to glory didn't come easy. Less than two years before his momentous day on the track, Frank was standing in a line, waiting to drink 90 milligrams of methadone, something he did every day back then. How he wound up on methadone and how he worked to achieve sobriety is a story about power—the power of heroin and the power of recovery.

This was not the first time Frank had earned recognition in his life, nor was it the first time he knew the rewards sobriety offered. In 1978 he left a life of crime and drugs, slowly recovered, and went on to help others as a drug and family counselor for ten years. Then he lost it all to heroin: all the state certifications he'd worked so hard to attain, the ten years of sobriety, his self-respect, and his reputation as a professional in the field of recovery.

The road back this last time was fraught with haunting voices of self-doubt and futility. Once you climb the mountain, stand at the top and look at the world in all its majesty, the fall back down to the bottom can be devastating. Climbing back from the valley of despair called addiction can seem impossible the second time around. Many never even attempt the climb again, but Frank did. It was a testament to his courage and humility and proof that following simple directions can restore an addict to life. In Frank's own words, "Two years sober, it's no big deal; I've been here before. I'm sober today, but if I don't do the right thing, I could lose it all again tomorrow. I'm not scared; I don't live in fear of it like something hanging over my head. But I know how easy it was to wind up on the methadone line. And the line is still there if I want it. Today my life is good, and if I stay sober today, there's no telling how fast I can run tomorrow."

The Path to Addiction

Frank's story began forty-six years ago in the sleepy little town of Chatham, New Jersey. Situated on the eastern border of Morris County, Chatham is one of the more affluent towns in New Jersey and serves as a bedroom community for the many professionals living there. Predominantly white, it is home to many business executives who commute daily to New York City, just forty minutes away by car, and to Morristown, the county seat, ten minutes west, where several large corporations have established headquarters as a result of tax breaks and vigorous courting by state and county officials.

Companies like AT&T and Allied Signal, both of which employ thousands and lubricate the state economy, make their homes in Morristown, a stone's throw away from the lush rolling hills of Bedminster, Mendham, and Far Hills. It is horse country, where the gentleman farmers of the eighteenth century settled, and where Jackie Onassis occasionally retreated to ride her horses. Mike Tyson owned an estate in this bucolic area. It was here that he had his infamous flare-ups with Robin Givens—which were usually followed by vehicular assault on innocent trees.

Chatham is the kind of town where the American dream was alive and well during the 1950s and 1960s. It still is today.

It is the kind of place you don't worry about locking your back door, a town where an immigrant family could work hard, buy a piece of land, and settle down to raise children. The school system is judged to be one of the best in the state year in and year out.

Frank's mother and father were married just after World War II when his father returned home a decorated war veteran. First-generation immigrants from Sicily, they had grown up in the melting pot of Newark, New Jersey. For a wedding present, Frank's grandfather bought them a house in Chatham, for less money than what today would be a down payment on a new car. His grandfather had made the voyage to America from Sicily in the 1930s. He settled in Newark, worked hard, and took care of his family.

Frank was born on October 17, 1952, the third of six children, three boys and three girls. The family lived in a modest house with three bedrooms on the edge of town. In an area known for its gentility, the little home was in the less expensive part of town, though in Chatham there really is no bad part of town. Nonetheless, Frank was always aware that his family was blue-collar in a white-collar world.

His early years were occupied with the daily adventures common to almost any red-blooded young boy in the 1950s. He busied himself climbing trees, building forts in tall oaks, watching *Davy Crockett* on the small black-and-white TV, playing soldier, and exploring the woods that led to the Passaic River behind his house. His father was a machinist by trade and made the daily commute to the Ballantine Brewery in Newark, just twenty minutes away, while his mother cared for the children. They were trying to live the American dream, striving to help their family climb up another rung on the social ladder, confident that if they worked hard they might see their sons and daughters graduate college and have a better life.

As Roman Catholics, Frank's family attended mass every Sunday at St. Patrick's, the one and only Catholic church in the predominantly Protestant town. His parents entrusted the Benedictine nuns of the small parochial school with the responsibility of educating Frank through his first eight years of grade school. He found the disciplined world of the nuns stifling, creatively repressive, and he was happy to finally graduate from the eighth grade and enter the public school system in the ninth grade.

During his first eight years of school Frank was not very big on sports, unlike most of the other boys his age. He enjoyed reading tremendously and took refuge in it, finding he could journey to faraway places and escape the confines of his structured world. He became subconsciously aware of his athletic talent for running at an early age but never really thought much of it. Whenever they played tag on the school playground no one could catch him, and when they tested the boys' speed during gym he was always the fastest. It was just something that came naturally to him. When Frank was twelve he took part in a track meet sponsored by the town recreation department and won a medal. Finally, he discovered that although he was terrible at baseball, football, and basketball he had a natural ability for running. He was tall, long legged, and very thin, what he would later discover to be a natural runner's body.

Winning his first race filled Frank with pride. He began to think more seriously about racing and took to running over the town's steep hills. Running was joy, an escape from the drudgery of schoolwork. It felt good to finally excel at something athletic. It was also an escape from pain. When Frank was in the eighth grade, his younger brother was killed, the victim of a hit-and-run accident. The loss drove Frank, an already quiet young man, further inside himself and blanketed the rest of his family with an overwhelming and, at times, stifling sadness.

It's not surprising that Frank started drinking at this time in his life. He was about twelve or thirteen. His best friend worked after school at the liquor store in town, sweeping up and taking out the garbage. The clever young man would occasionally hide a pint or two of liquor among the garbage boxes, and he and Frank would retrieve them later. They usually went into the woods by the river, where they would drink, become intoxicated, and talk of life and adolescent wisdom. They laughed and acted silly, as most young men do when they begin experimenting with alcohol. Frank remembers not liking it at first, but he soon learned to enjoy the effects of alcohol and looked forward to those times when his friend could sneak a bottle. It was also a thrill. It felt like he was doing something bad, and he enjoyed playing the renegade.

It was a role that came naturally to him. As a boy, he watched cowboys and Indians battling each other on TV and always rooted for the Indians. The coolest were the renegades. There was no telling what a renegade might do, and there was just something exciting about the way the words *renegade Indians* sounded. "A frantic scout galloped into the fort shouting that there were renegade Indians headed their way and you just knew the best part of the movie was about to happen," Frank explained. This identification would prove significant later in Frank's short-lived criminal career.

Frank's high school days were filled with running, hanging out with the kids on the fringes (avoiding the athlete/jock crowd), girlfriends, and smoking pot. He started using marijuana in the tenth grade and immediately liked its effect. He quickly learned to moderate his use and began a three-year pattern of controlled use. In his sophomore year he didn't smoke during track season. By his junior year he drank during track season but only on the weekends. By senior year he was smoking pot once a week while in training for track. He found he just didn't want to stay away from it.

Each year, however, brought greater accomplishments on the track. Frank ran the 100-yard and 220-yard events, moving to the 440 in his senior year. He earned varsity letters in his sophomore and junior years, and in his senior year broke the school and Morris County records in the 440 with a time of 49.6 seconds. His running ability drew the attention of college scouts. Twenty-one colleges and universities offered him full four-year scholarships.

Somehow, Frank was not motivated to see this for the opportunity that it was. By his senior year, he had come to feel that running was hard work; it had lost its earlier thrill. When Frank graduated high school in 1970, he turned his back on all the college scholarships and took a job as a landscaper, choosing to stay home in Chatham.

It was during this time that his drug use began to escalate. Frank worked alongside a twenty-six-year-old man who was a heavy drug user. He befriended the man, smoking pot with him occasionally, and learned about drugs like cocaine. In May 1971, *Time* magazine ran a cover story about cocaine. Frank found the story so alluring that when his landscaping buddy offered to take him to New York to buy some cocaine, Frank was more than ready to go.

They went to cop on the Lower East Side of Manhattan— ironically, in the area where Frank now lives. After several inquiries they found there was no cocaine available, but there was heroin. Frank tried the heroin and didn't like the way it made him feel nearly as much as he enjoyed the thrill of searching and copping, and the ritual of using. The anticipation he felt on the drive over to New York was a turn-on.

Within a short time Frank was making the trip to New York two or three times a week to buy heroin and occasionally cocaine. It only took a few months before he began injecting the drugs. His friend instructed him in this ritual, and eventually he learned to inject himself. Weekly use became his pattern and way of life. He enjoyed nodding off and listening to music in his room at home, his parents none the wiser. The heroin made him feel warm and carefree. It became an object of obsession, and he'd anxiously look forward to the times he'd have the money to buy more.

As winter set in and the landscaping business slowed, Frank's thoughts turned to warmer climes. He packed up his few belongings and headed for Santa Cruz, California, where he lived the life of a beach bum, smoking pot, drinking wine, swallowing Seconals, and surviving on the communal atmosphere that prevailed in the posthippie days of southern California. Free love was everywhere, as were free drugs—which was even better in Frank's mind.

Frank is not sure whether it was homesickness or boredom with the constant fog in which he lived, but by the summer of 1972, he decided to return home. Once back in Chatham, he picked up where he had left off with his heroin use. While in California, he did not have as much contact with heroin as he'd had at home, and when he did it was always the "black tar" heroin from Mexico, which he found to be inferior to the heroin he got in New York City. Back home, he almost immediately found himself using heroin three or four times a week. He quickly developed a habit and decided to try enrolling in a methadone program to curb his cravings and sickness.

Frank signed on with a program in Millburn, New Jersey, a neat, suburban town one would not envision supporting a methadone program. He learned from other patients how to boost his methadone with cocaine or benzodiazepines such as Valium and Xanax. Between 1972 and 1977, he was a regular patient at the clinic and rarely used heroin, but he discovered that he liked the methadone high even better than the heroin high, especially when boosted by Valium or cocaine. He was drinking 100 milligrams of methadone daily and complementing his dosage with pills, alcohol, and an assortment of other drugs procured from patients in the program. It seems every methadone program spawns an outlet for illicit drugs, and a resourceful addict can always find ways to get a supply of drugs to go along with the methadone. Frank occasionally bought methadone and doubled up his daily dose, sometimes drinking as much as 200 or 300 milligrams a day. At first he was on a six-day schedule, but eventually he worked his way to just three visits per week. He reported every Monday, Wednesday, and Friday and was given a take-home dose along with the 100 milligrams he drank in view of the administering nurses. Once outside the clinic, however, he promptly drank his take-home dose and enjoyed that old, familiar narcotic nod.

Caught in a cycle common to many methadone patients, Frank was still very much controlled by the ritual of drug-seeking to satisfy his escalating dependence. He worked a factory job for a couple of years during his methadone maintenance period, but his income and attendance were intermittent, at best. So he did what many heroin addicts do: he turned to nonviolent crime.

Viewed in a historical and social context, Frank became part of a wave of crime that plagued America between 1970 and 1975, a time during which the shift of global heroin processing from Marseilles to the Golden Triangle of Southeast Asia flooded the streets of America's major urban areas with high-quality heroin. Returning Vietnam veterans who had sampled pure heroin during the war joined many young Americans who began experimenting with drugs in the 1960s, smoking pot and dabbling in cocaine and hallucinogens, and had progressed to heroin by the 1970s. A rash of theft across the country resulted when addicts needed money for heroin. It is significant that the heroin epidemic of the 1970s was largely nonviolent in comparison with the cocaine epidemic of the 1980s, when cocaine psychosis and crack violence ruled the streets. The heroin addict of the 1970s stole. He broke into houses and cars. Anything that could be pawned or traded for heroin was taken. This is the kind of activity Frank got caught up in. He began breaking into houses.

Frank is ashamed of this period of his life and views it as an example of how powerless he was over heroin. He broke into homes and took whatever was light—cameras, jewelry, cash. He then sold the stolen goods to fences or gold stores in Manhattan. The social network of the heroin culture educated him as to where to go, how much various pieces of jewelry were worth, who could be trusted and who couldn't.

His short-lived criminal career came to a crashing halt in 1977. Frank had broken into a home, stolen an income tax refund check, some jewelry, and the car in the driveway. He drove the stolen car to the local bank and tried to cash the check. Apparently, the bank teller knew the man Frank had stolen the check from and alerted the police. It seemed to Frank that the entire police force of the small suburban town swooped down on him. He was summarily handcuffed and given a free ride to the county jail.

Locked up, Frank became acquainted with the agony of kicking methadone cold turkey. He spent four months behind bars before his family made bail, suffering the withdrawal and the shame and powerless frustration that come with having your physical freedom taken away. Staring at the bars, he couldn't believe it had been less than seven years since he graduated high school. He paced back and forth, swearing he'd never touch drugs again, but on some level he knew he was kidding himself and would probably get high the first chance he got. And that is exactly what he did.

The day he made bail, Frank bought a bottle of methadone and some pills. Unaware that four months of not using drugs had lowered his tolerance, however, he overdosed. His parents rushed him to the hospital, where he was given last rites. Comatose for three days, he finally regained consciousness, but was diagnosed with pneumonia and hepatitis. His condition worsened and he was administered last rites a second time, only to evade death yet again. He wound up spending a month in the hospital before he was well enough to go home.

Lurching toward Recovery

Frank's family had planned an intervention for him when he got home. By this time they realized how serious the problem was and decided to force him into treatment. They packed his bags and shipped him off to Dismas House in Paterson, New Jersey.

Dismas House is a rehabilitation center that uses a traditional, therapeutic community model to modify addicts' behaviors. Discipline, routine, and a highly structured environment are key elements in the addicts' lives. Because the belief is that while using drugs they didn't have any self-discipline, it is drilled into them every day. Frank suddenly was thrust into a world where men were jumping into his face, confronting his behavior and bad attitude. His hair was shaved off and he lived a life very similar to that of a soldier at boot camp. Too scared to resist, he threw himself into the daily routine and soon thrived under the discipline.

When the time came for Frank to go to court on the burglary charges, the judge allowed him to continue in the program and sentenced him to a conditional probation. He had to complete treatment or do jail time. Given a choice, Frank knew that no matter how bad the rigors of Dismas House might seem, it was still better than jail. He stuck it out, one of the very few who complete such a program. Typically, only 25 percent of entrants finish this type of drug treatment. Although the dropout rate is high, those who manage to finish usually do well once released.

During his time at the therapeutic community, Frank began running again for the first time since high school. He began to regain his physical conditioning and felt better than he had in a long time. He grew to like the lifestyle of a drug-free ex-addict. Therapeutic-community participants do not necessarily believe they are *recovering* addicts, because they don't believe in the disease concept of addiction; rather, they feel that addicts lack the discipline and ability to make rational decisions. Once clean, it is up to each participant whether or not to use again. So Frank learned how to be more powerful than heroin and methadone, with no exposure to AA/NA principles. He completed the program in eighteen months, lived in a halfway house with other addicts for a year, and maintained contact with Dismas House and its counselors. He volunteered time and helped out with new residents. While living in the halfway house he worked as a truck driver making local deliveries. Two years after he entered Dismas House, he was offered a job as a trainee counselor.

It was a good time in Frank's life. His family was pleased he was staying clean; he had nearly three years away from drugs. He began to study and take classes for certification as a drug counselor, and in 1980 he left Dismas House and went into the world of professional recovery. He worked at a succession of hospitals and treatment centers as a certified family therapist and drug counselor, eventually progressing to jobs as a clinical supervisor and clinical director. He worked his way up the ladder in the recovery world and in 1987 landed a job as the drug coordinator for the Maplewood-South Orange School District, responsible for designing drug education and prevention programs, as well as counseling and referring students who exhibited problems. Coming up on ten years without a drink or a drug, he was heavily involved in the local road-racing community and had regained the trust and support of his family and friends.

The Road to Relapse

Frank's recovery, even after ten years of sobriety, was more fragile than it appeared, and a series of seemingly minor decisions created a critical shift in his life's direction. Inexplicably, he drank a glass of wine with dinner at a restaurant on one occasion. Nothing happened. He decided to try it again, once again without catastrophic effect. Within a month he decided to try some pot. All this time he had stayed clean on discipline and willpower, telling himself he had too much self-respect to go back to dope, and had not availed himself of help from other addicts or the meeting rooms of AA/NA. By the end of that school year, when the board notified him that he had to be let go because he had failed to obtain a college degree (a condition of his hiring), his attitude had soured. Out of work, bitter, and feeling alone, he succumbed to the all-or-nothing mentality that had dominated his life for so long. He figured that because he had broken his clean time, he may as well go all the way. By 1988 he was back to swallowing pills, shooting heroin, and drinking methadone when he could buy it on the street.

The only way Frank could avoid his feelings of shame and disappointment was to use drugs, but even that failed to mask the overwhelming depression he felt when his certification was taken from him. He felt that his former colleagues were unwilling to help him in his hour of need, and he cursed everything recovery stood for. He thought, *If this is what it's all about, no one willing to reach out and say, "Hey Frank, here's a life preserver, let's get you back on track," then I want no part of any of it.* He used heavily for a year before winding up in treatment again.

Nineteen eighty-nine saw Frank in rehabilitation at Arm's Acres, in Carmel, New York. He completed a twenty-eight-day program there and was exposed for the first time to the Minnesota Model of treatment. He was informed that he needed to attend NA meetings if he was to stay clean and that he should get a sponsor to learn how to work the program's Twelve Steps. Frank skeptically attended NA meetings but sat on the fringes, failing to connect with the other addicts. He had trouble with many of the concepts he heard in the meetings and viewed the participants as religious fanatics thumping their ever-present black book, *Narcotics Anonymous*, and spouting claims of conversion. He didn't buy it but managed to stay clean for about a year, again through willpower.

By 1991, Frank had started seeing the woman to whom he is now married. He had again broken his abstinence, this time with marijuana. He smoked a joint and within six months was drinking methadone occasionally. He was living on the Lower East Side of Manhattan, down the street from a methadone clinic, where he made a few friends who gladly sold him their take-home doses. His girlfriend, a drug free, hardworking woman who loved him, had no idea of the roller-coaster ride on which she was about to embark. His methadone use was steadily escalating and in less than six months, he had become dependent again, six months after his first taste of methadone.

Once again, his life revolved around using drugs and figuring out ways to use more. Heroin, methadone, pills, cocaine— the vicious cycle started up all over again. The life he once had was a dream, as if it belonged to another man, not the haggard, lying addict who stared at him from the mirror. He thought often of the passage in the Bible that spoke of the spirit being willing, but the flesh weak. He was ashamed of what he had sunk to, but could not resist the daily temptations and urges to use more and more. He remembered being healthy, running fast, running long; the respect he earned was a long-ago memory that he could scarcely recall anymore, and now he was even beginning to lose the trust and respect of the woman he loved.

Climbing Back into the Race

In late 1993, under pressure from his girlfriend, Frank checked into the detox unit at Metropolitan Hospital. There he underwent medical withdrawal from the benzodiazepines to which he'd become addicted. After ten days, he was discharged and referred to a methadone clinic in lower Manhattan. He reasoned that at least he wouldn't have to buy heroin or methadone on the street, and he could buy some time to start yet another attempt at recovery, though he was still haunted by the ghosts of his previous failures.

The first six months of methadone maintenance were spent learning to trust his counselor, whom Frank liked right away. The counselor seemed to understand him, and Frank admired his straightforward style. He wasn't self-righteous or judgmental, and Frank felt the man actually respected him, treating him with dignity. Frank recalls, "One day it was as if the light switch had been turned on in the dark room of self-pity I'd been sitting in. I just realized that if this guy, who I respected, believed in me, then I could believe in myself. I thought at times he must be getting high to believe in me. He'd tell me things like, I could have it all back tomorrow, if I just didn't get high a day at a time. I complained all the time about what nonsense NA was, and he told me that was okay, I didn't have to believe in anything; just go for the coffee and don't judge anybody, just listen. So I went. And eventually it didn't seem so bad."

The relationship between Frank and his counselor matured. They talked about running and identified some of the things that Frank wanted from life. Frank began to take advantage of the open-door policy the counselor had, visiting with him three and four times a week. He still struggled with control, however, and dabbled in cocaine and pills to supplement his methadone doses. Frank remembers showing up at his counselor's door one day after an altercation on the street over a drug deal gone bad. He had blood on his hands and arms, and his pants were torn. His heart was still pumping, the adrenaline from the fight just beginning to wear off. The counselor, never one to pressure him, finally issued a directive: If Frank were to succeed he would have to once again go to a hospital and detox from the pills he'd built a habit on, then come back and follow a plan of recovery that prohibited illicit drug use.

Frank complied. He went to Staten Island University Hospital this time, for fourteen days. He kicked his Valium habit and returned to his clinic with a new resolve. Because of Frank's honesty, he and the counselor were able to identify a major roadblock to his recovery. By this point in Frank's drug history he had developed a distinct preference for methadone over heroin. Methadone had become his drug of choice. More significantly, Frank had a pattern of becoming involved with the other patients who sold pills, cocaine, or take-home doses of methadone. Frank had gotten himself into trouble before when he was spotted buying methadone on the street by the clinic's security personnel and written up for disciplinary action.

The dilemma became whether to keep Frank on methadone for the prescribed three- to five-year period before he began a therapeutic (long-term) detoxification, or to begin lowering his dosage and weaning him from methadone now. The latter strategy went against treatment protocol and research that showed many methadone patients did not fare well when weaned from methadone too soon in the rehabilitation process. Most methadone programs prefer the addict to be free of all secondary drug use for at least a year before they will consider him or her for reentry into a total-abstinence recovery process. Then the patient's methadone dose would be slowly titrated downward until he or she was drug free.

In Frank's case, however, the longer he stayed on methadone, the more temptation he had to either double up his dose or use secondary drugs. His home life was stable, he had a permanent residence, a relationship that was loving and supportive, and his own business that he worked at with his girlfriend. The biggest advantage Frank had was that he had stayed sober before for so long. It was really up to him. If he wanted to stay sober badly enough, he knew what he had to do.

The clinic's treatment team decided to take a chance on Frank. The team members would honor his request to begin a therapeutic reduction with the stipulation that if he began to show positive in the weekly urine tests for other drug use, the detoxification would stop and he would resume his normal

90-milligram methadone dose. He was also to have regular blood levels taken to assure them that he was not using additional methadone.

In December 1994 the clinic began to wean Frank off methadone. His dose was dropped by 5 milligrams every two weeks until late in April 1995, when he reached 40 milligrams. At this point Frank decided to bite the bullet. He checked himself into Beth Israel's Stuyvesant Square treatment facility and underwent a twenty-eight-day program, coming out on the twenty-ninth day totally drug free.

His first few days were rocky, but the inpatient program at Beth Israel set him up with a good, comprehensive aftercare treatment plan, consisting of weekly attendance at an outpatient satellite program and individual counseling. Frank immediately began attending NA meetings daily, got himself a sponsor, and slowly regained his physical strength. The protracted methadone withdrawal left him weak and discouraged about running, but the concept of living one day at a time became clearer to him. He decided to apply it to his running. At first he could barely walk a complete lap around the track, but eventually he was able to muster a sort of slow, shuffling jog. He began to make a little progress every day. It took six months before he felt comfortable running again. He was also making progress in his program of recovery and completed the outpatient program after a year. During the first year, he worked to rebuild trust in his relationships and to overcome the ghosts of the past that whispered, "You aren't good enough." He decided to put the past behind him. With the help of his sponsor he began working the Twelve Steps, and he felt better spiritually than he had in years.

In 1996, Frank began entering road races and a few indoor track events and performed well enough to draw encouragement from it. He stepped up his training and started finishing races with respectable times, drawing the attention of the Central Park Track Club, a by-invitation-only club. Frank felt honored when he was asked to train with the club. He got faster and faster as he trained harder, taking himself and his running more seriously now. Again, someone else had seen something in him that he couldn't always see in himself. Nonetheless, his accomplishments on the track began to feed his desire for greater success. One of his first thrills in recovery was representing the track club at the Millrose Games at Madison Square Garden. More than twenty-eight years after graduation, Frank was finally realizing some of his high school track dreams.

Frank's goals for now are to stay sober, build up his business, spend time with the woman who stuck by him and who is now his wife, and run fast. How fast? He doesn't really know, or won't say. He still struggles with being overly modest, but he has been able to post a personal-best time of 2:11 in the 800-meter distance, a 4:22 mile pace. He is confident he can go well below that. He hopes to drop his 400-meter time down to fifty-two seconds, a 3:46 mile pace. These are astounding times for any forty-five-year-old man, let alone one with a history of drug abuse. Most of all Frank hopes to continue building the relationships he now has in NA. For the first time in his life he feels connected—connected to NA, to his wife, to his running, and, above all, to himself.

PART

three

TREATMENT

6

Treatment for Heroin Addiction: The Behavioral Model

Addiction is a progressive, chronic, primary relapsing disorder generally involving compulsions, loss of control, and continued use of alcohol and / or other drugs despite adverse consequences.

"Addiction," as defined by the
Substance Abuse Mental Health Services Administration

Once an addict, always an addict. This is both a myth and a truth that addicts live by. Those who continue to use heroin behave as addicts do. Those who stop using and begin the recovery process must remember that once they use again, they awaken the disease of addiction. If you take away the heroin from an addict what you have is still an addict, complete with questionable decision-making skills and an assortment of psychological bruises sustained during his or her years of abusing drugs.

Treatment and recovery from heroin addiction is a long process. It is the rare individual who of his or her own volition decides one day to just put down a heroin habit and never use again. Most heroin users are coerced into treatment, either by the criminal justice system, intervention on the part of family members and friends, or as a result of personal calamities that force them to make life-changing decisions. The usual response by an addict when his or her behavior is confronted is an attempt at controlled use, which inevitably leads to failure and loss of control: "I knew I had a problem with heroin, but I didn't really want to stop using altogether; I just wanted to learn how to use only on the weekends." This is a familiar refrain to the professionals who treat heroin addicts. It is part of the denial of the disease—just as the first thought of the person diagnosed with cancer often is, "It can't be." The person who becomes addicted to heroin has to go through a process, often requiring several attempts at treatment, before the addiction becomes *manageable* and he or she is able to get on in life without heroin. American society expects the heroin addict to be treated once and be forever cured. This is not realistic and seldom occurs, leading many to view the efficacy of treatment skeptically.

"Once an addict, always an addict" can be heard in the meeting rooms of Twelve Step fellowships like Narcotics Anonymous and Alcoholics Anonymous across America. It reminds addicts that unless they are vigilant, they can easily use drugs again, and that once they use, they quickly return to their old ways. The idea of controlled drug using is debunked; the only hope for a life not controlled by heroin is through total abstinence from all drugs. The slogan reinforces the belief that it is the first drink or drug that will do the damage. Addicts learn to accept this concept and embrace the sober lifestyle of recovery from addiction. The slogan has been echoed, however, by those who do not understand addiction in order to disparage any treatment attempt: if "once an addict, always an addict," they say, then a drug addict can't be cured, so why waste time and money trying?

Defining addiction as a relapsing disorder bolsters the belief that treatment does not work. What many fail to see is that although relapse is part of the disease of addiction, it does not *have* to be part of the recovery process, and in fact is *not* a part of the lives of many recovering heroin addicts.

How did the myth that treatment doesn't work get started? Does it have a basis in the accumulation of statistics that document failed treatment and recovery attempts?

Personal bias against addicts and resistance to the concept of heroin addiction as a disease color the perceptions of many. It is a tug-of-war that those who work in the drug treatment field struggle with almost daily. If many addicts don't fully grasp the disease concept, how can the layperson be faulted for having doubts about the effectiveness of treatment?

Early Government Treatment Efforts

The U.S. government's earliest attempts to modify heroin addicts' behavior took place at the Public Health Service Narcotic Hospital in Lexington, Kentucky. It opened on May 25, 1935, in response to studies conducted during the 1920s on America's growing opiate-addicted population. The hope was that heroin addicts' behavior could be modified and corrected enough that they could complete a treatment program and return to productive lives in society.[1]

The Public Health Service Narcotic Hospital in Lexington, Kentucky, also known as the United States Narcotic Farm, shortly before it opened its doors on May 25, 1935.

Audio-Visual Archives, Special Collections and Archives, University of Kentucky Libraries

Until the establishment of the Public Health Service Narcotic Hospital in Lexington, Kentucky, treatment options for heroin addicts were largely limited to the quackery of quick-fix spas such as the one advertised in the May 1, 1904 edition of the St. Louis Post-Dispatch.

The Lexington facility was a combination hospital, farm, and prison for its patients. The majority of the patients were in fact federal prisoners incarcerated under the sentencing guidelines of the Harrison Narcotic Act of 1914. Some were sentenced to probationary terms that called for completion of a treatment program; they were released once they were deemed to be cured. A small percentage (4 percent) were voluntary patients who underwent a recommended six-month treatment program. Those patients who were prisoners served the full term of their sentences at the facility.

Prison reformers in the 1920s advocated strenuously for a long-term prison/farm to deal with heroin addicts. The number of prisoners with heroin problems was also a growing concern to the wardens assigned to guard them. The wardens knew they did not have the appropriate facilities to manage addicts properly. However, the idea that prison could be a place where rehabilitation occurred was still relatively new. Prison reformers like Thomas Mott Osborne and Frank Tannenbaum proposed a prison system that was meant not just for punishment but that actually took steps to alter criminal thinking and behavior. They envisioned prisons as separate communities where inmates could acquire the skills necessary to be good citizens upon release. They believed that work ethics and values could be instilled in the offenders if given the proper environment.

The Public Health Service hospital in Lexington grew out of this prison reform movement. In 1928, Stephen Porter, a Republican congressman, introduced a bill that would establish a "narcotic farm"; the bill was approved in 1929, and Lexington opened its doors in 1935.

The surgeon general at the time, Hugh S. Cumming, hailed the new facility as a way to correct the behavior of heroin addicts. He described addicts as people who were unable to deal with the complexity of American society. The industrial age was in full swing, and the styles and mores of urban life were spreading across the country. Gone were the days when America was a predominantly agrarian society. But Cumming and others apparently felt that immersion in the cultural models of a bygone era could help heroin addicts of diverse backgrounds.

Each patient at the Lexington hospital was to have a job assignment that ranged from furniture repair and manufacturing to an assortment of farm-related activities. Patients tended to crops, slaughtered animals, and raised hens. The belief that America's agrarian past held the key to personal and civic health was evident in the design of the hospital as a farm. The problem inherent in the concept is that the hospital was supposed to be preparing patients for a return to a modern industrial and urban society. Most of the patients were from the larger cities, had never been on a farm, and would never see a farm again. A review of the first year's patients showed that the voluntary patients were mostly farmers who had become addicted to opiates as a result of a medical condition. The rest were men from the cities, where heroin and the netherworld of organized crime reigned. It should not have surprised anyone that those patients who returned to the city upon release did not fare well.

In 1923, Dr. Lawrence Kolb, a psychiatrist who studied addicts extensively during the 1920s, was assigned to the Public Health Service Hygienic Laboratory in Washington, D.C., where he worked with 200 addicts. In 1925, after two years of research, he published his findings in a series of articles stating that the cause of opiate addiction was a preexisting psychoneurotic deficit. As discussed in chapter 4, Kolb described addicts as individuals who suffered from inferiority complexes and used drugs to soften or mask feelings of inadequacy. The implication was that these were people who were not particularly talented or capable and were unable to compete in a changing society.[2]

Kolb also felt that there was really no need for a long-term prison hospital. He believed that given two weeks without opiates, an addict could be detoxified, achieve abstinence, and be adequately treated psychiatrically. Ironically, this was the man whom the government chose to be the first medical director of the Public Health Service Narcotic Hospital.

It is hard to imagine the thoughts or reservations Kolb must have had concerning his new assignment, given his belief that such an institution was unnecessary. But he had been a psychiatrist with the Public Health Service since 1909, and as such was accustomed to following orders and accepting assignments, as any career bureaucrat must do. Being a conscientious public servant, Kolb must have put his personal philosophies aside and assumed the responsibilities entrusted to him.

Kolb instituted a three-phase treatment. The first phase lasted thirty days, the first ten of which were dedicated to withdrawal, or detoxification. During this time the patient was interviewed and assessed, and a profile was pieced together. The patient's relatives and friends were also interviewed to gain as much information about the patient as possible. A treatment plan was then written from medical observations, psychosocial information, and the patient's criminal history.

The second phase of treatment lasted the major part of the addict's stay. During these months patients were given work assignments, lived highly structured lives, and built themselves back up mentally and physically. The Public Health Service hospital was described as a healing environment, where new values could be learned. The third phase was preparation for the addict's return to the outside world. Ideally, the social services staff members at the hospital helped in returning the addict to a softer, gentler, more supportive environment than the one from which he came. Gainful employment was a stated goal. The reality, however, was that very few patients returned to jobs and supportive families. Most went right back to their old haunts, unemployed and devoid of any meaningful support network. This was arguably a setup for failure and led to high rates of relapse among early patients. The failures were heralded as evidence of the futility of the effort by those who were skeptical of treatment for heroin addiction. Many, including Kolb, labeled these relapsers as thrill seekers, incorrigibles incapable of recovering. The onus for failure was placed on the addict, not the treatment protocol.

Studies of relapse rates were conducted during the 1940s and 1950s. In 1965, John O'Donnell, a sociologist who worked at Lexington, analyzed these studies and concluded that an 80 percent relapse rate was the norm for heroin addicts. He cited problems with the methodology of the follow-up data and with how relapse was defined, taking exception to the idea that even short episodes of drug use qualified as a relapse. His findings were used by the pessimists who believed that treatment didn't work, and that addicts were primarily antisocial types who were better off in prison. These same pessimists supported the theory Kolb had expressed: that addicts were thrill seekers incapable of even modest accomplishments, such as staying away from drugs.

By the 1970s, other treatment facilities had sprung up around the country, and in 1974 the Lexington hospital was closed and turned over to the Federal Bureau of Prisons. The program failed despite the social, psychological, and medical services offered. Even the low patient-to-staff ratio (2 to 1) could not overcome the prisonlike setting. The attempt to instill traditional agrarian social values and work habits proved ineffective with hardened addicts from the inner cities. The result was that addicts were more likely to wind up in prison than in treatment.[3]

Synanon and the Therapeutic Community Model

In the early 1950s a group of narcotic addicts banded together to form Synanon, one of the first therapeutic communities, in Visalia, California.[4] The group was led by Charles Dederich, a narcotics addict who believed that addicts were better off without the establishment medical and psychiatric communities. Synanon members resented that doctors and society had branded them as incurable criminals as a result of their drug-seeking and using behaviors.[5]

Synanon borrowed aspects of Alcoholics Anonymous and devised an aggressive group therapy style that confronted the manipulative behavior of heroin addicts. Group members did not believe in employing professionals, whom they viewed as the enemy; all of the counselors and leaders were ex-addicts themselves. This approach, which came to be known as the therapeutic community model, was a response to the unwillingness or inability of the health care system to help the hard-core heroin addict.

Therapeutic communities became known for using rather severe tactics in confronting addicts' behaviors. Stories abound of addicts being forced to shave their heads, wear signs, and even submit to the occasional diapering, in which an addict was asked to sit in a corner wearing a diaper and a sign that proclaimed him a baby.

Synanon flourished into the 1960s and was acclaimed for its tough-minded approach to treating heroin addiction. The organization began to fall apart in the 1970s, however, when Dederich's increasingly bizarre behavior drew the attention of law enforcement officials. In 1978 Dederich and two members of Synanon were accused of placing a rattlesnake in the mailbox of a lawyer, Paul Morantz, who was involved in several lawsuits against Synanon. Dederich and the two members were convicted in 1980 of conspiracy to commit murder. Dederich was sentenced to a five-year probation and the other defendants received jail terms.

In 1985 Synanon found itself in court again, this time for allegedly defrauding the Internal Revenue Service. In a twenty-two count indictment, nine of the top Synanon officials were charged with falsifying records and avoiding taxes. They were slapped with liens totaling $55.6 million in back taxes and penalties. Among those charged was Cecilia Dederich, daughter of the founder.[6]

Synanon's ability to raise money was highlighted in 1986 in *Forbes* magazine, which detailed how the organization pulled in an estimated $30 million per year "manufacturing and selling ballpoint pens, coffee mugs and desk clocks customized with corporate logos" to major corporations.[7] Synanon clients included Western Union, IBM, RCA, and H. J. Heinz. The group reportedly used the pitch that it was doing good work with its profits and that the Synanon products generated funds for treatment. The magazine reported that Synanon's sales force was particularly aggressive. One of the group's prospective clients said, "Once they have you as a sales prospect they don't let go."[8]

The combination of legal problems and mismanagement eventually led to Synanon's demise. Dederich, who once proclaimed Synanon a religion, died at eighty-three in March 1997.

The Twelve Steps

Just as Synanon was in its infancy, another group of narcotic addicts in southern California founded Narcotics Anonymous in July 1953. This Twelve Step fellowship was closely modeled after Alcoholics Anonymous, with the same guiding principles of anonymity and self-help. The major difference from AA was that addiction was seen as all-inclusive. They believed they had a problem not with a specific substance, but with the disease of addiction. Any mood-altering substance was to be avoided. The first step of Alcoholics Anonymous reads: "We admitted we were powerless over alcohol—that our lives had become unmanageable."[9] Narcotics Anonymous amended this to: "We admitted we were powerless over *our addiction*, that our lives had become unmanageable."(Emphasis added.)[10]

Membership in Narcotics Anonymous grew rapidly throughout the United States, and in 1972 a central office, called the World Service Office, was opened in Los Angeles. Narcotics Anonymous meetings can be found throughout the world today with a membership estimated to be in the millions.

The most influential organization in the world of treatment has been Alcoholics Anonymous. It is *the* self-help organization upon which Narcotics Anonymous and numerous other anonymous fellowship groups base their programs. AA traces its roots to Akron, Ohio, and the chance meeting of two men, a stockbroker from New York and a local physician. The history of how Bill Wilson, a struggling alcoholic businessman, met Dr. Robert Smith, known as Dr. Bob, in Akron has been well documented in print and in the film *My Name Is Bill W.,* starring James Woods as Bill Wilson and James Garner as Dr. Bob. For a complete history of the early days of AA, read *Not-God: A History of Alcoholics Anonymous,* by Dr. Ernest Kurtz.

Bill Wilson, co-founder
of Alcoholics Anonymous,
at the gravesite of Dr. Bob Smith
in the Mount Peace Cemetery,
Akron, Ohio, 1958
Photo: Mel Barger

Bill Wilson had been fighting a losing battle with alcohol his whole life and was sober just six months when he met Dr. Bob in June 1935. Wilson had stopped drinking only after his exposure to the Oxford Groups of the time through a friend who was alcoholic. His friend had become sober following the principles of this small religious group that had its beginnings in England. Impressed by his friend's abstinence from alcohol, Wilson investigated the group's tenets. He didn't accept everything the group espoused but agreed with some of its beliefs, such as the need for taking a moral inventory, sharing it with another person, making restitution to those he had harmed, helping others, and the need for faith and dependence on God. For Wilson, who had become prejudiced against conventional religion, the key was coming to accept his own perception of God, a God of his personal understanding as opposed to a God of conventional religious thought.

Despite this revelation, Wilson continued to drink and, as had happened before, he wound up in the hospital, suffering again from delirium tremens. He reportedly had a life-changing spiritual experience during that hospital stay. He describes the experience in the book *Alcoholics Anonymous*, the basic text of AA: "There I humbly offered myself to God, as I then understood Him, to do with me as He would. I placed myself unreservedly under His care and direction. I admitted for the first time that of myself I was nothing; that without Him I was lost. I ruthlessly faced my sins and became willing to have my newfound Friend take them away, root and branch. I have not had a drink since."[11]

Wilson immediately began talking to other alcoholics about his experience, though with no success other than that he stayed sober himself. That, however, was a significant discovery in and of itself. Wilson realized that by sharing his story with other alcoholics, he could stay sober. He followed this strategy for six months until the day he met Dr. Bob in Ohio. Wilson had gone to Akron on business, but when his deal went sour, he became fearful that he might start drinking. He sought out another alcoholic to talk to and was directed by local clergy to Dr. Bob, whose drinking exploits were well known among the locals.

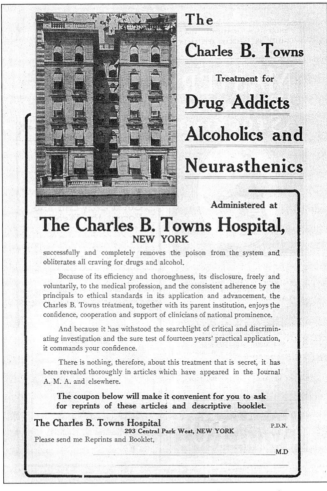

An ad for the Charles B. Towns Hospital in New York City,
where Bill Wilson had the spiritual awakening
that later led to the formation of AA

Hazelden-Pittman Archives

Dr. Bob was deeply affected by the talk he had with Wilson and shortly thereafter stopped drinking. He had his last drink on June 10, 1935, and remained sober until his death in 1950. He was the first man Wilson was able to enlist to his way of thinking, and the date of Dr. Bob's last drink marks the advent of Alcoholics Anonymous. The two men joined forces and began making calls to hospital wards, where they shared their experiences with hopeless alcoholics. They soon reached alcoholic number three and kept on until their ranks numbered close to one hundred.

The newly sober alcoholics met in each other's homes and later in church basements. Eventually, groups spread to New York and Chicago. By 1939 they published their "Big Book," or

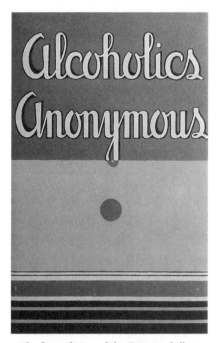

The first edition of the "Big Book,"
Alcoholics Anonymous
Photo: Dennis Becker

basic text, *Alcoholics Anonymous*, which served as a guidebook for getting sober. It included personal stories and "steps" that needed to be taken in order to remain sober.

The two most important concepts of Alcoholics Anonymous are the beliefs that there is a Power greater than oneself, and that the alcoholic is powerless over alcohol. Wilson, Dr. Bob, and the first AA members devised a set of guiding principles by which to live. They believed it was the only chance they had for staying sober, and that in order to live a fulfilling life they had to live by those principles. Below are the guiding principles—the Twelve Steps—of Alcoholics Anonymous:

Step One: We admitted we were powerless over alcohol—that our lives had become unmanageable.

Step Two: Came to believe that a Power greater than ourselves could restore us to sanity.

Step Three: Made a decision to turn our will and our lives over to the care of God *as we understood Him.*

Step Four: Made a searching and fearless moral inventory of ourselves.

Step Five: Admitted to God, to ourselves, and to another human being the exact nature of our wrongs.

Step Six: Were entirely ready to have God remove all these defects of character.

Step Seven: Humbly asked Him to remove our shortcomings.

Step Eight: Made a list of all persons we had harmed, and became willing to make amends to them all.

Step Nine: Made direct amends to such people wherever possible, except when to do so would injure them or others.

Step Ten: Continued to take personal inventory and when we were wrong promptly admitted it.

Step Eleven: Sought through prayer and meditation to improve our conscious contact with God *as we understood Him*, praying only for knowledge of His will for us and the power to carry that out.

Step Twelve: Having had a spiritual awakening as the result of these steps, we tried to carry this message to alcoholics, and to practice these principles in all our affairs.[12]

These steps were to be taken one at a time and in the order in which they were written. The biggest stumbling block for many was the idea of God. Simply saying that God could be whatever the alcoholic believed Him to be, a Power greater than oneself, enabled many to overcome prejudice against conventional religious associations with the word *God*. AA is not a religion but a spiritual way of living. The distinction between spirituality and religion is important, making it possible for atheists and agnostics to belong to AA. For many, their AA group is their Higher Power, while for others it is everything living around them. Some choose to view God as good, orderly direction provided by their sponsor or confidant in AA.

Bill Wilson was able to achieve what the medical profession had failed at. He discovered that alcoholics helping each other could remain sober. An alcoholic could stay sober by working with other alcoholics, sharing his or her own experience. Wilson wasn't successful with everyone, but at least he was staying sober himself. This discovery is the guiding principle that many treatment centers today use in designing their programs.

Today, Narcotics Anonymous, Sex Addicts Anonymous, Overeaters Anonymous, Gamblers Anonymous, Debtors Anonymous, and many, many more self-help groups are based on the Twelve Steps. The Twelve Step way of life seems to work for those suffering from addiction. Some members of AA believe that the Big Book was divinely inspired, that everything they need to know to stay sober is contained in those pages. Whether or not this is true, the words offer hope and direction for addicts who seek a more spiritual way of life. For those willing to go to any lengths to achieve sobriety, the Big Book shows the way to live. Wilson's belief in the near-infallibility of the Big Book as a guide to recovery is revealed in a now-famous anecdote. When asked if he would have changed anything in the Big Book, Wilson replied that there was nothing, except for one word. In chapter 5, titled "How It Works," the first sentence reads: "Rarely have we seen a person fail who has thoroughly followed our path." Wilson said he would have changed the word *rarely* to *never*. This was how sure he was that recovery from addiction was possible if the addict or alcoholic was willing to *thoroughly* follow the AA path.

Undoubtedly, AA and its principles have been a major influence in the recovery of millions around the world. One of the most prominent organizations in the field of recovery that bases its program of treatment on the Twelve Steps of AA is the Hazelden Foundation.

Hazelden and the Minnesota Model

Hazelden was incorporated as a treatment center on January 10, 1949. Hazelden's history is closely linked to Alcoholics Anonymous, the Catholic Church, and members of the early AA groups in Minnesota and Wisconsin. B. Patrick Cronin (1897–1965) was an alcoholic who read the AA Big Book during the summer of 1940 and was able to stop drinking by November of that year. He was one of the first AA members in Minnesota, and his influence and work with AA was far reaching. He is credited with establishing approximately 450 AA groups throughout the Midwest. He was an indirect force in the Hazelden story as the result of an introduction he made between two other alcoholics.

Cronin put together an alcoholic priest, Father M., who had

been struggling to stay sober, and Austin Ripley, a newspaper writer, author, and recovering alcoholic. Ripley had been asked to help alcoholic priests before; his religious conversion to Catholicism and his sympathy for the burden the alcoholic priests had to bear inspired him to champion the idea of a treatment center for priests.

Ripley offered to help Father M., who was in danger of being dismissed from the priesthood because of his alcoholism. He approached Lynn Carroll, an attorney and fellow recovering alcoholic for advice. He also spoke to Archbishop John Gregory Murray of St. Paul on the priest's behalf. Archbishop Murray was sensitive to the plight of alcoholic priests and was grateful to Ripley for the work he had done before in helping other priests through AA. The archbishop agreed to donate money toward Ripley's idea.

In 1947, Lynn Carroll met with Ripley and Robert McGarvey, a prominent Minneapolis businessman, to discuss the prospect of a center for professionals and clergy. Carroll and McGarvey felt they had a better chance of raising money if it were open to professionals as well as clergy, but were not able to dissuade Ripley from his view that it should be a facility strictly for members of the cloth. Ripley was adamant about this and Carroll and McGarvey relented. What eventually became the Hazelden Foundation was initially envisioned as a treatment center for Catholic priests and Protestant clergymen.

The three were able to raise money and pledges from Archbishop Murray, Father Edward Flanagan from Boys Town, and Father John Cavanaugh, president of the University of Notre Dame. They looked at property owned by the Power family in Center City, Minnesota. The beautiful, sprawling estate covered more than two hundred acres. Charles Power had bought the property from a man named Andrew Porter in 1925, the same year he married Hazel Thompson. Power named the estate Hazelden after his wife, and, according to their son, Charles Power, the "den" had no particular meaning other than being a natural elongation of her name. When the time came to incorporate, the board members used the title on the letterhead of the Powers' farm, Hazelden, and the name was never changed.

The philosophical differences among Ripley, McGarvey, and Carroll splintered the group before the treatment center ever opened. In the end it was Ripley's inflexibility and inability to appear accountable and fiscally responsible that moved him out of the plans for what would become the Hazelden Foundation. McGarvey and Carroll were able to obtain the backing of a prominent Minnesota banker, Richard Coyle Lilly (1884–1959), who was instrumental in putting together the financing for purchase of the Power property. Lilly served as the board of trustees' first president; Carroll, McGarvey, and Jack Kerwin were the first vice presidents. A friend and adviser to Lilly, A. A. Heckman, was also on the first board.

Lynn Carroll, the first director
of the Hazelden treatment center
Hazelden Foundation

Carroll was the general manager of the newly formed rehabilitation center and began the work of curing alcoholics on
May 1, 1949. It was McGarvey who suggested that the center
should be open to all men and women who were deserving of
treatment, rather than to professionals and clergymen only. At
first only men were treated. In 1956, however, women were admitted to a separate residence known as Dia Linn in White
Bear Lake, Minnesota.

Carroll's vision was to make Hazelden a place where alcoholics could heal themselves through the principles of AA. He
encouraged them to stay three weeks, which seemed to be
enough time to begin absorbing the concepts AA espoused
and to regain their physical strength. He worked tirelessly
with a small staff. He was the only counselor for the first few
years and wondered whether he had the proper background
for the task. He questioned whether the center should employ
psychiatrists and psychologists, but when he looked at his
own recovery he realized that no one in the medical profession
had ever been able to reach him. In the end it was one alcoholic
talking to another over a cup of coffee that had helped him, so
he began the work of healing alcoholics with a small staff consisting of himself; a cook, Ma Schnabel, who was also a registered nurse; a groundskeeper, Jimmy Malm; and a utility man
who helped with a variety of assignments.

In the beginning it was Carroll's experience with recovery
in AA that shaped the daily curriculum for the alcoholics who
made their way to Hazelden. Carroll believed in AA, knew that
it worked for many, and he applied its principles faithfully.
The course of recovery was straight AA philosophy. Carroll
talked to the men about the Steps and explained the process of
a recovering life to them, with great success.

From Hazelden's inception, its board of trustees was concerned with achieving results and with follow-up studies. In
his first report to the board, in January 1951, Carroll wrote
that after eighteen months 156 men had been treated at

Hazelden and that 78 percent had recovered and made progress in their lives. He noted that some had experimental, post-treatment drinking bouts, but that shortly after experimenting they had returned to the recovering lifestyle they had been taught; Carroll's approach was proved effective. Today, Hazelden is still known for achieving results where others have failed, and it is the haven of last resort for many desperate addicts and alcoholics.

During the 1950s, A. A. Heckman's vision and foresight proved to be important. Heckman had several concerns, one of which was that Hazelden should not rely solely on Lynn Carroll's abilities. He believed Carroll should take on understudies who could learn his method of treatment. If something were to happen to Carroll, the organization would be in trouble. So Hazelden began to take on trainees. Today, Hazelden has one of the world's finest counselor-training programs, with participants coming from all over the globe.

Another of Heckman's recommendations was that Hazelden not be run solely on AA principles. He suggested a multidisciplinary approach with cooperation between the professional and nonprofessional fields. An experiment that had begun in the 1950s at Willmar State Hospital in Minnesota, with alcoholics learning AA philosophy and being treated by members of the medical profession, was expanded and carried out at Hazelden during the 1950s and 1960s. This multidisciplinary approach came to be known as the Minnesota Model.[13]

Hazelden began to treat alcoholics with psychiatrists and psychologists, nurses, chaplains, social workers, and alcoholism counselors, all while keeping the AA Twelve Steps as the core of its treatment philosophy. This model proved to be the most well-rounded, holistic approach that had ever been used, producing effective results. The Minnesota Model has in some way affected virtually every treatment modality since and remains the basis for treatment at Hazelden today.

Hazelden is one of the few U.S. treatment facilities still able to offer a traditional twenty-eight-day course of AA treatment. The twenty-eight-day time period was arrived at by experiment at first—it seemed to be enough time for alcoholics to detoxify and begin absorbing AA education while rebuilding their physical strength. When Hazelden started treating needy cases who couldn't pay for treatment, grants were obtained from supporters. The donors usually paid for a four-week stay; thus, Carroll's initial recommendation of three weeks as an optimal recovery period was extended to four weeks, which became a standard for rehab treatment. When managed-care health care philosophies became preeminent in the early 1990s, however, insurance companies balked at paying for extended treatment, and time limits were imposed on inpatient stays. Many treatment facilities, and the alcoholics and addicts they treated, began to feel the pinch and were forced to resort to either outpatient treatment or seven to fourteen days in a treatment center. Many managed-care companies insist on even shorter stays, as less expensive solutions to addiction are sought, with not much concern for addicts' long-term well-being.

Although Hazelden's reputation was built on treating alcoholics, since the late 1980s the center also has become known for its treatment of patients addicted to heroin. According to Hazelden counselor Don Gargaro, the center is seeing more individuals from all parts of the country addicted to heroin. The addicts are younger than they used to be—mostly in their twenties and thirties, as opposed to late thirties and forties, as was typical ten years ago. Gargaro states that many smoke heroin or develop heroin-sniffing habits, and that the stereotypical needle user has become less common.

The patient begins the admission process with an interview to assess the extent of his or her heroin usage and to ensure that he or she receives proper medical attention during withdrawal. If the patient is in withdrawal, he or she will usually be given catapress, a medication to lower the blood pressure.

Hazelden does not use methadone to detoxify heroin addicts. The new patient will be given a bed in the medical unit where he or she will be monitored before being transferred to a primary rehabilitation unit. Heroin addicts are usually kept in the medical unit for just a day or two unless they are exhibiting severe withdrawal symptoms. Because heroin withdrawal is not life threatening, addicts are moved into the rehab phase as quickly as possible.

During these first days of treatment, a psychological assessment and medical examination are done, and a drug history is written. From this assessment a treatment plan is devised. The new patient is assigned to a room in a residential unit where he or she will live with twenty to twenty-four other men or women. Patients are not segregated by drug of choice; thus, for example, alcoholics, heroin addicts, and methamphetamine abusers all would be part of a single unit. Men and women are separated during treatment, and fraternizing with the opposite sex is not allowed.

In the residential units there are four-person, two-person, and single-person rooms. The singles are for those patients who might have a physical problem that requires privacy, or for those nearing completion of the program who have acquired "senior peer" status, which carries additional responsibility. New admissions usually start in a four-person room, work their way to a two-person room, then move into a single toward the end of their stay.

There are four men's and two women's residential units in the rehab center, with each unit housing up to twenty-four patients. In Center City, Hazelden can accommodate up to 150 patients at a time. Each unit is a self-contained community with its own head counselor and staff. The units eat, sleep, and work separately. Fraternization among the units is discouraged—again, particularly between men and women. This allows for closer bonds to be knit with members of the patient's own little community.

There are four counselors per unit, including the head counselor, enabling each counselor to carry caseloads of four to seven patients and thus ensuring proper therapeutic relations between patient and counselor. Each patient also receives the services of a recreation therapist, a chaplain, a psychiatrist, and social workers.

A typical treatment day will start with breakfast, followed by a group meditation with a reading from the "little black book," Richmond Walker's *Twenty-Four Hours a Day,* which has helped alcoholics start their days for decades and is a source of strength for the millions who use it. Each patient receives a "therapeutic duty assignment," which could be anything from vacuuming to taking out the trash. A sense of collectiveness and humility can be gained from these TDAs, as they are called.

After the assignments are completed the units break into smaller groups of six to ten patients each for group therapy sessions led by the counselors. The groups are nonconfrontational. A supportive, nurturing, and solution-oriented style is used. All of the patients attend a lecture after morning group sessions. The didactic lectures can be on any number of topics, such as one or more of the Twelve Steps, relapse prevention, or

The original Hazelden farmhouse
Hazelden Foundation

AA history. Lunch is next, and the food is good as far as rehab food goes, with special attention paid to the importance of proper diet for the newly recovering person. For example, substances like caffeine are not available to patients in the cafeteria. The afternoon consists of another lecture and another group therapy session. Individual counseling sessions also take place throughout the day, but the emphasis is on group therapy because it has been found to be more productive and therapeutic for addicts. Dinner is followed by an evening lecture and then free time.

During free time patients write. They work on any one of the many workbooks that Hazelden publishes on topics such as living skills, anger management, or dealing with shame. Many heroin addicts struggle with shame and guilt as a result of their desperate drug-seeking and using behaviors. Patients write about whatever issues were identified in their treatment plans. They may write essays about powerlessness, for example, describing how their lives became unmanageable. They work through the first three Steps, do the Fourth Step in writing, and complete the Fifth Step by sharing the Fourth Step

Hazelden today
Hazelden Foundation

with another person, usually a chaplain. Patients might be asked to write a short essay on a passage from a book such as *The Road Less Traveled* by M. Scott Peck. There is much to do and the image of treatment as addicts lying around in hospital beds smoking cigarettes is not applicable at Hazelden.

Recreational therapy is available at the athletic center, which has a heated indoor swimming pool, basketball courts, indoor running track, and weight room complete with barbells, treadmills, and Universal weight-lifting equipment. The philosophy is that the whole being needs nurturing and rehabilitation and that recovery time can be used to begin rebuilding physical strength and instilling healthful habits that a heroin addict can use to stay sober. Many heroin addicts wind up exercising almost passionately once they stop using and find that exercise can release endorphins, creating a natural euphoria.

By the end of the twenty-eight-day treatment period the heroin addict will have learned about the Twelve Steps of AA and completed the first five; ideally, he or she will have had a spiritual awakening that will give him or her the extra push needed to face the world again. The addict will have gone through peer evaluations in which his or her blind spots to recovery were pointed out, and he or she will have spent considerable time reflecting on his or her life. Patients are taught to embrace the program of recovery offered by NA and AA and are given help in finding a Twelve Step group following discharge. At Hazelden, the addict is treated with respect and dignity, perhaps for the first time in his or her life. He or she leaves the center prepared to reenter the human race as a proud, sober member.

Hazelden focuses on healing the psychological, spiritual, medical, and social facets of addiction. The center teaches the addict to rely on the Big Book of Alcoholics Anonymous for inspiration and guidance, and shows him or her how to live a spiritual life, directed by the Twelve Steps. When it is time for a patient to leave, Hazelden recommends a halfway house where the addict can live for anywhere from a few months to a year. Hazelden stresses that the keys to success upon discharge are establishing relationships with other recovering people, giving oneself enough time away from drugs to change life habits, and following the directions of people in AA/NA.

The high success rate Hazelden realizes with its patients could be due to the thoroughness of the Minnesota Model. Many who have been through this type of program say it was the spiritual healing and their involvement with AA/NA that saved their lives. They claim that being treated with respect was new to them, and that it gave them a sense of dignity. One thing seems clear: an addict who shows up physically, spiritually, and emotionally bankrupt can turn his or her life around in a program that spiritually awakens a belief in himself or herself and some sort of Higher Power. It seems this belief is needed in order to address and heal the physical and emotional bruises and scars left after life as a heroin addict.

The Haight Ashbury Free Clinics and the Community-Based Treatment Model

Not everyone makes it to a treatment center like Hazelden, however. Some may be caught without insurance, forcing them to rely on community-based treatment programs funded by local, county, or state funds. There are many of these programs around the country. The advent of managed care has made them the only recourse for many addicts trying to recover. It is to such programs that those on public assistance, for example, are most often referred. Many cities throughout America have provided services to heroin addicts via freestanding treatment centers, like the Haight Ashbury Free Clinics in San Francisco, California.

Founded in 1967, the Haight Ashbury Free Clinics have provided treatment to addicts for the past thirty years under the leadership of Dr. David Smith, the clinic's founder. In three decades the clinics have seen drug trends come and go, and in the last five years they too have seen an increase in the number of heroin addicts they treat.

Treatment at the Haight Ashbury Free Clinics is administered, as the name implies, free of charge. The clinics currently treat an average of 300 patients a month with approximately 150 more on their waiting list. According to Richard Seymour, information and education director at the Haight Ashbury and managing editor of the *Journal of Psychoactive Drugs,* heroin addicts present a unique challenge in treatment. The clinics use a modified medical model in combination with a behavioral science approach. Seymour says that "the more tools there are available to treat addicts with, the better chance the addict has of recovering."[14]

The heroin addict who enters treatment at Haight Ashbury is usually in some state of withdrawal, so he or she receives clonidine, which lowers the blood pressure and alleviates some withdrawal symptoms. Once the addict is past the withdrawal stage, he or she is prescribed naltrexone, an opioid antagonist that will block the effects of a heroin dose and diminish cravings for opioids. The addict could be on naltrexone indefinitely, if needed, but will be weaned off of it if he or she proves able to manage cravings.

Treatment is open ended and delivered on an outpatient basis. The first two weeks are devoted to stabilizing the patient physically so that he or she is able to take part in group therapy sessions, where the work of recovery begins. Patients receive psychosocial counseling individually and in groups. The program consists of five full days per week and Seymour describes it as "diagnosis-driven treatment," meaning that each case is different and that what might work for one addict will not necessarily be effective for another. Each individual requires a specific treatment plan for his or her own circumstances. "Motivation is the key," Seymour reports. As an example, he describes two patients, one an airline pilot, the other a homeless person living on the street. What motivates the pilot to recover may not have any significance for the homeless individual. Figuring out a patient's motivators is essential to designing a successful treatment plan.[15]

All of the clinics' patients are educated about NA/AA and are encouraged to attend meetings regularly. Most patients wind up going through about a year of treatment, then resume their lives and return to work or school. While they are in treatment, random urine tests are given to check their sobriety. While Haight Ashbury requires total abstinence as part of its program, it does not use the urine tests to police or discharge patients; rather, it uses the tests as a diagnostic tool to see where the patient is in his or her recovery program.

Haight Ashbury has long been known for its population of hard-core drug users. The clinics have been successful in treating many, but they lose many others. Seymour believes that applying the best of the medical and behavioral models helps achieve results, and that it sometimes takes a combination of modalities to reach an addict and arrest his or her disease.[16] In essence, whatever it takes is in order. At Haight Ashbury a combination of the medical and behavioral approaches with a Twelve Step model meets the needs of a wide range of individuals. Treating hard-core users, the clinics have done "whatever it takes" for thirty years.

Dr. David Smith, a former president of the American Society of Addiction Medicine, is not surprised by the most recent heroin epidemic. He explains that an opiate epidemic naturally occurs after a stimulant epidemic like the one the United States experienced during the 1980s with cocaine. What comes after an opiate epidemic? Another speed epidemic, this time methamphetamine. Working on the front line, Smith and the staff at the Haight Ashbury Free Clinics will continue to use all the tools available from both the medical and the behavioral toolkits. The drugs used by addicts may change, but the nature of addiction never does.

Does treatment work? There are skeptics who feel it does not. Dr. Herbert Kleber, of Columbia University's Center on Addiction and Substance Abuse, believes "the skepticism about treatment effectiveness arises from misunderstandings about improvement vs. cure, chronic relapse, the failure to distinguish rehabilitation from habilitation, and the visibility of failures and anonymity of successes."[17] Kleber states that it is probably more accurate to say that treatment *can* work rather than to say that treatment *does* work.

There are many variables in the treatment of heroin addiction, as we have seen, and there is probably no one sure way to treat it effectively. To some extent, our society's problems in judging the effectiveness of treatment modalities come as a result of our preconditioning. For example, the Food and Drug Administration judges a medicine to be effective if it improves the symptoms of a disorder by 30 percent. Kleber points out that in judging addiction treatment, laypeople and professionals alike expect a combination of the effects of penicillin and a smallpox vaccine, with lifetime immunity after one dose. It would be unfair to judge the effectiveness of any treatment modality based on the expectation of instant cure.

Addiction is a chronic relapsing disorder. It is also a progressive disease. In the same way, recovery is progressive. Many times, addicts learn from their relapses and improve with each failure and new treatment attempt. They might not get it on the first try but find success on the third or fourth. It must be remembered that for many active addicts the goal is learning how to control using. Many relapses are exercises toward this end. With each uncontrollable episode, or relapse, the addict grows closer to accepting his or her powerlessness with respect to the drug. Because success is measured by total abstinence, it is no wonder that many view treatment skeptically. Many experts argue that *progress* should be the barometer for gauging drug treatment success.

If not for the sake of the addict, treatment makes sense for the sake of society. Treatment's cost benefits and its positive impact on society make it worth the money. An untreated drug abuser costs society $43,000 per year in social services, medical care, and crime. To incarcerate that addict costs about $40,000 per year. Residential treatment costs, on average, $16,500 per year.[18] Reductions in criminal activity, drug use, and risky sexual behavior are but a few of the positive impacts treatment can have on society.

For too long, issues surrounding drug policy have been influenced by politics. In the words of Hebert Kleber, "Treatment is not a conservative or liberal approach—it is simply a cost-effective approach."[19]

CHAPTER

7

The Politics of Methadone Maintenance

Each of us has a responsibility to be intolerant of drug use
anywhere, anytime, by anybody. . . . We must create an
atmosphere of intolerance for drug use in our country.

NANCY REAGAN

Methadone is a synthetic opioid compound used in the detoxification of heroin addicts and in long-term daily maintenance of
their physical cravings for the drug. It binds to the same receptors in the body that bind with morphine molecules and is referred to as an opioid agonist.[1] A heroin addict receiving a
therapeutic dose of methadone on a daily basis will be relieved
of his or her craving for opiates, and the methadone will in effect "block" a dose of heroin if the addict tries to get high. It is
a long-acting (twenty-four to twenty-six hours) drug that can
be administered orally; in contrast, morphine needs to be given
every four to six hours in order to stave off withdrawal symptoms, and it must be administered intravenously for optimal effect. Many in the medical field view methadone as the drug of
choice both for treating heroin withdrawal syndrome and for
use in a well-administered daily maintenance program, but its
use, especially in daily maintenance, is often viewed skeptically
by laypeople and even some professionals in the field of substance abuse as a mere substitution of one opioid for another.

Methadone is one of the most controversial subjects that
will arise in any discussion of treatment for heroin addiction.

Some believe it to be nothing more than an immoral substitute for heroin, with equally addictive qualities. Others see methadone maintenance as a valid pharmacological approach, an effective first step on the road to total abstinence, and for some addicts a way of life less traumatizing than heroin addiction because it enables them to feel less socially marginalized. There are many myths and misperceptions surrounding methadone, and in order to understand the differing views it is essential that we look at the history of the drug as well as societal perceptions of who becomes addicted to heroin.

There are currently between 750,000 and one million Americans who use heroin regularly.[2] Approximately 120,000 of these users are treated in some form of methadone maintenance program.[3] This means that only 10 to 15 percent of heroin addicts have access to what many doctors and researchers consider to be the most effective treatment modality for heroin addiction. Skepticism abounds, however, among government policy makers, the public, and substance abuse counselors about this option. Some addicts themselves are leery of using a drug they feel is harder to break away from than heroin. Among addicts, the myths about methadone are that it "gets in your bones," makes your teeth rot, and makes you impotent. Those in the medical community who are proponents of methadone dispute these myths and point to the results of long-term studies. They believe extensive research has shown that methadone is medically safe to use over extended periods of time.

Methadone was first synthesized by the Germans during World War II when their supplies of morphine started running low.[4] A popular myth has circulated that the chemists named the drug Dolphine after Adolph Hitler. This is not so; the name derives from the Latin *dolor* (pain) and the suffix *phine* (as in morphine). The Germans used Dolphine as a painkiller for their wounded and found it to have the same qualities as morphine, with the added benefit of a longer duration of analgesic effect.

After the war, methadone was first studied in America at the Public Health Service Narcotic Hospital in Lexington, Kentucky, for its possible use in treating heroin withdrawal syndrome. It was used in place of morphine with a slow, seven- to ten-day tapering of the dose until the addict was detoxified.

Methadone Maintenance

In the 1960s the idea of using methadone as a maintenance drug, or daily substitute for heroin, was researched for the first time by a team of pioneering doctors in New York City. The concept of maintaining heroin addicts with a daily supply of opiates, however, was not new. As early as 1912, a clinic in Florida dispensed morphine to addicts every four to six hours. A similar clinic opened in Tennessee in 1913, and by 1919 there were forty-four opiate clinics in municipalities across the country, primarily where large populations of addicts existed. Some operated as detoxification centers; others prescribed and dispensed heroin and sometimes cocaine. Two of the more famous programs were in New York City and Shreveport, Louisiana. In New York, the Department of Health clinic detoxified addicts with decreasing doses of morphine and heroin; in Louisiana, the clinic run by Dr. Willis Butler also maintained addicts on morphine.[5] A now famous anecdote about the commissioner of public safety in Shreveport illustrates the theory that perceptions of who can become addicted can influence public attitudes. The commissioner is reported to have strongly objected to the presence of a maintenance clinic in his town, until he discovered that his own mother was a patient of Butler's. He then apparently had a sudden change of heart about the matter.[6]

Maintenance clinics were able to operate legally because of the wording in the Harrison Narcotic Act of 1914. The legislation was not intended to outlaw opiates, cocaine, and their derivatives, but rather to regulate their manufacture, distribution, and prescription. An amendment to the law in 1919 allowed physicians to prescribe narcotics for legitimate medical purposes. However, an overzealous attitude on the part of the Treasury Department's Narcotics Division thwarted the efforts of doctors working in the early maintenance programs. The Treasury Department's position was that addiction to opiates was not a disease; therefore addicts were not real patients, and doctors who prescribed narcotics to them were in violation of the term "legitimate medical purposes" in the amendment. Treasury agents thus went on to harass and imprison doctors and addicts alike. The final blow was dealt to early maintenance clinics by two Supreme Court decisions in 1919, *Webb et al. v. United States* and *United States v. Doremus*. Both decisions upheld the Treasury Department's position. Later, however, two cases went against the *Webb* decision: *Lindner v. United States* in 1925 and *Boyd v. United States* in 1926. They came too late, though, to save the early maintenance programs. The Treasury Department's Narcotics Division had adopted the antimaintenance position set forth in the *Doremus* and *Webb* decisions and continued its harassment of physicians until the last clinic, Butler's in Shreveport, closed its doors in 1923, two years before those controversial decisions were overturned. Most likely the pressure of harassment, fear of imprisonment, and lack of public support deterred doctors from opening maintenance clinics after 1926.

Not coincidentally, the period between 1923 and 1936, when there were no governmental programs for heroin treatment, saw a dramatic increase in drug-related crime in almost all major cities across the country.[7]

As discussed in chapter 1, by the turn of the twentieth century, the faces of opiate addicts had begun to change from those of middle-class white women to those of lower-class European and Asian immigrants. It was this shift in the addict population that spurred the enactment and enforcement of the new narcotics laws. One could argue that the change of focus was both racist and sexist in nature because heroin use became of great concern to white middle-class men only when the fear became widespread that white women were becoming ensnared by drugs and thereby involved with the new immigrant minority underclass that was flooding the country.

After World War II, another change in the makeup of the addicted population occurred as many African Americans from the country's rural south migrated to the industrial northern cities in search of work. At the same time, Latinos from Puerto Rico, the Caribbean, and Central and South America immigrated to the United States, settling in major cities across the country. "White flight" followed as the European immigrants left urban tenements for the suburbs that were springing up across America during the 1950s and 1960s. They left behind decrepit buildings in neighborhoods where there often existed narcotics trafficking and an assortment of other inner-city social problems.[8]

By 1960, the public attitude toward addiction was not one of compassion, but one of intolerance. The targets of that attitude were the poor white, Chinese, African American, and Latino immigrants who found themselves locked in urban ghettos that offered them little hope of improving their lives and presented many obstacles for them to overcome in the daily struggle to survive. As a refuge and comfort, many turned to the euphoria that heroin offered, a temporary escape from the harsh reality in which they were forced to live.

This is arguably the root of the stigma that heroin has carried, a stigma conceived in the cultural and ethnic prejudices of the dominant white culture. It was this stigma that was passed on to the early methadone patients. The face of heroin addiction by 1960 was decidedly one of color, so it is no surprise that the pioneers of methadone maintenance met severe criticism, skepticism, and lack of compassion for their clients, who were largely members of the underclass.

It was in this social climate that a New York doctor, Vincent P. Dole, a specialist in metabolism at Rockefeller University, was asked to begin experiments with heroin addicts. Dole felt an urgency for this work and considered it to be of extreme importance, because the leading cause of death for young adults between the ages of fifteen and thirty-five in New York City was, by the 1960s, heroin related.[9] In 1962 he was appointed chairman of the Narcotics Committee of the Health Research Council of New York City by Dr. Lewis Thomas. Dole assembled a research team that included Dr. Marie E. Nyswander, a psychiatrist who had worked at the Public Health Service Narcotic Hospital in Kentucky. Nyswander had also worked with heroin addicts in private practice and in a clinic she established in East Harlem. She was convinced that heroin addicts could be treated in private practice as long as their craving for the drug was eliminated. It was her published article, "The Heroin Addict as a Patient," that convinced Dole she should be involved in the research. She joined the team in 1964. The team was completed by Dr. Mary Jeanne Kreek, a clinical investigator doing work in neuroendocrinology at the New York Hospital-Cornell Medical Center.[10]

Initially, the team focused on injecting low doses of morphine into its first two patients, but found this ineffective because the patients required several doses a day in order to be stable. The patients were also unable to function normally on morphine since they were high or euphoric and tended to nod off. They also remained preoccupied with drugs and required increasingly higher doses. The researchers tried synthetic opioids, such as heroin, oxycodone, codeine, and meperidine, with similarly unsatisfactory results.[11] In retrospect, it may seem paradoxical to use heroin to treat a heroin addict, but not when viewed in light of what were then the goals of maintenance:

controlling addicts' criminal, drug-seeking behavior and minimizing health risks addicts posed to themselves and society.

The research team then began to consider using methadone. Little was known scientifically about methadone because the technology to measure blood levels of heroin and methadone had not yet been invented; researchers had to rely on careful observation in clinical settings. Through clinical testing, the team found that once tolerance to a dose of between 80 milligrams and 120 milligrams of methadone had been achieved, the patients no longer exhibited the physical craving for and preoccupation with drugs they had when using the shorter-acting opioids. This meant it was now possible for addicts to resume normal, socially acceptable patterns of behavior, such as looking for work or caring for a family.

Because of the Narcotics Committee's initial research, six major findings regarding methadone maintenance were brought to light:

1. The patients' behavior was normalized; they did not experience euphoria once a tolerance to methadone had been developed. This enabled them to function productively in society without nodding off.

2. At a methadone dosage of between 80 milligrams and 120 milligrams, tolerance to heroin and other opioids was high enough to block any euphoric effect, thus discouraging the addicts from using illicit opioids.

3. There was no increasing tolerance to the methadone itself, which enabled addicts to remain on a constant dosage daily.

4. Methadone was effective orally and its influence lasted for twenty-four hours, eliminating the need for injections, which in turn eliminated unsterile practices and needle sharing.

5. Methadone relieved the craving for heroin, which had been cited as a major cause of relapse in past trials.

6. Methadone was nontoxic and had few side effects. The most common patient complaints regarding methadone use included constipation, sweating, and decreased libido. These side effects could be treated, however, and eventually normalized.

In 1965, buoyed by the findings of the research team, Dr. Ray Trussell, commissioner of the New York City Department of Hospitals, expanded the research to Manhattan General Hospital, where a detoxification program was in place. An independent committee was created under the guidance of Dr. Frances Rowe Gearing at the Columbia University School of Public Health and Administrative Medicine to evaluate the progress of methadone maintenance. That group's work was reviewed by another independent committee under the leadership of Dr. Henry Brill, who recommended expansion of methadone maintenance programs in the city and further research.[12]

The behavior of patients treated with methadone maintenance was found to be socially acceptable; the patients ceased criminal behaviors associated with heroin addicts. They began to think of looking for work and becoming integrated into mainstream society. Of course there were those who were polysubstance abusers and others who did not respond immediately with socially acceptable behaviors, but the research was found to be successful enough that methadone maintenance was hailed as the treatment modality of choice for heroin addiction.

A combination of social and historical factors helped to expand methadone maintenance over the next few years. The first was that returning Vietnam veterans began to show up at VA hospitals with heroin-related problems and addiction. It should be noted that the popular perception that the vast majority of Vietnam veterans were addicts was simply not true. There were veterans who became addicted while overseas and who resumed their addiction upon returning to America, but the great majority did not use heroin while in Vietnam and did not become addicted after discharge. Their near-universal characterization as heroin addicts was one of several myths the veterans had to endure in the troubling postwar years of the 1970s.

Another factor in the expansion of methadone maintenance was President Nixon's growing concern about evidence linking crime in the cities to an upswing in heroin addiction. In 1970 domestic advisers began to look for solutions to the problem by visiting treatment programs in the Washington, D.C., area. One of the more successful ones they looked at was run by Dr. Robert DuPont, who was using the methadone maintenance modality with considerable success. The advisers recommended setting up committees to provide suggestions on how to combat the rising number of heroin addicts. A government-led group consisting of staff members from the National Institute of Mental Health, the Office of Economic Opportunity, the Drug Enforcement Administration, and the Department of Housing and Urban Development recommended that methadone maintenance treatment not be approved, but rather be further evaluated and tested. Another group, led by non-government professionals working in the field of addiction as program directors and researchers, recommended rapid expansion of methadone maintenance as a form of treatment.

Nixon took the advice of the nongovernment group, and in 1971 methadone maintenance treatment became federal policy. The president appointed Dr. Jerome Jaffe director of the Special Action Office for Drug Abuse Prevention.[13] This office devised and coordinated strategy for drug policy, except law enforcement. Nonprofit community-based methadone maintenance programs, as well as private clinics run by doctors for profit, began to spring up across the country rapidly during the remaining years of the 1970s.

It was during this time that many of the myths the public came to believe regarding methadone were developed. There was much controversy surrounding the placement of clinics

*A community protest at a proposed methadone clinic site
in Elizabeth, New Jersey, October 1973*

Photo: Humberto Fernandez

near residential neighborhoods. Many residents objected to the daily traffic of unsavory looking individuals. Concerns about loitering, drug dealing, and crime around the clinics were key reasons the public resisted the use of methadone treatment. The image of an unkempt person of color nodding in midstride on the sidewalk in front of their houses was not what most middle-class Americans envisioned for their neighborhoods. As a result, many clinics wound up in buildings or offices in the less desirable parts of inner cities, or on the outskirts of towns in areas often inaccessible by public transportation. Patients who used additional drugs, such as benzodiazepines and alcohol, *were* seen in somnolent states, leading the public to believe that methadone was merely a legal substitute for heroin, that the two were essentially the same drug, and that therefore the addicts' drug supplies were being doled out at taxpayer expense. In addition, the government was accused of being pro-methadone at the expense of other modalities; but in fact, methadone programs were outnumbered by programs treating heroin addiction with nonpharmacological traditional approaches. The problem was that "model," or compliant, methadone patients were invisible; they acted normally, with no apparent signs of being heroin addicts. They went to work, raised families, and went about their business quietly. It was the addicts who continued in addictive behavior patterns, often with other drugs, who were extremely noticeable and who created a bad impression for methadone treatment. Unfortunately, this is still true today. Among the more serious problems plaguing methadone programs are perceptions resulting from secondary drug abuse by some patients.

The purpose of methadone maintenance was to eliminate the need to use heroin, and in that regard the treatment has been successful, as evidenced by the statistics. A study conducted during the 1970s in New York City, with more than 10,000 patients participating, showed that 85 percent stopped using heroin within the first year of treatment. The patients showed a 94 percent reduction in heroin use after three or more years.[14] Based on this and additional research, it is generally thought that the optimum length of time for a heroin addict to receive methadone treatment is three to five years. Some manage to put their lives together in shorter time frames; others require longer periods before they are ready to address the root causes of their addiction and begin to wean themselves off methadone. Still others find that they cannot endure life without opiates and stay on methadone indefinitely, supporting the theories of researchers who believe that heroin addiction is a metabolic disease. They believe that once the brain becomes dependent on opioids, an irreversible chemical imbalance occurs; the brain will require continued opiate use.

In the 1980s, the national focus moved away from heroin as cocaine from South America began to flood the country. Crack cocaine and violent crime in the cities became more pressing concerns to Americans, particularly to professionals working in the substance abuse field. It was during this decade that the abstinence model patterned after the Twelve Steps of Alcoholics Anonymous had its heyday. Twenty-eight-day treatment programs sprang up everywhere, and insurance companies began to finance rehabilitation for alcohol and cocaine addictions with a conviction that these programs were the most effective way to treat addicts. It heralded a dramatic shift away from pharmacological approaches like methadone maintenance to more spiritually oriented approaches with heavy emphasis on self-help groups.

By the mid-1980s, however, the AIDS epidemic was taking a serious toll on intravenous drug users and their sexual partners, so that by 1989, methadone was once again being considered as a control mechanism, or tool, to stem the spread of disease and HIV infection. Funding for methadone that had been cut during the late 1970s and early 1980s started to return as communities restored programs for heroin addicts. Despite the lingering popular perception that methadone treatment was an embarrassment and ineffective, its use in combating the spread of AIDS was generally accepted.

Research has borne this theory out. In a study of methadone programs in Baltimore, New York City, and Philadelphia, it was found that 71 percent of 388 patients in treatment for over a year had ceased intravenous drug use. By contrast, 82 percent of 105 patients who left nonmethadone treatment programs relapsed rapidly to needle use.[15] Another study showed that patients in methadone treatment before 1983 were significantly less likely to test positive for HIV infection than those entering treatment after 1984. Yet another study revealed an absence of HIV infection in all of 58 socially rehabilitated, long-term methadone patients who had been enrolled in methadone maintenance an average of 16.9 years; before treatment, the same patients had engaged in an average of 10.3 years of intravenous drug use with many reporting that they had shared needles.[16]

The Current State of Methadone Maintenance

Despite indications that methadone plays a valuable role in the prevention of disease, federal money has dwindled over the last two decades, making it increasingly difficult to provide addicts with treatment slots in methadone programs. During the 1980s federal money for methadone programs was reduced by one-third.[17] In the 1990s, with the shift to place Medicaid patients into private managed-care programs, a resurgence in heroin addiction has occurred. This could be one of the reasons why only 10 percent to 15 percent of all heroin addicts receive methadone treatment. Prejudicial stigma still haunts a viable treatment modality because of preference for a total abstinence model over harm reduction via methadone maintenance.

Currently there are only eight states that do not provide methadone maintenance treatment. New Hampshire, Vermont, Mississippi, and West Virginia arguably have a need—that is, they have documented populations of heroin addicts of significant numbers—but claim otherwise, and provide no public funding for such treatment despite federal guidelines that permit them to do so. Montana, Idaho, North Dakota, and South Dakota offer no methadone treatment but have not opposed it either, as the other four states have. This can be attributed to the fact that there are indeed few addicts in those states or that heroin users in those states tend to choose abstinence model treatment.[18]

There are advocates who struggle to solve the problems facing methadone maintenance treatment today. One of these, the American Methadone Treatment Association, with offices in Washington, D.C., and New York City, focuses on issues surrounding public health policy making. The association's president, Mark Parrino, says that one of his key concerns is the expansion of methadone treatment slots available to heroin addicts in the 1990s. The impact of managed-care policies on treatment is being felt as states begin to look at limiting time in treatment for addicts and at defunding public programs in favor of private clinics; both trends run counter to the concept that not everybody recovers at the same pace and in the same way. While some addicts may become habilitated in three to five years, others may require fifteen. The question arises: Should society arbitrarily cut off an addict from methadone treatment after three years, perhaps sending him or her back out to the street in search of heroin? This strategy seems contra-indicated by clinical studies that show the effect of limited-duration methadone treatment to be a 71 percent relapse rate within the first six weeks for those prematurely discharged.[19,20] Furthermore, a study conducted in 1993 showed that shorter stays in treatment were the strongest predictor of high-risk behaviors, leading to the spread of addiction, disease, and needle sharing.[21] The biggest problem faced by addicts seeking treatment in privately owned clinics is their inability to pay for the treatment. Many are forced to continue a "hustle," or illicit means of supporting their treatment, which is contradictory to accepted treatment aims such as honesty and law-abiding behavior. In a study conducted over a five-year period in the San Francisco Bay Area, it was found that the leading cause of addicts being unable to access treatment was their inability to pay.[22]

So, organizations like Parrino's struggle to convince public policy makers of the efficacy of methadone treatment. One of Parrino's primary goals is to use existing methadone treatment programs as hub sites for new rapid-intake admission and for networking among satellite entities, including hospitals, general medical practitioners, and possibly HMOs. The idea is to move the more stable methadone patients into privatized medical treatment in the care of doctors who would treat them as they would any other patient with a life-threatening disease. This would accomplish two things: it would restore a level of dignity the patient doesn't have in many clinical settings, and it would free up an additional six thousand treatment slots nationwide for new patients.[23] One problem is that many clinics now have guidelines dictated by zoning ordinances limiting the number of patients they may treat. This is a direct result of community pressure. If a clinic is treating four hundred heroin addicts, the last thing the neighborhood wants is for the patient list to increase by 25 to 50 percent. So we see that even though many addicts would like to have a more normal life via treatment with methadone, there are real obstacles in their path.

Parrino presents an interesting question: If heroin addiction is real, and if addiction is in fact a disease, doesn't it make sense to treat it with the most effective tools at our disposal? He feels the lack of public support for this modality is due to prejudice and misperception, and he offers an example to back up the theory that we as a culture do not value treating heroin addicts because of their color or socioeconomic status: if a white middle-class businessman smokes cigarettes, drinks excessively, eats red meat, and doesn't exercise, which can lead to heart disease or cancer, we do not question whether he should be given the best medical treatment to save his life when he's wheeled into the emergency room with a heart attack. We treat the health problem. Yet when a heroin addict presents himself for treatment, the public and even some substance abuse professionals feel entitled to pass judgment because "he did it to himself." Parrino says we have a tendency to deny the disease concept as it applies to addiction, in much the same way that medical insurance companies did during the early 1980s. A heroin addict could be admitted into a hospital for a twenty-eight-day stay, but had to proclaim that he was also an alcoholic because insurance companies paid for alcoholism treatment and heroin detoxification but not twenty-eight-day heroin addiction treatment.

The following are some of Parrino's recommendations to address the problems facing methadone maintenance treatment in America today:

- Offer comprehensive medical and counseling services on-site to respond to the immediate needs of the current patient population and develop a network of ancillary referral services.
- Plan medical, case-management, and counseling caseload

numbers around the specific needs of the program's
patient population.

- Configure caseloads to provide better access to HIV
  counseling and intensive clinical support for patients
  using alcohol and other drugs.
- Encourage patient peer-support and self-help groups to
  meet in methadone maintenance treatment programs.
- Take patient loitering seriously; prevent loitering by
  establishing policies that are integral to the treatment
  process and are maintained by stable personnel.
- Educate the public about the value of methadone
  maintenance treatment.
- Use cooperative "good-neighbor" projects, open houses,
  and educational forums to engage the community.
- Use treatment resources as efficiently as possible; this
  goal will become more achievable as policy-driven
  research increasingly suggests how to use the best mix
  of personnel in treating patients at different phases of
  their care.
- Develop models of care that respond to individual patient needs during different phases of the methadone
  maintenance treatment experience. Newly admitted patients will require access to a broad range of services,
  whereas successfully stabilized patients who have been
  maintained on methadone for several years may require
  less intensive services.[24]

As stated earlier, the original concept behind methadone
maintenance was to use it as a control mechanism: to control
and diminish criminality and drug-seeking behavior, and to
eliminate the cravings for heroin. Richard Nixon's primary
concern was crime reduction when methadone maintenance
was instituted as federal policy. The political agenda of the
day had less to do with relieving the hard lot of heroin addicts
than with the war on crime. Nixon may have been trying to

relieve the plight of heroin addicts, but his agenda was first and foremost crime reduction.

Providing effective treatment is something that many programs still struggle with today. It would be an oversimplification and a generalization to say that methadone is used as a control device, or Band-Aid, but since the AIDS epidemic arrived in the 1980s, we are once again talking about methadone as a means of "controlling" the spread of HIV. Some well-administered clinics do use the opportunity methadone maintenance provides for intervention, and they deliver valuable service; sadly, many more merely control addicts' behavior.

Establishing methadone clinics accomplished two things: it reduced crime and it registered the heroin addicts. We "knew where they lived," so to speak. And although federal confidentiality laws protect methadone clients, those laws can easily be outmaneuvered. For example, while working at a methadone program in Manhattan, I was approached by two police officers from the "fugitive squad" who were looking for an individual. They had been to his residence and had learned from his landlord that he was in a methadone program and that he needed to go to his clinic every day. The landlord gave them the location of the clinic. When confronted by the officers and asked whether the individual in question was a client there, I was bound by the confidentiality laws to neither confirm nor deny his status. I advised them of this and asked that they leave; however, they merely waited in an unmarked car in front of the clinic for several hours until the fugitive showed up. They were able to identify him from a mug shot and arrested him as he tried to enter the clinic. They were, however, decent enough to allow him to be medicated with his daily dose before escorting him to jail. Needless to say, it caused quite a commotion in the waiting line before the nurse's station, as two police officers escorted the handcuffed client to the front of the line and held a cup of methadone to his lips while he drank. Procedure prohibited them from taking off the man's handcuffs so he could drink the methadone himself. It was truly a humanitarian gesture on the part of the officers; they knew that to not medicate him would have been cruel. Heroin addicts and police are not normally the best of friends, but in this situation I overheard some of the addicts who witnessed the incident say that the "cops were square dudes" who had done the right thing. Certainly, the individual who was arrested was relieved that he would not be sick for at least another day or two.

Many of the counseling staff members I interviewed for this book expressed frustration with the way some clinics are administered. Methadone patients come in daily but are in and out in ten minutes; they do not want to be hassled with counseling efforts and "just want to drink their methadone and go." Hence, it is sometimes difficult to establish therapeutic relationships with the patients. Many facilities are severely cramped for space and workers and find it difficult to conduct group therapy. Some clients do not want to bother with group or individual therapy sessions even if space is available.

A common patient complaint is that there is a high turnover among counseling staff members—"they come and go." Given the fact that many patients remain on methadone for ten, fifteen, and even twenty years, it is easy to see how they could say this. Another complaint is that many of the counselors are much younger than the addicts. A fifty-two-year-old addict with a twenty-five-year drug history, for example, could wind up on the caseload of a twenty-four-year-old college graduate with a psychology degree, and even if that staff member had state certification as an addictions counselor, the addict might still feel somewhat disconnected. "What can she possibly tell me? I've been shooting heroin and in and out of jail longer than she's been on this earth" is a common attitude that young drug counselors have to contend with, and it can be a barrier to establishing a relationship. It can take between eighteen and twenty-four months of trust building, with monthly ten-minute visits, before anything that resembles a therapeutic relationship can be established. By that time, the counselor is usually ready to move on to a better paying job within the field, or is ready to escape burnout from handling caseloads that can average as many as fifty to sixty patients. Then the addict will have to deal with feeling abandoned. Abandonment and neglect are common threads in heroin addicts' stories. Many suffered childhood traumas and have problems with trust. A new counselor will take over a caseload and wonder why some patients resist establishing a trusting relationship. From the addict's viewpoint, he is forced to once again go over his life story and help the new counselor understand who he is and how he got there, perhaps for the fifth or sixth time in ten years. It is no wonder that some hardened methadone patients say, "I'm just here to drink my methadone."

Continuity of clinical counseling staffs is a vital issue in administering effective, therapeutic methadone treatment, and unless better pay and lucrative incentives are offered to counselors as a means of keeping them in one clinic for three to five years, it will remain difficult for patients to receive the maximum benefits of this form of treatment.

Public skepticism and bias, community resistance, legislative constraints, lack of treatment slots, long waiting lists, prohibitive costs, and administrative deficiencies all are obstacles that heroin addicts who desire treatment have to overcome before they can confront their personal obstacles. Many do persevere. Their stories are heart-wrenching testaments to the strength of their will to survive.

CHAPTER

8

Case Histories: Methadone Maintenance

The following are four case histories of patients
currently in methadone treatment in New York City.

Allison

Allison is a white female, forty-nine years of age, who has been in methadone treatment off and on over the past twenty-five years. A high school graduate, she has attended college and reports having earned sixteen college credits. She was born in Brooklyn to a working-class couple: her mother was a homemaker and her father a salesman. An only child, she studied dance from the age of three and one of her early dreams was to be a ballerina. A major disappointment in her life was an injury to her ankle during her early teens that ended her dancing career. Her first major trauma was the death of her mother when Allison was nineteen. She reports being devastated by her mother's death and that things were never the same after her mother died. She regrets not having been able to make amends with her mother over an argument they had just before her mother died. Apparently, her mother was unhappy with the direction in which Allison was heading and didn't like the fast crowd Allison hung out with.

Allison's drug use began at age eleven or twelve with alcohol. She and a girlfriend stole some liquor from her mom's house and drank it secretly. She reports feeling sick and vomiting but recalls being strongly attracted to the initial feelings of intoxication. At age fourteen she tried methamphetamine with friends in order to feel "part of the crowd." Her pattern of use during her teen years was occasional drinking and pot smoking, mostly on weekends, but there were periods of time when she drank or drugged every day.

Her first exposure to heroin came at age twenty. She was with a boyfriend who was sniffing heroin, so she tried it. She reports that she felt nauseated but that the high was everything she had been looking for. She was feeling despondent over the recent death of her mother and the heroin made her feel warm, able to forget the emotional pain. She sniffed occasionally for a few months and then graduated to intravenous use, again with her boyfriend, and within one year was using up to seven bags of heroin daily. She went into her first detox in 1969 at age twenty-one, but failed to stay clean, so by 1971 she enrolled in a methadone maintenance program in Brooklyn, where she was treated from 1971 to 1979. During this period, she worked intermittently but was often on public assistance. She also continued occasional use of heroin and other illicit drugs.

She dropped out of treatment in 1979 and stayed relatively clean at first, with only occasional heroin use. But her use gradually escalated, and she returned to methadone treatment in 1982. After three years at a methadone program in Queens, New York, Allison again left treatment, citing the "nuisance" of her daily visits to the clinic as her reason for dropping out. As before, she had been unable to abstain from other drugs, such as cocaine and alcohol, during her treatment, and she had even indulged in occasional heroin use on weekends, when she would sell her take-home methadone dose. From 1985 to 1991, away from any formal methadone program, Allison resumed full-time heroin use. She was reportedly arrested twenty-seven times during this period for offenses ranging from larceny and writing bad checks to car theft. She did prison time at Rikers Island in New York City for some of these offenses and a stretch at a women's prison in upstate New York.

She resumed methadone maintenance in 1991 to avoid going to jail and has been in treatment since then.

Currently, Allison has her own apartment and is attending college, working toward a degree in psychology with aspirations of becoming a substance abuse counselor. She feels her life is more stable now than it ever has been, but she's not sure that she can ever live totally drug-free, and sees methadone maintenance as a vehicle for stabilizing her life and thereby helping her achieve her life goals.

Allison deeply regrets the years she lost to her addiction, particularly a failed marriage and the loss of a relationship with a son by that marriage. Her son is currently in his early twenties, and Allison takes pride in the way he has turned out—by her description, a straight, normal kid. She expresses concern over rumors that methadone treatment in the future will be limited in duration; she feels she needs another three years of stability before she could attempt methadone detoxification, a process she views with trepidation.

Mitchell

Mitchell is an African American male, fifty-nine years old, who has used heroin and has been in and out of prison for most of his adult life. Born in Manhattan at Bellevue Hospital, he was the older of two boys in his family. His father died when he was only two years old and his mother never remarried. He says it was tough growing up without a father, but that quite a few of his childhood friends also were fatherless, and that he was very close to his mother and younger brother while growing up.

His mother was a domestic worker who always held multiple jobs to make ends meet and to provide for Mitchell and his brother. He expresses admiration for how hard she worked, and one of his deep regrets is that his mother died in 1977 before she could see the birth of Mitchell's own son.

Mitchell grew up in Harlem and attended public schools

until the eleventh grade. He reports that his early childhood and teen years were similar to those of his peers, with a considerable amount of time spent alone while his mother worked to pay the bills. He spent time hanging out with friends "on the stoop," usually playing "the dozens," a game of verbal one-upmanship, and looking for things to do. He first drank beer in 1951 or 1952 at age thirteen. Shortly afterward, he started smoking marijuana. He claims alcohol and marijuana use helped to pass the time and that he enjoyed the way they made him feel; "plus, all of my friends were doing it." He drank and smoked pot for several years but remained, nonetheless, active in sports, particularly basketball. Basketball enabled him to get out of Harlem by his senior year, when he earned a scholarship to a private high school in North Carolina from which he obtained a high school degree. His basketball abilities earned him a scholarship to a college in Durham, North Carolina, but he only played through his freshman year; his career was cut short because of drug use.

While in North Carolina, Mitchell had initially stayed away from drugs, but during school recesses he returned home to New York and inevitably "hooked up with his boys," with whom he smoked marijuana. It was during such a school recess that he tried heroin for the first time. He recalls feeling nauseated and vomiting from the effect of the drug which he'd used by sniffing, but that once his stomach calmed down he felt a peaceful euphoria unlike anything he had ever experienced. "It was what I had been looking for all along," he says.

During the summer break between his freshman and sophomore years of college, Mitchell was arrested in New York for possession of heroin. He cites this as the reason he failed to return to college in the fall. Back in New York for good, his college and basketball careers over, he began to sniff heroin on a daily basis. To support his use he began selling heroin. It was a couple of years before he graduated to needle use, at first "skin popping," then intravenous injection. He was twenty or twenty-one years old. Because he was selling heroin and using the profit to support his habit, he was able to build up a high tolerance to the drug, injecting up to three "Harlem quarters" per day. (A "quarter" was a unit of measurement named for the measuring tool, a quarter tablespoon; it was usually available only in Harlem. In other parts of New York the more standard "bags" of heroin were sold. A quarter yielded approximately six to ten bags of heroin and sold, in the 1950s through the 1970s, for around $15 to $25, depending on the purity.)

Mitchell was unaware that the colds and the flulike symptoms he frequently suffered from were actually heroin withdrawal symptoms; he reports that he needed one quarter each time he injected just to feel "normal." Eventually, however, he came to realize that he was seriously dependent on heroin.

Drug selling eventually got him involved with the criminal justice system. A convicted felon, he has reportedly been arrested nineteen times for possession and possession with intent to sell, and once for a weapons violation. He was incarcerated from six months to five years at a time on numerous occasions throughout his life. His usual pattern was to be arrested for possession, convicted and sentenced to three to six years of jail time, then released on parole after serving three years. While on parole he would invariably be rearrested for possession, charged with parole violation, and sent back to prison for another two to four years, only to repeat the pattern all over again. Mitchell reports that he has stayed out of trouble since his last incarceration, largely because of methadone treatment. He recently completed his first successful parole period.

Mitchell estimates that he has spent about twenty-five years in prison; at this point, he states that he is tired and scared of going back to jail. He says that his last stint behind bars left him terrified of current prison conditions. "The kids, the young guys, don't have no regard for life. They'll stab you or cut you just as soon as look at you, and for no good reason. I'm too old to survive another incarceration," he says.

Mitchell has been on methadone maintenance since 1991, and he says that his life would not be the same without it. Upon his last release, he almost immediately got back into using heroin, but rather than continuing to risk violating his parole, he enrolled in a methadone program. He reports that his life has been stable since that time and that he has been able to resume his education.

While in prison Mitchell was able to earn an associate's degree and is now only eighteen credits shy of a bachelor's degree in psychology. Although he's not exactly sure what he will do when he finishes his degree requirements, he expresses amazement that he has been able to accomplish this, and it is a great source of pride for him.

Mitchell believes he owes his rehabilitation to methadone treatment. He has been able to maintain his own residence, a small one-bedroom apartment on the Lower East Side of Manhattan, and he works a steady job at a bakery to support himself. He is trying to reestablish relationships with his grown daughter and teenage son. He regrets the years away from them, years he spent chasing drugs or locked up, but feels that there is hope if he can stay clean.

"If they limit my time on methadone, I don't know what I'll do," he says. "I know I won't survive because I ain't never been able to stay away from heroin without it. I'm too old to stand the detox from methadone, and too old to survive in prison. I have to have my methadone, that's all there is to it."

Louise

Louise is an aspiring musician in her early thirties. She was born in Queens, New York; her mother is Italian American and her father is of Puerto Rican heritage. Both of her parents were heroin addicts and she says that her mother was on methadone maintenance throughout Louise's early childhood years.

Louise's first exposure to drugs came at age seven when a friend of her mother's introduced her to marijuana. By age eleven she was smoking pot and drinking alcohol on her own. She reports that her parents broke up when she was four years old and that she was raised by her mother until she was thirteen. At thirteen she went to live with one of her mother's friends in what she describes as a softer, gentler environment. She attended private school and seemed to flourish. This period lasted for only about a year, however; she was back with her mother by the time she was fourteen. She remembers feeling depressed because she didn't like living with her mother, who was an active drug user and a source of embarrassment to her.

By age sixteen Louise dropped out of high school. She had been drinking and using marijuana since she was eleven and reports being an alcoholic drinker by age sixteen. Between her seventeenth and nineteenth birthdays she began experimenting with LSD and other hallucinogens. Her pattern consisted of smoking pot, drinking daily, and using LSD on weekends. She almost always used with friends and was depressed whenever she was alone.

One of her early traumas was the disappearance of her father. He vanished from her life when she was nine years old, and no one would say where he was. It was not until she was thirteen that she discovered in a rather abrupt and dramatic fashion that he had been sent to prison for murdering his girlfriend. Apparently, her father escaped from the hospital for the criminally insane in which he was incarcerated and showed up in Louise's bedroom one night. He told her to pack her bags and come with him. She went along with him initially but, after becoming frightened by his bizarre behavior, such as looking through garbage cans on the street and talking loudly to himself, she convinced him to take her home. She has not seen him since. She says he was returned to prison and that she communicates with him periodically through letters. She claims he is very poetic and encouraging to her, and she admits that consequently she tends to romanticize and idolize him.

Louise began using heroin at age twenty-one with a musician boyfriend. She reports sniffing half a bag and feeling euphoric like she had never felt before. Initially she vomited, but after the nausea wore off she felt extremely flushed and warm, uninhibited and loved, and that everything was all right with her world. She continued sniffing heroin over the next three years until she first used intravenously at age twenty-four. She says that she enjoyed the rush of sensation tremendously and never went back to using heroin any other way. She admits to being fixated on needles.

Louise has been on methadone maintenance for six years and has never been able to stop using secondary drugs; she admits to repeated episodes of bingeing with cocaine during her methadone maintenance treatment. She also occasionally resorts to using heroin when she can't get to the clinic to be medicated.

During her methadone treatment Louise has had only one arrest, for fare evasion on the subway, for which she was sentenced to community service. She has not spent any time in jail.

Her goals are to stabilize her life and to pursue her career as a rock musician. She envisions herself one day being free of methadone and heroin, but smoking pot and drinking occasionally in a controlled manner.

Louise has drifted from one male companion to another and currently resides in Brooklyn. She has had no significant contact with her mother over the past ten years and says that if she does get off methadone she would like to someday have a child and "do the right thing."

When asked what "the right thing" meant, she replied, "Not mess up my kid's life the way my mother did to me. I never really got a square shot at this, you know."

Kent

Kent, a forty-five-year-old African American male who is currently on methadone maintenance, was born in Elizabeth, New Jersey. His father was a truck driver who had migrated from

North Carolina in the late 1940s. It was in Elizabeth that his father met his mother. They married and had five children, of whom Kent is the second. He reports that his mother never really worked due to poor health and the responsibility of raising five kids. He remembers his father as being a very big, strong man and he says he felt closer to his mother, who died when Kent was a young boy. His father never remarried but had girlfriends who would stay with them occasionally.

Kent's earliest memories are of good times on Friday and Saturday nights when his parents would have friends over to play cards. He remembers peeking out from his room with his older brother and watching the men and women dancing to music, having a good time. In the morning he and his brother would sometimes look for half-empty glasses of liquor and drink whatever was left over from the previous night. This was his first exposure to alcohol. He recalls feeling woozy and enjoying the giddiness that the alcohol produced. His father caught him on one occasion and gave him a beating, admonishing him to never drink again. He reports that after this he and his brother gave up the practice.

Kent romanticizes his childhood as idyllic, especially the time he spent with his mother. He gives the impression that he was her favorite, and he gazes off with a dreamy look whenever he speaks of her. He claims that he didn't really get into doing drugs until after high school, which he completed.

After graduating from high school, he began hanging out in New York City, mostly around Eighth Avenue and Forty-second Street, where the sex trade was a thriving industry at the time. Elizabeth, New Jersey, is a twenty-minute train ride from midtown Manhattan, so it was possible for him to live at home with his father and spend his nights in New York City. This continued for a couple of years until his father grew tired of Kent's lifestyle and forced him to either get a job or move out. Kent chose to move out. He was making money running errands and purchasing drugs for some prostitutes he had befriended. He says that he never pimped, but that he did enjoy being around the people involved in that kind of life, with sex, liquor, and drugs easily available.

It was in this setting that he first tried heroin at age nineteen. One of the "girls" he knew from the street provided him with the drug. After sniffing a full bag, he felt like he'd "found what he was looking for." Within six months he was using a needle, at first shooting into the muscle in his arm and eventually graduating to intravenous use.

Within two years he was using as many as five to ten bags of heroin daily. He supported his habit by buying drugs and selling them to the girls from the sex trade with whom he had become friendly. He was arrested at age twenty-one on a possession charge, the first of what he reports to be at least nine arrests. He did time (six to twelve months) in the city jail on a few occasions and was sent to a prison in upstate New York for seven years on one charge, the longest stretch he served on any single conviction. Even while in prison, however, he was unable to stay away from heroin.

After his release in 1983, Kent faced another three years of parole time, and he knew that unless he did something, like enrolling in a methadone program, he would inevitably return to prison. The first thing he did upon release was to buy heroin, so his fears were not unfounded. During the mid-1980s he began methadone maintenance treatment. Before this he had only been treated in detox in city hospitals whenever his habit became too much to bear, so he thought the only hope he had was to register in a methadone clinic.

Even while on methadone maintenance Kent has been unable to avoid using heroin. He occasionally sells his weekend take-home dose and buys heroin with the money. He says that he does this because he misses the rush of injecting heroin; he looks forward to it on Saturdays and Sundays. He also uses cocaine on a weekly basis, or whenever he can afford it, mixing the cocaine with heroin in a "speedball" injection. Sometimes he complements the daily methadone dose with Valium because, he says, that this makes him feel quite euphoric. He admits that he is not trying to rehabilitate himself and that he is still involved with addictive behaviors, but he feels he cannot cope with his life circumstances any other way. He "just likes to get high."

Kent has lost touch with his brothers and sisters, and his father died several years ago. He now lives alone in a single-room-occupancy hotel managed by the city of New York for people with AIDS. He was diagnosed HIV positive in 1990, and his health has deteriorated rapidly over the last two years. He has lost forty pounds, has trouble climbing stairs or walking even short distances, and suffers from inflammation of the legs and feet. He has numerous abscesses on his legs and arms from unsterile injections and has undergone two skin grafts to replace tissue on his right calf.

Kent exhibits a sadness in his face and expresses himself with slow, drawn-out speech patterns. He readily admits that his lifestyle is the cause of his demise but feels that it "all just kind of snuck up on me." He feels he doesn't have a whole lot of time left to live and claims he is trying to stay away from heroin and cocaine. But he says that sometimes life just becomes too much to bear, so he uses heroin to escape and glimpse a bit of happiness from earlier days. He reports that the hotel he lives in is infested with drugs, making it difficult to stay away from the dealers, who offer credit and come around to collect their money on the days that public assistance checks arrive. Some months he is left with very little cash and has to scrounge or rely on the generosity of others to feed himself. He reads the Bible and is involved in a study and prayer group that he finds comforting at times. Kent knows it is only a matter of time before he passes on, and he seems to look forward to it. He expresses fear of death but says that at last he will be reunited with his mother.

The following was recorded during a conversation with Kent in 1996:

I was very close and protective of my mother. She was a very beautiful woman with long black hair. She must have had some Indian blood in her. I remember being eight or nine years old and coming in the house and she would ask me, "You gonna comb mommy's hair today?"

See, she used to let me comb her long beautiful hair, and I would take care of her. She would get sick a lot; she drank and didn't take care of herself too well. So she'd have to go away sometimes. Sometimes for six months, sometimes for as long as a year, she would go to the mountains and recover from the TB.

My father, he would take me to visit with my brothers and sisters once in a while. I remember her there in a place with maybe fifty other people, all lined up in beds, all in a row. They were all sick with the TB too. And we would have to wear these gowns, and padded slippers, and face masks. We'd just stand there looking like doctors in a operatin' room, ten feet from her bed, and we'd just look at her. Then after a while we'd go back home. It was a long drive, I remember that. And I missed her all the ride home.

I was so happy when she would come home! She loved to do puzzles of beautiful landscapes with a lot of different colors. She would spend hours just sitting there putting together jigsaw puzzles that filled up the whole room. When she was done she would glue the pieces together and put them up on the walls and even the ceiling. So I'd just lie on my back and gaze at these beautiful colors that hung up on our walls.

When she got sick the last time, I knew I wasn't going to see her again. They took her to the hospital, and two days later my father told me that she had passed on.

I didn't cry. I didn't cry during the three days of the wake and funeral. I just sat there and looked at how beautiful she looked. And so young. She looked so peaceful like she was just asleep and would wake up any minute.

I was glad she died. I used to pray for her to hurry up and die 'cause I didn't want her to suffer no more. . . . I should have taken a lock of her hair then. I wish today that I had some of that beautiful straight hair. I don't know why I didn't think of it then. I must have been in a state of shock or something. But I sure wish I had a lock of that beautiful hair today to touch.

I didn't cry. I also didn't say a word. I didn't speak a word for four days from the moment my father told me she died. When we came home from the funeral, my father said, "Boy, you stop carryin' on that way—mommy gone now. It's over."

I wasn't being difficult. I just didn't know what to say.

I didn't cry until a month later one day. I don't know why I started crying, I just did. I was in her room and I picked up her hairbrush. It suddenly swept over me like a strong wind. She was gone and wasn't ever coming back. I'd never brush that long, beautiful, straight black hair again, and I started to cry.

I cried all day that day, until my insides hurt. I missed her then, and I miss her now, more than ever before.

If only I had cut a lock of her hair.

CHAPTER

9

Pharmacological Approaches
to Heroin Addiction Treatment

Everyone is looking for simple answers to a very complex
problem. . . .

HOWARD LOTSOF,
heroin addiction researcher and treatment advocate

While Ronald Reagan was president in the early 1980s, the
federal government's annual budget to fight the drug war was
approximately $1 billion. Almost two decades later that figure
has climbed to more than $16 billion. The combined federal,
state, and local effort toward the drug war has cost nearly
$290 billion. Despite this, worldwide production of cocaine
and heroin has more than doubled, making the drugs cheaper,
more plentiful, and of increasingly higher purity levels.[1]
These are some of the statistics put forth by those who pro-
pose that the drug war is not working. Law enforcement
sources themselves admit that we cannot arrest our way out of
the problem. Many experts point to a three-part approach
consisting of enforcement, treatment, and prevention as the
most effective way to combat the havoc that drugs have
wreaked on our society. Some say that the nearly 70 percent of
available funds that are spent on enforcement and interdiction
is too much, that more money should go toward treatment and
prevention efforts. If we were to allocate more money for
treatment, where would it go? What research is being

conducted to find the most *effective treatment* of heroin addiction? As we have seen, behavioral programs, such as the therapeutic-community approach and those based on the Minnesota Model, have produced varying degrees of success in treating heroin addiction. This chapter will look at some of the drugs being considered as *pharmacological* solutions to the problem of heroin addiction.

Ibogaine

Ibogaine is one of the most controversial drugs to have been offered as a treatment for heroin addiction. It is derived from a flowering shrub, *Tabernanthe iboga*, primarily found in the West African country of Gabon. It is an alkaloid that was first purified by French chemists in the early 1900s.[2] The indigenous people of Gabon use it as a stimulant while hunting and in larger doses during religious ceremonies. The Gabonese tribesmen are practitioners of the Bwiti religion and believe that ibogaine assists them in speaking to the spirits of those who have died.[3] The drug is also used ceremonially in a rite that marks adolescents' passage into adulthood.[4]

The person who uses ibogaine enters a dreamlike, hallucinatory state lasting twenty-four to forty-eight hours. Proponents of ibogaine as a cure for heroin addiction believe the user is able to examine his or her life in a way that is possible only with hallucinogens. Researchers at the University of California at Berkeley have reported that it unlocks repressed childhood memories.[5] Given to heroin addicts, it seems to help them look at their early lives and examine their current life circumstances, and it provides a cathartic experience from which they are able to muster the resolve necessary to change addictive behavior. Addicts reportedly walk away free of heroin withdrawal symptoms, with no craving for the drug, and are able to stay clean for years, all from a single ibogaine administration. If the addict relapses or has urges to use again, he or she can undergo another ibogaine treatment, with no danger of developing a dependence on the drug.

Ibogaine's effectiveness in treating heroin addiction was discovered by accident in 1962 by Howard Lotsof, at the time a heroin addict living in New Jersey. He took the drug just looking for another high, but discovered that after the experience he didn't need a heroin fix. He was straight, without a dose of heroin for over twenty-four hours, yet surprisingly was not sick. He was devoid of the familiar signs of withdrawal. Amazed, he gave the drug to seven of his heroin-addicted friends. He found that five of the seven quit heroin immediately without any withdrawal symptoms. Having struggled for years with his own heroin addiction, Lotsof, deeply affected by his discovery, was filled with a sense of purpose. He felt strongly that the ramifications of this experience, and what it could mean to the hundreds of thousands who suffered from heroin addiction, should be earnestly and vigorously explored. So he set out to convince the U.S. government of the efficacy of using ibogaine in treatment, urging them to begin conducting experiments with heroin addicts. His ardor was met with skepticism for more than twenty years. It was not until 1991 that he began to get the serious attention of the world's scientists. That year he began working with Jan Bastiaans, the Dutch psychiatrist known for his work with LSD therapy in treating Holocaust survivors. Their initial joint effort consisted of treating a group of thirty American heroin addicts who were flown to Holland for ibogaine therapy.

Lotsof reported that two-thirds of the addicts treated with ibogaine remained clean and sober for periods ranging from four months to four years. The scientific community's response was that the information was anecdotal and the sample group too small to be conclusive. But the results piqued scientists' interest because conventional treatment modalities were reporting relapse rates as high as 75 percent for heroin addicts.

In 1993, a delegation of American addiction researchers arrived in Amsterdam to study the experiments of Lotsof and Bastiaans. The researchers were so impressed that shortly after their visit, the National Institute on Drug Abuse started experimenting with ibogaine on rats and began to seriously consider ibogaine as a possible treatment therapy for heroin addiction. The Food and Drug Administration approved experiments on humans in 1994, but only at levels high enough to test ibogaine's safety thresholds, not its effect on addiction. Research is in progress at the University of Miami, with FDA approval, under the supervision of Dr. Deborah Mash and Dr. Juan Sanchez-Ramos, two neuroscientists.

According to Lotsof, a therapeutic dose of ibogaine is safely measured at 18 milligrams per kilogram of body weight. A 180-pound man would require 1,500 milligrams of ibogaine to bring on the hallucinatory dreamlike state required to effect a psycho-pharmacological, spiritual experience. Not surprisingly, the medical establishment has expressed reservations, which may not be unfounded. There have been two deaths possibly attributable to ibogaine therapy, though in fairness both may have resulted from heroin overdose and not the ibogaine.[6] (The details surrounding the deaths are murky, and it is not known whether the addicts' use of heroin while taking ibogaine resulted from fear of withdrawal or a desire to overcome the effects of the ibogaine.) The only known dosage threshold for ibogaine was tested on rats in clinical experiments. Both deaths—one in Switzerland in 1990 and one in Holland in 1993—were caused by respiratory arrest, and both patients had heroin in their blood. They both were given less than 10 percent of the known ibogaine rat threshold, so it is at best unclear whether or not their deaths were caused by ibogaine. Lotsof claims that ibogaine is totally safe when its use is supervised properly.

It was in the 1980s that Lotsof began to gather clinical

proof that his theories about ibogaine had merit. In 1988, Dzoljic et al. verified that ibogaine attenuated narcotic withdrawal in rats.[7] Clinical observation showed that opiate-dependent rats stopped self-administration of opiates after an ibogaine experience, with no visible signs of withdrawal. Glick et al. (1991) expanded on Dzoljic's experiments and also concluded that rats would stop taking opiates after being given ibogaine.[8] In some cases, a single administration was not enough, and the experiments conducted by Glick concurred with what Lotsof had theorized in 1985, that in these cases a second or third administration would indeed interrupt opiate self-administration.

How exactly does this wonder drug work? To understand the phenomenon it is necessary to delve into the world of neuroscience. Ibogaine purportedly moderates use of not only opiates, but also cocaine, a stimulant, and alcohol by affecting the body's ability to produce dopamine, the substance believed to be responsible for reinforcing the pleasurable effects of drugs. This was found after experiments conducted by Maisonneuve et al. in 1991.[9] Studies by Popik et al. (1994) showed ibogaine to bind to the NMDA receptor complex.[10] Deecher et al. (1992) demonstrated that the drug binds to the kappa opiate receptors as well.[11] In addition, ibogaine has been proved by Dr. Deborah Mash et al. (1995) to target serotonin transporters and to elevate serotonin levels.[12]

Another clinical experiment, conducted in 1996 by Hough et al., helps explain why the effects of ibogaine are so long lasting.[13] The researchers found that ibogaine clings to the fat cells in the body and is excreted very slowly.

If these results are correct, we have in ibogaine a drug that binds to the body's opiate receptors, allowing a painless heroin withdrawal, while elevating serotonin levels (as drugs such as Prozac are known to do), reducing the desperation usually accompanying the first few days of withdrawal. Furthermore, the addict walks away with no cravings, because the ibogaine is slow to leave the body. Perhaps the most significant part of this potential treatment option is the psychological catharsis the addict undergoes during the ibogaine experience, which is difficult to measure or document in purely clinical terms.

In addition to the positive results in treating heroin addiction, ibogaine has been successful in treating methadone-dependent individuals. Lotsof reports that clients who had been maintained on doses as high as 120 milligrams of methadone daily successfully detoxed in two to four days without the agony of methadone withdrawal, which would normally last six to eighteen months.[14] Most important, as reported by Kaplan et al. (1993), addicts themselves advocate it as the most effective way to break the chains of addiction.[15] In addition, in a study published in 1990 (Woods et al.), ibogaine, unlike methadone or any of the other opioid agonists, has proven to be nonaddictive.[16]

So why don't we have ibogaine treatment available on demand to those who want it? According to Lotsof, who holds patents on this form of treatment and on the use of ibogaine in the treatment of nicotine, alcohol, and polydrug dependence, the problems are politics and money. He has had to do his work in Panama, Europe, and Israel, where the Albany Medical College is conducting treatment on demand. It seems the FDA and the politics surrounding new drug approvals have moved at a snail's pace, forcing him out of the country to conduct his treatments.

Lotsof reports that NIDA, the National Institute on Drug Abuse, which finances much of the research in the field of addiction, is too financially invested in other pharmaceutical approaches to consider ibogaine treatment seriously. "What would you say if you had been working on a vaccine for heroin and cocaine addiction for the past ten years, and someone comes along and proves that your research and effort are moot? You probably wouldn't be too receptive, and you'd be more than a little skeptical of ibogaine," Lotsof says.[17] At the present time, ibogaine research on humans in this country is being conducted at the University of Miami with the cooperation of Lotsof and his company, NDA, Intl., but work has become mired in contract disputes over future profits. The researchers at the university, Mash and Sanchez-Ramos, have placed experiments on hold until these issues are resolved. Again, their research centers primarily on the safety thresholds of the drug and not its efficacy in treating heroin addiction.

Another reason that ibogaine may not be in NIDA's plans has to do with the influence of the large pharmaceutical companies. "This is not a maintenance drug, hence not as profitable to the larger pharmaceutical companies," Lotsof says.[18]

Only time will tell whether this treatment modality will be approved. In the meantime, the only place to receive ibogaine treatment is abroad. Lotsof's vision for ibogaine, however, clearly extends beyond the current limitations on its use. "If we could set up a national outreach program, providing ibogaine treatment on demand, in conjunction with psychosocial follow-up counseling, we could un-addict persons faster than they could re-addict themselves," he says. "Everyone is looking for simple answers to a very complex problem. We may have to spend some social service dollars on the older, career addicts for follow-up, but think of the future generations, and the ability to nip addictive behaviors in a person's early twenties. Think about that if you ask: Is it cost-effective?"[19]

Ibogaine is only the second psychoactive drug to be approved by the FDA for clinical experiments. The first was MDMA, better known as ecstasy, which is now a sought-after and much-abused black-market drug. Many young people who frequent the club scene make ecstasy their drug of choice. They report that it enables them to dance all night and that it heightens sexual performance. This hallucinogen, with its reported aphrodisiac qualities, has even been marketed as a legal drug under the guise of an herbal product. Although the herbal product contains no MDMA, its effects are reportedly similar, as a result of the high ephedrine levels found in the Chinese herb mahuang, one of the product's main ingredients. Many states have recently passed legislation making it illegal to sell this herbal product as a result of deaths attributed to its abuse. Considering the problems the FDA found with MDMA, it is not surprising that the agency is hesitant to approve another psychotropic substance like ibogaine for fear of its potential for abuse.

Buprenorphine

Buprenorphine hydrochloride is the latest analgesic to undergo extensive clinical testing in an effort to gain FDA approval for treatment of opiate addiction. It joins methadone, naltrexone, and LAAM (l-acetyl-alpha-methadol), which will be discussed later, as the fourth medication available for treatment.

Buprenorphine is a narcotic derivative of thebaine, an opioid agonist, and is classified under the Controlled Substances Act.[20] It is manufactured by Reckitt and Colman Products in England and is distributed by Reckitt and Colman Pharmaceuticals in Richmond, Virginia, under the brand name Buprenex.

An opioid analgesic, it is as addictive as methadone and the other derivatives of morphine. In relation to morphine, .3 milligrams of Buprenex is equal to 10 milligrams of morphine sulfate in painkilling ability and respiratory depressant effect in adults. The effects of the drug occur as soon as fifteen minutes after intramuscular injection and last for six hours or longer. Buprenex affects the central nervous system, causing a drowsy euphoria with respiratory depression similar to the effects of morphine.[21]

Three major studies have been conducted on buprenorphine. The first, by Drs. Rolley E. Johnson, Jerome H. Jaffe, and Paul J. Fudala, was part of NIDA's intramural research program in Baltimore, Maryland. Their results were published in the

Journal of the American Medical Association in 1992. They conducted a random, double-blind, parallel group study with 162 heroin-dependent patients at the outpatient facilities of the Addiction Research Center in Baltimore.

The 180-day study consisted of 120 days of induction/maintenance followed by forty-nine days of gradual dosage reduction and eleven days of placebo dosing. The primary outcome measures were retention time in treatment, urine samples testing negative for opioids, and failure to maintain abstinence.

The 162 patients were males and females between the ages of twenty-one and fifty, with an average of two or more heroin use episodes per day and self-reported habits of $50 per day or greater. To qualify for participation the volunteers had to present at least three consecutive daily urine samples that were positive for opioids, but negative for methadone.

Patients were excluded if they presented with medical or psychiatric conditions. All of the women were tested for pregnancy both before and during the study and were denied entry if pregnant.

The study, conducted between September 1988 and November 1989, divided the patients into three groups. Fifty-three patients received 8 milligrams per day sublingually (dissolved beneath the tongue) of buprenorphine, fifty-five received 20 milligrams per day of methadone, and fifty-four received 60 milligrams of methadone per day. Patients could participate in thirty- to sixty-minute weekly counseling sessions, but this was not required.

Upon completion of the study the researchers concluded, "Buprenorphine was as effective as methadone 60 mg/day and both were superior to methadone 20 mg/day in reducing illicit opioid use and maintaining patients in treatment for 25 weeks."[22]

In the research and pharmaceutical communities, the experiments were considered a success because not much difference was noted between those patients who received 60 milligrams per day of methadone and those who received 8 milligrams per day of buprenorphine; the tests also proved that more methadone worked better than less methadone. "Throughout the maintenance phase . . . the percentage of urine samples negative for opioids was significantly greater for buprenorphine and methadone 60 mg/day, than for methadone 20 mg/day. Failure to maintain abstinence during the maintenance phase was significantly greater for methadone 20 mg/day, than for buprenorphine. During the detoxification phase, no differences were observed between groups with respect to urine samples negative for opioids. . . . All treatments were well tolerated, with similar profiles of self-reported adverse effects," the researchers said.[23]

Upon closer inspection of the statistics, confusion arises as to how this study can be termed successful, unless we are simply looking at a comparison of methadone use versus buprenorphine use. Thirty percent of the individuals given buprenorphine completed the twenty-five-week study; 20 percent of those who received 60 milligrams per day of methadone completed the full twenty-five weeks; and the group treated with 20 milligrams per day of methadone had a 6 percent retention rate.

"Over the 17 weeks of the maintenance phase of the study, buprenorphine treatment was associated with an average of 53% of urine samples negative for opioids, methadone 60 mg/day with an average of 44%, and methadone 20 mg/day with an average of 29%," the researcher said.[24]

So, not many stayed and most continued to use opioids such as heroin. The researchers addressed this by stating that "because counseling was available but not mandatory, patients probably formed fewer emotional ties than in a treatment program emphasizing psychosocial components. Probably the most significant difference between the procedures of this study and those of most methadone treatment programs was that patients were informed at the time of recruitment that their participation in the study had a finite duration and would end with detoxification. . . . These study characteristics may help to explain the relatively low retention rates and the continued illicit opioid use observed."[25]

Two studies have been completed since the one described above: a sixteen-week study chaired by Dr. Walter Ling of the Los Angeles Addiction Treatment Research Center and a NIDA-funded clinical study by Dr. Eric Strain of the Behavioral Pharmacology Research Unit at the Johns Hopkins University School of Medicine in Baltimore. Assisting Strain were Drs. Maxine Stitzer, George Bigelow, and Ira Liebson.

In Ling's study, 733 patients were monitored at twelve sites throughout the United States and Puerto Rico. Although complete analyses of the findings were not available, Doralie Segal of NIDA's Medications Development Division declared that buprenorphine significantly reduced the patients' craving for heroin. Segal stated that "regardless of the dose, heroin craving dropped dramatically within four weeks and remained very low for the remaining twelve weeks of the study." Patients were randomly assigned doses of 1, 4, 8, or 16 milligrams per day of buprenorphine. Those who completed the sixteen-week study were then allowed to continue on buprenorphine for another thirty-six weeks under a flexible dosing schedule, during which time they could be increased to as much as 32 milligrams per day or as little as 1 milligram per day.[26]

In the Johns Hopkins study, researchers observed 164 patients admitted to a six-month research treatment program. Patients were given either 50 milligrams per day of methadone or 8 milligrams per day of buprenorphine on a flexible dosing schedule. If a patient's urine tests showed repeated opioid use, his or her dose could be increased to a maximum of 90 milligrams per day of methadone or 16 milligrams per day of buprenorphine. This more closely simulates clinical practice than fixed dosing. Strain reported that 56 percent of the patients in each group stayed in treatment for the sixteen-week dosing period.[27]

Because buprenorphine reportedly causes a certain euphoria, although not as strong as that of heroin, morphine, or methadone (methadone euphoria ceases once the patient reaches a tolerance level), there is the danger of it being diverted by program participants, making it unsuitable for take-home medication. This is a big problem today among methadone maintenance programs. Researchers claim that they may be able to administer buprenorphine every other day; they are also considering seeking approval of a buprenorphine-naloxone combination tablet being developed by NIDA and Reckitt and Colman Pharmaceuticals. The thinking is that naloxone, an opioid antagonist, would render the buprenorphine-naloxone tablet unusable for all but treatment purposes. If a heroin addict tried to dissolve it and inject it, he or she would experience unpleasant withdrawal symptoms as a result of the naloxone. However, when taken sublingually, the buprenorphine-naloxone tablets do not produce these effects. The problem is that the buprenorphine abuser could just ingest the drug sublingually. A nontolerant person could in this way experience sedation and euphoria, just as methadone tablets provide a high to street purchasers. Not everyone will be looking to inject the buprenorphine.

Over the coming years it is expected that buprenorphine will be used to maintain and detoxify addicts, in much the same way that methadone has been used. Researchers do not intend for it to replace methadone. It is yet another drug in the treatment provider's arsenal of pharmacological weapons.

Naltrexone

Naltrexone is categorized as a synthetic opioid antagonist with the ability to bind to the same opiate receptors as heroin. The opiate receptors have been identified by neuroscientists as the mu, kappa, and delta receptors. Naltrexone, like heroin and morphine, has the greatest affinity for the mu receptor.[28] Once attached, it reverses the effect of heroin in the body, causing instant withdrawal, and attachment cannot be displaced by additional heroin use.

The irreversible nature of this drug is what makes it effective in treating heroin addicts. Once a detoxified addict is administered naltrexone, the craving for opiates is diminished, if not eliminated.

Naltrexone is nonaddictive and normally used daily, for three months in most cases. It does not produce euphoria or any noticeable effects, although the side effects reportedly include nausea, difficulty in sleeping, anxiety, nervousness, abdominal pain/cramps, vomiting, low energy, joint and muscle pain, and headaches. Many of these effects are mild, they are reported by a minority of patients, and they usually disappear in a short time. Naltrexone can cause liver damage when taken in excessive doses, and it is not recommended for use by individuals who suffer from liver or kidney damage.

Approved by the FDA in 1984, naltrexone was originally marketed under the brand name Trexan by DuPont Merck Pharmaceutical. Studies prior to approval showed the drug to be helpful in preventing relapse among heroin addicts. A detoxified addict could take a daily dose (therapeutic dose was determined to be 50 milligrams) and not suffer from cravings. If the addict got an urge to use heroin, and tried it while on naltrexone, he or she would not feel any euphoric effect because the opioid antagonist was closing down the very receptors to which heroin binds.

Over the past ten years, naltrexone has been reevaluated, and clinical experiments have shown it to be as effective in treating alcoholism as it is in treating heroin addiction. Tests conducted in 1992 by Joseph Volpicelli at the University of Pennsylvania showed that "naltrexone helped to prevent early return to heavy drinking in a significant proportion of treated patients."[29]

A separate trial experiment conducted at Yale University, by Dr. Stephanie O'Malley and her colleagues, showed similar results. The FDA considered data from these studies and a private study by DuPont and granted approval for use of naltrexone as an adjunct to conventional alcoholism treatment in December 1994.

DuPont rechristened the drug Revia and began to market it to a whole new audience. With more than one million Americans treated each year for alcoholism, DuPont sees a great need for Revia.[30] Studies have shown that more than 50 percent of alcoholics relapse within the first few months of treatment. With the aid of a drug that reduces cravings and takes away the pleasurable effects of the first drink, many more patients stand a chance of making it past the first three months of abstinence.[31]

Although the daily use of naltrexone for heroin addicts during early abstinence has diminished somewhat, the advent of a new form of treatment has revitalized its use. The new treatment, termed "ultrarapid opiate detoxification under general anesthesia," relies on naltrexone to instantly flush, or rid, the patient's body of opiates.

A Spanish firm, CITA, claims to have detoxified more than 1,000 addicts this way since 1992.[32] Although radical and still experimental, it has been hailed as the quickest and most painless way to break away from heroin addiction. The patient is first sedated with general anesthesia, then administered naltrexone, causing instant withdrawal. Because he or she is sedated, the symptoms of withdrawal are not felt or remembered upon awakening. The patient's vital signs are monitored, and breathing is controlled as oxygen is pumped into the lungs. After approximately six hours the withdrawal is complete. The patient is given more sedatives, and after a twenty-four-hour period is able to go home, totally detoxified without having suffered terribly.

All of the treatment providers using this technique point out that in order for it to be effective, proper psychological counseling and peer support are necessary if the patient is to successfully abstain from heroin.

In 1995, when the news media picked up on its usefulness in treating alcoholics, Revia was hailed as the "magic bullet" and "the cure." Although Revia (naltrexone) has proved to be a useful tool, it should be noted that there are *no* magic cures for addiction.

LAAM

LAAM, which stands for l-acetyl alpha methados (the acronym is pronounced "lamb"), is a synthetic opioid with characteristics very similar to methadone. It is highly addictive and causes sedation and euphoria in patients who have not developed a tolerance, but when taken as part of a maintenance treatment program, it does not cause euphoria. It blocks the euphoric high of opioids and suppresses the symptoms of withdrawal. The major difference between LAAM and methadone is that LAAM's effects are longer lasting, usually between forty-eight and seventy-two hours. (Methadone's duration is about twenty-four hours.) With patients in a maintenance program requiring fewer visits, LAAM enables the program to treat more patients on a daily basis and allows the patients to lead more normal lives. A look at the numbers will attest to the need for more outreach to heroin addicts. There are currently between 115,000 and 120,000 heroin addicts being maintained on methadone, whereas it is estimated that from 500,000 to 1,000,000 Americans use heroin regularly.[33]

After more than twenty years of experiments and studies, LAAM was approved for treatment use on July 20, 1993, only eighteen days after the FDA received the new drug application. The reasons for the quick approval were the many years of studies that had been conducted and the drug's full backing by NIDA's Medications Development Division.

In 1990, the FDA requested that NIDA reassemble the information it had gathered on LAAM during the early 1980s and submit new studies under the guidelines of the FDA's "investigative new drug" application procedures.[34]

NIDA contracted with twenty-six Department of Veteran's Affairs medical centers and university clinics and came up with results that pointed to LAAM's effectiveness as a maintenance drug for heroin addicts.

"If your goal is to reduce drug abuse," says Nicholas Reuter, a consumer safety officer in the FDA's Office of Health Affairs, "a properly administered maintenance program appears to be the most effective treatment."[35]

What is effective treatment? Government agencies have established three measurement criteria: reduced heroin use, retention in treatment, and perceptions by both patient and doctor of improved well-being.

Federal officials believe in methadone maintenance, and they expect LAAM to improve results and patient outcomes. They point to findings that show methadone patients have a death rate ten times lower than untreated addicts, and an incidence of needle sharing of only 14 percent, compared with 47 percent before treatment. In a recent study of heroin addicts with HIV infection, 24 percent of maintenance program cases progressed to AIDS, compared with 41 percent of untreated heroin users.[36]

In treating heroin addicts, perhaps maintenance is the most effective modality we now have. Treatment professionals point to the direct line between time in treatment and improvements in general health and social productivity along with decreases in drug use and criminal activity.

If one accepts that addiction for some heroin addicts is a lifelong struggle, then LAAM may help provide such addicts with the opportunity for a less controlled and regimented life than methadone maintenance offers; the addicts would be better able to plan daily routines without having to go to a clinic on a daily basis.

The most recent report on LAAM's effectiveness comes from the *Journal of the American Medical Association*. In an article published on June 25, 1997, the journal reported on research showing that LAAM reduced heroin use in maintained patients by up to 90 percent.

NIDA Director Dr. Alan Leshner says that "this study reinforces the fact that heroin addiction can be treated effectively. . . . When higher doses of LAAM are used in combination with other drug abuse treatment methods, such as behavioral therapies and psychosocial care, we may see even more positive outcomes for persons who are opioid dependent."

The recent findings Leshner refers to were compiled from a seventeen-week study conducted with 180 heroin addicts (70 females, 110 males) at the Behavioral Pharmacology Research Unit of the Johns Hopkins University Bayview Medical Center in Baltimore. Upon admission, patients were randomly assigned to high-, medium-, or low-dose therapy groups. It was reported that LAAM reduced heroin use most in the high-dose group. Before treatment, patients reported having used heroin on 29 of the previous 30 days. After sixteen weeks of LAAM treatment, the same patients reported using heroin on an average of 2.5 days in the previous 30; patients in the medium-dose group reported using on an average of 4.1 days, and those in the low-dose group reported using on an average of 6.3 days. The reports were corroborated by urine testing.

Dr. George Bigelow, director of the Behavioral Pharmacology Research Unit at Johns Hopkins, says, "The completion of this dose-comparison study of LAAM will allow clinicians to base their dosing decisions on empirical data and may help to increase LAAM's therapeutic effectiveness."[37]

Over the coming years, continued research and clinical studies will undoubtedly provide us with insight into more sophisticated ways to curb heroin addiction. Is pharmacology the best answer? It seems that even those who feel daily maintenance is the most effective way to address heroin addiction and its accompanying social problems are quick to point out that a well-rounded treatment protocol—psychosocial counseling, peer support as found in Twelve Step fellowships, and the full backing of the social services and educational systems—is essential to the successful treatment of today's heroin addict. Belief in the addict as a person worthy of redemption is a necessary value if we are to employ all of the resources available in this difficult task. Historically, control of the addict and his or her criminal behavior has been the assigned role of pharmacology. If we are to succeed in bringing addicts into the mainstream, pharmacology needs to be seen as but one of the components in an effective treatment strategy and not merely as a politically expedient solution.

four

SOCIETY

CHAPTER

10

Heroin and the AIDS Epidemic

If an infection is spread from person to person by an inanimate object, you can prevent it by removing that object. . . . This is not rocket science.

DR. PETER LURIE,
Center for AIDS Prevention Studies, University of California

January 1996. Injection drug use is the second most frequently reported risk behavior among AIDS patients; intravenous drug users accounted for 184,359 AIDS cases through December 1995.[1]

April 1988. Louis sits alone with his thoughts more often than he'd like to these days. He sits and stares from his window, moves slowly, bringing a cigarette to his lips. He blows out a cloud of smoke and says quietly, almost whispering, "It was the darkest day of my life. . . . I was clean for five years, put my life back together again. Good job, nice apartment, good woman. We went on a vacation, my girl and I, down to the Bahamas. That's when it started. We smoked some pot. . . . I forgot how bad it used to be, started dabbling, and within three months I was back to shooting dope again. I know exactly when, and who, I caught the virus from. He was a guy from the neighborhood I used to run with. We went to cop together one night. . . . I had two bags of dope and nothing to do it with, so I borrowed his works. I had a feeling, but I just shook it off. I can't explain it. I didn't care about anything

187

right then but getting high. But now I know, in that moment I changed my life. Turns out I caught the virus and a case of syphilis too. Now I lost my girl, I can't work 'cause I feel too tired all the time, and I can't stop getting high. I don't know that I want to anyway. . . ."[2]

Louis was dead by the summer of 1993. His is but one story. There are too many more stories to tell of addicts who died with AIDS, the result of using an infected needle. Why would an addict share a dirty needle at the height of an AIDS epidemic? To understand this is to know the desperation, hunger for the drug, and disregard for risk that addicts live with. Sometimes the answer can be as simple as, "I just wanted to get high."

In the early 1980s, the vast majority of AIDS cases reported were confined to the gay male community, who transmitted the disease among themselves via sexual contact. America was slow to react to the crisis. The limited population it affected and widespread negative perceptions of and attitudes toward homosexuals slowed the government's response to the emergency. At the time, we were not prepared and could not imagine the way this blood-borne disease would affect heterosexual intravenous drug users. There were warnings from the medical community, but politics and society's inherent prejudice toward addicts and homosexuals prevented us from establishing safeguards against the spread of AIDS through needle sharing. Two inexpensive items, condoms and sterile needles, could have saved many lives.

In this chapter we will explore the efficacy of needle exchange programs, look at why they have not been well received at the local community level, and examine why today many of the new HIV infections reported are among intravenous drug users and their sexual partners.

In 1995 the Centers for Disease Control and Prevention in Atlanta reported that 36 percent of all AIDS cases were IDUs (intravenous drug users), their heterosexual sex partners, and children whose mothers were IDUs or sex partners of IDUs. By comparison, in 1981 only 12 percent of reported AIDS cases were associated with injection drug use.[3]

Research conducted by Dr. Peter Lurie at the Center for AIDS Prevention Studies, University of California, San Francisco, and Dr. E. Drucker with the Department of Epidemiology and Social Medicine, Montefiore Medical Center, Albert Einstein College of Medicine, showed that anywhere from 4,394 to 9,666 HIV infections could have been prevented between 1987 and 1995. They report that the health care costs to treat those infected will be between $244 million and $538 million, an expense that could have been avoided had there been a federal needle exchange program for America's heroin addicts.[4] Unless the federal law banning needle exchange is lifted, the doctors estimated, an additional 5,150 to 11,329 individuals will be infected with HIV by the year 2000.

An examination of those at risk shows a disproportionate number of minorities being infected with HIV and progressing to full-blown AIDS. "The rate of IDU-associated AIDS per 100,000 population is 3.5 for whites, 21.9 for Hispanics, and 50.9 for African Americans."[5]

For the past six years the Centers for Disease Control has estimated that between 40,000 and 80,000 individuals are infected with HIV annually.[6] A 1996 study conducted among ninety-six large metropolitan areas estimated that nearly half of those HIV infections would occur among intravenous drug users and their sex partners.[7]

A federal ban passed in 1988 prohibits federal funding for needle exchange programs unless it can be proved that they reduce the transmission of HIV and do not increase illicit drug use. The law is in keeping with the history of U.S. drug policy, which stems from the Harrison Narcotic Act written more than eighty years ago. The focus has always been on enforcement, interdiction, and eradication of the "problem." For more than eighty years, at the federal, state, and local levels, laws have been written and interpreted to criminalize the addict's behavior and any paraphernalia necessary for the use of illicit drugs, that is, syringes.

Forty-seven states, the District of Columbia, and the Virgin Islands have antidrug paraphernalia laws.[8] Only Alaska, Iowa, South Carolina, and four territories have no state or territory-wide drug paraphernalia statute.

Many drug paraphernalia laws were amended in a decidedly conservative direction in response to the burgeoning subculture of drug use in the 1960s and 1970s, when so-called head shops proliferated. The shops sold cigarette-rolling papers, bongs and fancy pipes used to smoke marijuana and hashish, and, later, glass pipes for cocaine. The laws were tightened further when the Federal Mail Order Drug Paraphernalia Control Act was passed as part of the Anti-Drug Abuse Act of 1986.[9] Its purpose was to prohibit use of the U.S. mail to receive or ship equipment that could be used for illicit drug purposes.

That law did not affect IDUs as much as the 1988 federal ban on needle exchange funding, however. With the ban, the federal government sent a message to the states: needle exchanges promote and encourage hard-core drug use. Naturally, for politicians at the state and local levels it became unwise to endorse or advocate the distribution of clean needles. Most politicians, concerned with their own political survival, hesitated to align themselves on the side of anything that would make them appear to be "soft on drugs." Anything that made it easier for addicts to abuse drugs was seen as counter to the "get tough on drugs" attitude of the nation's drug-war policy. Thus, the laws were strictly enforced and many addicts caught in possession of syringes were arrested. As a result, addicts became even more leery of carrying syringes with them. It is one thing to carry two or three bags of heroin, which are small and can be easily swallowed to avoid arrest. A syringe, however, is virtually impossible to conceal during a search. To carry a needle was to run the risk of being arrested and sent to jail, where the addict would have to endure an agonizing cold-turkey withdrawal. This fear led many to share needles. Others simply used their own unsterile needles over and over again, exposing themselves to the risk of getting abscesses, hepatitis, and endocarditis. The result was that needle sharing became even more prevalent than it had ever been before, at precisely the wrong time—during the height of the AIDS epidemic.

The 1988 federal ban stipulates that if needle exchange programs can be proved to reduce HIV transmission while not increasing drug use, the government would then be free to help finance and establish a national needle exchange program. To date, six government-funded studies have concluded that needle exchange does reduce the incidence of HIV infection and does not increase drug use.

Researchers with the National Institutes of Health, the General Accounting Office, the Centers for Disease Control and Prevention, and the National Academy of Sciences all arrived at the same conclusion: "that well-implemented needle exchange programs can be effective in preventing the spread of HIV and do not increase the use of illegal drugs."[10]

In June 1997 the American Medical Association voted to work with Congress to revoke the 1988 federal ban and to work toward relaxing state paraphernalia laws, making it easier for users to legally buy needles.[11] Dr. Nancy Dickey, chairperson of the board of trustees and president-elect of the association said, "There is more and more evidence that the advantages of needle exchange outweigh the disadvantages. . . . We're addressing a public health epidemic."[12]

It seems logical to think that if government-funded studies find needle exchanges to be effective in reducing the transmission of AIDS, then a redirection of policy should follow. But this has not happened.

President Clinton has had his share of problems with public perception as it relates to his stance on drugs. His gaffe about smoking but "not inhaling" marijuana quickly became fodder for comics and cartoonists. Not wanting to be seen as being soft on drugs, he enlisted the help of a retired Army general, Barry McCaffrey, to lead the war on drugs as his "drug czar" and head of the Office of National Drug Control Policy. That Clinton chose a military man to lead the *war on drugs* is very much in keeping with the tough, combative stance government policy has always dictated. The administration's first perceived threat was a fast-moving grassroots campaign to amend the marijuana laws in California and Arizona to allow medicinal use of the drug. The administration took its typically hard-line stance of zero tolerance, claiming that relaxing the marijuana laws would open the door for heroin and LSD to be legalized next. It was an awkward stance to take, because being against this amendment was equated with being unwilling to help people dying of cancer and AIDS and those suffering from glaucoma and arthritis. The voters of California and Arizona prevailed. Public sentiment overcame the federal government's efforts, and both states passed referendums legalizing the use of marijuana for medical purposes. Not willing to admit defeat, McCaffrey threatened to prosecute doctors under federal marijuana laws. How this standoff plays out in the years to come will be interesting to see, but the significance is that Clinton now must consider whether he wants to be remembered as the president on whose watch the nation took a turn and got soft on drugs.

When asked to consider needle exchange as a way to diminish the spread of AIDS, the administration has been, not surprisingly, slow to move. The deeper political implications make this a more problematic question than it is when seen only as a public health issue. It is hard to imagine that an administration that opposes the use of marijuana by cancer and AIDS patients could tolerate the thought of heroin addicts being supplied needles at government expense.

For years Donna Shalala, Health and Human Services secretary, has been unconvinced that needle exchanges reduce HIV transmission and that they do not increase illicit drug use. In March 1997 however, she softened a bit. She admitted that exchanges *might* reduce the risk of HIV transmission, but remains unconvinced that they don't encourage illicit drug use. She believes, therefore, that there is insufficient evidence to repeal the ban.[13] The impact of her belief is that needle exchange programs remain ineligible for a piece of the more than $600 million available in AIDS prevention money.[14]

Clearly, Congress and Secretary Shalala do believe that needle exchange programs add to illicit drug use and that they make it easier for addicts to use heroin. These are prejudices that are hard to overcome. The point that officials seem to be missing is that needle exchange programs have at the very least been proved to prevent the spread of HIV, a public health hazard that is affecting unsuspecting, innocent Americans such as the babies of IDUs and sexual partners of those users. Americans must ask themselves whether it has become more important to make it harder for addicts to inject heroin than to consider what is best, in the midst of a national health crisis, for the country as a whole.

In 1995, President Clinton created the Presidential Advisory Council on HIV and AIDS, and after a year of studying the problem, the council called on the White House to "show greater courage and leadership" and do what really needs to be done to reduce HIV transmission. Although it praised the administration for funding efforts like the Ryan White Comprehensive AIDS Resource Emergency Act, the thirty-member council faulted the administration's lack of support for needle exchanges.[15] According to *The New York Times*, "The council did not go so far as to call for federal spending but said that government policy was not consistent with current knowledge regarding the impact of such programs on HIV prevention."[16]

At the state level, a similar politically entangled scenario has played out in New Jersey. Governor Christine Todd Whitman is not shy about advocating that the state should neither condone nor fund, in any way, heroin addicts' lifestyle of injecting drugs. She is a proponent of referring addicts for treatment but is dead set against spending state money on needle exchanges. She says that she has a responsibility not only to prevent AIDS, but also to prevent crime and create safe neighborhoods, and that "illegal drug use is at odds with those goals."[17]

Whitman herself appointed a thirty-five-member panel in 1994 to study and recommend solutions to the AIDS crisis in the state. New Jersey ranks fifth in the nation in number of AIDS cases, IDUs accounting for 51 percent of the state's cases.[18] After studying the research and visiting an exchange program in New York, the panel voted to recommend that New Jersey allow needle exchange and legal sale of syringes without a prescription. Despite Whitman's very vocal opposition to such measures, the panel clearly found merit in providing easier access to clean needles. It reported, "There is nothing that we can come up with as effective as a clean-needle program and the retail distribution of needles."[19] As of this writing, Whitman has been reelected to a second term and still opposes needle exchanges. The likelihood of any change occurring for another four years seems dim.

Where do we go from this standoff? It seems that opponents of needle exchange programs are unconvinced of the scientific findings. They claim that the results of the studies completed thus far are inconclusive, but are there simpler, more practical reasons behind their stance on the issue? For example, in addition to the political risks of supporting needle exchanges and a general cultural disdain for heroin addicts, there is also a not-in-my-backyard aspect to needle exchange opposition. The residents and businesspeople of the neighborhoods where needle exchanges exist have not been supporters of such programs; they resent the daily traffic of addicts who are attracted to their streets. They say crime, illicit activities such as prostitution, and declining real estate values are problems in areas where programs are implemented.

Yet, despite politics and local opposition, there are more than 100 needle exchange programs in operation throughout America and Puerto Rico today; they hand out more than ten million syringes per year. The first program was started in Boston in 1986, and similar programs began to appear in other major cities afflicted by heroin addiction.[20] Most of them have operated in defiance of state laws, though some municipalities have made exceptions to state law or have chosen to look the other way.

Most programs provide clients with identification cards that permit them to be in possession of syringes should they be stopped by police. In some instances, the workers at the exchanges have been arrested for handing out syringes, but most of the time the police look the other way. This has not been the case in Oakland, California, however. Alameda County leads the nation in needle exchange prosecutions. Activists have been arrested and prosecuted for exchanging needles with and distributing condoms to addicts. They are constantly forced to move their exchange locations to avoid arrest.

Recently, local politicians, including Oakland City Council member Nate Miley, staged a protest and handed out needles themselves on a street corner in West Oakland. They did it to point out that the law is "unjust and immoral" according to Miley.[21] The county's district attorney has felt it is his obligation to pursue prosecution, despite the objections of the Oakland City Council, the Alameda County Board of Supervisors, and the mayor of Oakland, all of whom believe in the efficacy of needle exchanges. Often, even the police perform their duties reluctantly. The office of Police Chief Joseph Samuels, which would rather not be placed in the position of enforcing this law, issued a statement saying that it just wants the law to be changed so needle exchanges are not illegal. There is little chance of that occurring in the near future, however, because California Governor Pete Wilson has vetoed needle exchange bills for several years in a row.[22]

Other states and municipalities currently operate success-ful exchange programs without fear of being shut down. One of the more studied programs is in Connecticut, where in 1992, state laws were changed to allow purchase of syringes without a prescription and to allow possession of up to ten syringes without medical need.

Beth Weinstein, director of Connecticut's Bureau of Com-munity Health, part of the Department of Public Health, has reported that since the law was changed in Connecticut, the sharing of needles has decreased by 39 percent.[23]

New Haven, Connecticut, is a city with a large population of Hispanics and African Americans, two of the groups hardest hit by AIDS. Here needle exchanges have proved to be effec-tive in reducing the transmission of HIV. A twelve-member panel chosen by the National Institutes of Health found that in New Haven, needle sharing was reduced by as much as 80 per-cent, leading to a 30 percent overall reduction in new HIV in-fections.[24] More significantly, the panel went on to say that the exchanges did not increase illicit drug use or present a prob-lem with discarded needles in residential areas. It is this kind of scientific evidence that needle exchange opponents, groups like the conservative Family Research Council, reject as faulty. That group's senior policy analyst, Robert L. Maginnis, when confronted with evidence that needle exchanges and sex edu-cation were effective in reducing HIV transmission, was quoted as saying, "I completely reject this."[25]

New York City has long been home to many of the nation's heroin addicts, and as such, would naturally be one of the places one might expect to find needle exchanges. But even there, needle exchange workers were prosecuted in the early 1990s, though there are now six free city exchanges, financed in part by New York state. Research conducted by the Chemi-cal Dependency Institute at Beth Israel Medical Center showed that these programs have reduced new HIV cases by 50 percent, as a result of clean needle distribution and exchange.[26] The laws in New York still do not allow pharmacies to sell syringes without a prescription; needles are considered drug paraphernalia under state law. Members of New York City's exchange programs are given anonymous ID cards that *usually* assist them in avoiding arrest when stopped by police.

Even if New York and the rest of the country followed Connecticut's lead and made nonprescription syringe purchases legal, addicts would still have to contend with the prejudices and whims of their local pharmacists. In Michigan, for example, where state law does not require a prescription for the purchase of syringes, pharmacists have the right to exercise discretion. Harry Simpson of the Detroit-based Community Health Awareness Group reported that "[pharmacists] often deny sale to a person who they do not feel has a legitimate medical need."[27] In Maine, prescription laws were repealed in 1993, but in a telephone survey of pharmacists only 44 percent reported that they would sell syringes to someone they thought was a drug user.[28]

When a government-funded syringe exchange program was set up in Amsterdam in 1984, the Netherlands became one of the first countries to set up such an operation. Since then, other countries throughout the world have followed suit. Australia currently has approximately 2,000 exchange programs, compared with the reported 111 in America. The experience of the European programs has been consistent with findings of studies conducted in the United States: syringe exchange programs reduce the risk of HIV transmission and do not promote additional drug use.[29]

One area of the world worth watching is Myanmar. Until recently, the Southeast Asian country supplied most of the opium used to make heroin, and it is known for producing heroin of a high purity level. Myanmar, too, has begun to experience the spread of HIV and AIDS as a result of intravenous drug use. Estimates are crude, but nearly 450,000 people were thought to be infected with HIV as of 1995, according to the Myanmar National AIDS Program. The rate of infection is said to be unusually high because there is a little-acknowledged but widespread domestic heroin market. Estimates are that nearly 4 percent of adult men engage in intravenous drug use. An unpublished United Nations report in 1994 estimated that 60 percent to 70 percent of IDUs in Myanmar were infected with HIV. The following figures reflect the percentages of IDUs infected with HIV in three of Myanmar's cities: 74 percent in Rangoon, 84 percent in Mandalay, and 91 percent in Myitkyina.[30]

It is currently illegal to possess syringes in Myanmar, except for medical purposes, and they are in extremely short supply. The cold reality: Addicts share needles because they have to, which helps explain the country's high rate of HIV transmission.

As long as we continue to criminalize heroin addicts' behavior and build prisons to warehouse those we arrest rather than address the issue as a public health epidemic, we will see the spread of HIV and AIDS across the country. This can only lead to heavy concentrations of HIV and AIDS in our prisons. How we meet this challenge will directly determine how many more people will die of this disease.

CHAPTER

11

Organized Crime, Heroin Distribution, and the War on Drugs

American concern with narcotics is more than a medical or legal problem—it is in the fullest sense a political problem.

DAVID F. MUSTO,
The American Disease: The Origins of Narcotic Control

Early Rumblings of War

For the past thirty years the U. S. government has waged a battle against drugs. Although it is not a war in the conventional sense of the word, with an opposing country as a declared enemy, it has come to resemble a true war in many ways. It has been fought in the air, on the seas, and along our borders. Pitched battles in this war take place every day on our streets. Soldiers die in war. In the drug war, as in other wars, the foot soldiers, law enforcers, die tragically and, often, heroically. Innocent people also die in war, and the war on drugs is no exception. Bystanders are gunned down during shoot-outs over drug sales territories. Children are recruited as addicts, runners, and enforcers, and many overdose or are murdered. To the many families who mourn the loss of loved ones, this is no less a war than any other conflict in which America has been involved. The war on drugs has lasted longer than any other American war: for thirty years the U.S. government has struggled to contain and eradicate the illicit drug trade. It is no closer to winning that struggle today than it was three decades ago; this is a war with no end in sight.

Who is the enemy? Is it the drugs themselves; those who import, distribute, and sell them; or those who create the demand for drugs, the users? Who are the heroes? Are they the local and state police or the federal drug agents or both groups? And who are the true victims? Contrary to popular perceptions, the answers to these questions are not always clear. What is clear is that there are casualties on all sides: police, users and sellers, innocent bystanders, and family members of all of the above. Some casualties languish in prison; wives, girlfriends, and mothers get sucked into the drug trade by their partners or children and end up serving prison sentences two to three times longer than the drug ringleaders—all because they refused to testify against a loved one.[1] The battle cry of the drug war is and always has been, "We must protect our children from the slavery of a life addicted to drugs." But as time passes and the casualties mount—including an ever-increasing number of the very children the war was supposed to save—one begins to wonder whether taking another road, one less combative, might have prevented the needless sacrifice of so many lives.

Although President Nixon is credited with starting the campaign against illegal drugs, rumblings and rumors of war were heard in the decade before he took office. In 1950, the U.S. Senate began investigating the impact of organized crime on American life. The Senate Special Committee, headed by Senator Estes Kefauver, a Democrat from Tennessee, along with hearings by the House Ways and Means Narcotics Subcommittee, headed by Representative Hale Boggs, a Democrat from Louisiana, fanned the flames of public sentiment against "the scourge of drugs." Millions of Americans watched the televised hearings and listened in horror as testimony revealed the extent of organized crime's involvement in the drug trade. The publicity created public support for passage of a bill sponsored by Boggs (House Resolution 3490) on July 16, 1951, that called for tougher federal sentences for drug offenders. The bill was signed into law (Public Law 82-255) on November 2, 1951, and established minimum and maximum sentences for all narcotics violations, including marijuana possession. At the time, no distinction was made between marijuana and heroin possession. Below is a table showing the sentencing guidelines:[2]

Offense	Fine	Minimum Prison Term	Maximum Prison Term	Suspended Sentence/ Probation
1st	$2,000	2 years	5 years	Permitted
2nd	$2,000	5 years	10 years	Forbidden
3rd & subsequent	$2,000	10 years	20 years	Forbidden

Some argued that the guidelines were flawed because they made no distinction between those who were arrested for possession of small quantities of drugs for their own use and those who were trafficking in illicit drugs. Representatives Emanuel Celler, a Democrat from New York, and Richard M. Simpson, a Republican from Pennsylvania, pointed out that judges should be allowed to hand down sentences that punished the trafficker more stiffly than the addict, who was merely feeding his habit.[3] The supporters of the new law pointed to public sentiment against the increasing use of narcotics and argued that severe measures were called for. A line was drawn in the sand. The government's inability to separate penalties for marijuana possession from those for possession of harder drugs would come back to haunt it in the following decade.

Throughout history, Americans' fear of narcotics users has been closely tied to how they perceive certain minorities. For example, in the nineteenth century the first opium laws were passed in response to fear of the enslavement by Chinese immigrants of white women lured to opium dens. Early in the twentieth century, Southern men feared the "cocainized" black man and set out to lynch and repress him whenever possible. Myth had it that blacks under the influence of cocaine could not be stopped with .32 caliber bullets, so many police departments switched to stronger, more powerful .38 caliber revolvers.[4] Prejudice against Mexican immigrants and the steady influx of

Latinos from the Caribbean led to the passage in 1952 of the Immigration and Nationality Act (Public Law 82-414), also known as the Exclusion and Deportation Act.[5] Under this law any immigrant who violated narcotics laws was subject to deportation. In practice, a Mexican immigrant convicted of possessing a small quantity of marijuana could be deported and barred from ever returning. Government representatives said they were merely carrying out the wishes of the people in their quest to rid the country of drugs and undesirables. Narcotics users were perceived to be people of color, immigrants, and disaffected whites, all of whom posed a threat to America's culture, values, and way of life. The low rumbling of public fervor against these drug users was quickly gaining volume.

By 1955 two congressional subcommittees had begun more hearings on the narcotics problem in America. Their purpose: to make the already severe penalties even harsher, so that drug users would be further deterred. The result of these hearings led to the passage in 1956 of the Boggs-Daniel Bill, sponsored by Boggs and Representative Price Daniel, a Democrat from Texas. The new federal laws severely increased the penalties for possession of narcotics and imposed even more severe sentences on traffickers.

Below are the sentences created by the law signed July 18, 1956:[6]

POSSESSORS	Maximum Fine	Minimum Jail Term	Maximum Jail Term	Probation/ Parole/ Suspended Sentence
1st offense	$20,000	2 years	10 years	permitted
2nd offense	$20,000	5 years	20 years	forbidden
3rd & subsequent	$20,000	10 years	40 years	forbidden
TRAFFICKERS General				
1st offense	$20,000	5 years	20 years	forbidden
2nd & subsequent	$20,000	10 years	40 years	forbidden

Special penalties were established for anyone convicted of selling heroin to a minor: a minimum ten-year sentence with maximum punishment of either life in prison or the death penalty. Sale of any other narcotic to a minor carried a mandatory minimum ten- to forty-year sentence. Once again, the law lumped marijuana in with narcotics, making it possible for a person to go to jail for at least ten years for selling a joint to a minor. Significantly, the Exclusion and Deportation Act was broadened after being tested in 1958–59 by two Mexicans convicted of marijuana possession.

The two Mexicans, Mendoza Rivera and Rojas Gutierrez, argued that the Boggs-Daniel Bill used the term *narcotic drugs* and did not specify marijuana. They contended that marijuana was neither legally nor technically a narcotic drug and therefore the government had no right to deport them for mere possession of marijuana. Their argument was upheld by a federal district court in southern California and again by the Ninth Circuit Court of Appeals on April 3, 1959.[7] The two avoided deportation but their victory spurred action by Congress to close the loophole in the law. A bill was quickly drafted, passed, and signed into law (Public Law 86-648) July 14, 1960, making it clear that "illegal possession of marijuana" or any narcotic was grounds for deportation. The defect in the wording of the law was taken care of, the loophole closed, and the penalties for marijuana once again were equal to those for heroin. The legislators could not have known then of the social change the 1960s would bring. But once again, their failure to distinguish marijuana as a more benign drug than heroin brought the country another step closer to war.

In the news of the day, the Interdepartmental Committee on Narcotics, a federally sponsored study group, reported that there were an estimated 60,000 addicts in the country.[8] The committee reported that nearly all were addicted to heroin and characterized the addicts as mostly males between the ages of twenty-one and forty; 60 percent were black, 24 percent white, 6 percent Mexican, 8 percent Puerto Rican, and the remaining 2 percent were described as "all others." The group said that the majority of these addicts lived in New York City,

Los Angeles, Chicago, and Detroit and that nearly all of the heroin they used was coming into the country from Mexico or in ships docking at the major ports, such as New York.

The solution to the heroin problem seemed simple enough. Push hard in these four cities with tough law enforcement strategies, lock up the users and sellers, deter others with stiff prison sentences, provide treatment to those who asked for it and mandate treatment for the captured addicts at facilities like the Public Health Service Narcotic Hospital in Lexington, and the heroin problem would be under control. Law enforcement did its part. For example, on February 14 and 15, 1959, the New York City Police Department conducted a massive drug sweep, arresting twenty-seven importers and distributors, and seized 28.5 pounds of heroin with an estimated value of $3.6 million.[9] Similar efforts took place in the other major heroin cities, but the buying and selling of heroin went on. The police efforts did nothing more than create the occasional shortage—and panic among addicts resulting from those shortages.

Despite law enforcement efforts heroin continued to make inroads into the country. One of the early driving forces behind the heroin trade was Salvatore C. Lucania, better known as Charlie "Lucky" Luciano.

The Mafia and the U.S. Heroin Trade

Luciano, born in Sicily in 1897, emigrated to America as a child in 1906. He rose through the ranks of the Italian Mafia on the Lower East Side of New York and became a prominent gangster during the Prohibition era. His association with the conspicuous Jewish criminals of the day, Meyer Lansky and Benjamin "Bugsy" Siegel, has become legend and the subject of many films and books. During Prohibition, Lansky and Siegel were part of one of the Jewish gangs involved in bootlegging and gambling. Lansky would go on to become one of the most powerful figures in organized crime as a result of his friendship and association with Luciano.

Lansky and Luciano prospered during Prohibition, building reputations for themselves as cunning and ruthless gangsters. By 1930–31, Luciano had earned the respect of many underworld figures and was seen as one of the Young Turks, a man who was smart, knew how to make a dollar, and was not afraid to use violence when necessary. Many crime historians believe that Luciano orchestrated a war between Salvatore Maranzano and Joe Masseria, the leading Mafia figures of the time, in order to assume leadership himself. This theory can be neither proved nor disproved, but what did happen, as happens in many organizations, was that the Mafia underwent a changing of the guard. More than sixty gangsters died in a war that exploded on the streets of New York during 1930–31. Luciano survived the internal struggles and, when the dust

Lucky Luciano (center) with associates
Historical Collections and Labor Archives,
Pennsylvania State University

settled, proposed in a series of meetings with the surviving Mafia leaders that they organize their illegal businesses into one national enterprise. He pointed out how previously, one Mafia head assumed leadership as the *capo di tutti capi,* or boss of all bosses, by killing his predecessor, only to be knocked off himself by the next aspiring leader to come along with sufficient vengeance and greed in his heart. He illustrated how the violence and internal warfare was ultimately bad for business, how it drew attention to themselves and brought the wrath of law enforcement upon them. He proposed that the twenty-four Mafia "families" in the country could cooperate with one another, share information and profits, and work together as one "syndicate." This was a radical concept at the time. He applied modern business techniques, explaining how each family head could become a member of a *board of directors*, and how this commission of leaders could control crime in an organized fashion throughout the country, with increased profits for everyone. This unprecedented move marked the birth of organized crime as we know it today. Luciano was appointed head of the commission, naturally, but each family head had an equal voice, or vote, on matters concerning the new "corporation."[10]

Luciano was known for his vision and business acumen as well as his courage. He saw the end of Prohibition coming before it happened and prepared by diversifying into the heroin business. Although there were fewer customers in the heroin market than in the bootleg liquor market, the addictive nature of heroin kept the clientele coming back for more. Heroin was less bulky than liquor, making it easier to smuggle, and the profits were even higher. Heroin was also a valuable tool in another of Luciano's business ventures. During the 1920s, he put many small-time pimps out of work as a result of his organization of the prostitution business. He was believed to control as many as 1,200 prostitutes working in two hundred New York–

area brothels by the mid-1930s.[11] The prostitutes often doubled as heroin customers. Once addicted, it was difficult for the prostitutes to leave Luciano's employ because they had to have the heroin, and selling their bodies was the only way to maintain their expensive drug habits. It is estimated that Luciano was raking in close to $10 million a year from his brothels alone. This, combined with profits from heroin, gambling, and labor racketeering made him one of the most powerful figures in organized crime. Unfortunately for Luciano, it also drew the attention of the government.

In 1936, a young New York state district attorney, Thomas Dewey, successfully prosecuted Luciano not for narcotics but for running a prostitution ring. Alfred McCoy, in his book *The Politics of Heroin*, writes that Dewey felt the public would be more outraged over the prostitution than the heroin trafficking, making it easier to obtain a conviction. Dewey pressured some of Luciano's prostitutes into testifying against him, and he obtained a conviction and a sentence of thirty to fifty years. This would not be the end of Luciano, however, even though he was exiled to an upstate New York prison. Luciano kept his criminal empire going with the help of Meyer Lansky and other associates who continued to distribute heroin and run the gambling and other rackets the mob controlled.

By the time America declared war on Japan and joined the Allied forces in World War II, Luciano had served nearly five years in Clinton State Prison. Even in prison, Luciano's life seemed to take turns that worked in his favor; ironically, the war proved to be an opportunity for Luciano to serve his country. During the war the Office of Naval Intelligence (ONI) had serious concerns about sabotage on the New York waterfront, particularly after the *Normandie* suspiciously caught fire while waiting in New York to be christened as a troop ship. The Navy's fear was that foreign submarines in U.S. coastal waters were surreptitiously being fueled by local fishing boats. The

ONI enlisted the help of New York District Attorney Frank Hogan in hopes of infiltrating the Mafia-controlled Fulton Fish Market to see whether there was any basis for this fear. Hogan coerced Joseph "Joe Socks" Lanza, the mob leader of the fish market who was under indictment for extortion, to help in the undercover venture. Lanza referred Hogan to Luciano. So the ONI contacted Luciano's attorney, Moses Polakoff, who placed them in contact with Meyer Lansky. Lansky worked as an intermediary between the ONI and Hogan's office on one hand and for Luciano on the other; together they were able to secure the New York waterfront and prevent any wartime sabotage. Luciano was also influential in obtaining the help of members of the Sicilian Mafia, providing the Allied forces with strategic information, maps of the Sicilian coastline, and direct help once Allied troops invaded the island.[12]

Not coincidentally, the close attention authorities paid to the waterfront, in combination with Luciano's imprisonment, resulted in reduced heroin smuggling. At the end of the war, America's heroin addict population was estimated to be at an all-time low of 20,000.

New York District Attorney
Frank Hogan
Archive Photos

Meyer Lansky
Archive Photos

After the war was won, Luciano's attorney pressed for a pardon, successfully obtaining one in 1946 from the very man who had sent Luciano to jail, Thomas Dewey, who by then was the governor of New York. After ten years in prison Luciano was released and promptly deported to Italy, where he established residence and ran a candy factory that he used as a cover for illicit business in Rome. Luciano's release had tremendous impact on the global heroin trade. From Rome, he engaged in what he did best, providing heroin for America's addicts and thereby maximizing the profits of the organized crime syndicate. Through his contacts in America, Italy, Marseilles, and the Middle East, Luciano established a global smuggling ring that flooded the streets of America with heroin. Just six years after his release, in 1952, the number of U.S. addicts had climbed from 20,000 at the close of the war to 60,000. As a direct result of his establishing links from Lebanon, where opium poppies were refined into morphine, to Marseilles where they were refined into heroin, to the United States through either Canada or Cuba, Luciano increased the supply of heroin available to a growing number of hungry American addicts. By 1965, despite the tough sentencing laws being passed by Congress, America's population of heroin addicts had swelled to an estimated 150,000. Once again, Luciano had taken the business of organized crime to a new level of efficiency, establishing a model for the global heroin trade that resulted in tremendously increased profits for him and his associates. When he died of a heart attack in Rome in 1962 at age sixty-five, he was a very wealthy man. In Mario Puzo's book *The Godfather* and the Francis Ford Coppola movie of the same name, the wise old Mafia don is portrayed as resisting the heroin business and its "dirty" money. Although this may have been true for some of the older dons, in Luciano's case there was no such thing as dirty money. His influence as a leader of organized crime facilitated the involvement of most of America's crime families in the business of heroin and cocaine smuggling and distribution.

Setting the Stage for the Drug War

By the time of Luciano's death, the Boggs-Daniel legislation had been in effect for six years, and despite the tough laws, Americans were using more heroin, in part because of the sophisticated smuggling rings that were a legacy of Luciano's modern Mafia. John F. Kennedy had been elected president in 1960; he was the youngest man and the first Catholic to hold the office. With his youthful good looks and charm, he called for the start of a new era in America. His famous "Ask not what your country can do for you" inauguration speech was a call to arms for the nation. Many of America's postwar baby boomers were reaching their teenage years, and the country was filled with a youthful enthusiasm and optimism. The race to put a man on the moon would be won by the United States in July 1969, new housing construction was booming, and business and the economy were going strong, as evidenced by a doubling of the gross national product between 1960 and 1970. There were also many problems in America. Green Berets—members of the U.S. Army Special Forces—were dispatched to Vietnam, the first of many Americans to fight in a troubling and soon to be unpopular war; social unrest and racial tension were brewing as the civil rights movement gained momentum. Black-and-white television reports captured images of black men and women being thrown against buildings by vicious torrents of water gushing from fire hoses used to break up protests, and of police dogs being unleashed on marchers. Civil rights activists, including James Meredith and Medgar Evers, were assassinated. President Kennedy himself would be assassinated in November 1963, with Lyndon Johnson, his vice president, assuming leadership of the country. Martin Luther King eloquently called for a day when his children could live in a better world. Black men and women refused to sit at the back of the bus anymore; they boycotted public transportation and, in asserting their economic power, brought the city of Montgomery, Alabama, to a standstill. Statistics concerning property crimes rose and heroin addicts were blamed for the increase. The perception that addicts caused crime was furthered by politicians who sought office by promising more law and order.

In 1964, Lyndon Johnson was elected president, promising to build a Great Society by enacting social programs to address the ills that faced the country. He worked to fix the root causes of crime: addiction, poverty, racism, discrimination, and poor education. While some remained optimistic about America's future, many others felt the country was a powder keg about to blow. Nightly TV news broadcasts brought into living rooms images of young men being killed in a war that was hard to understand, while the fiery speeches of Malcolm X had begun to overshadow the nonviolent approach advocated by Martin Luther King. The Black Panthers were arming themselves and talking of revolution. On college campuses protesters burned the American flag, young men burned their draft cards, and young women burned their bras. The sexual revolution was on; it was the dawning of the Age of Aquarius, and nearly eleven million baby boomers between the ages of fifteen and twenty-four made their presence felt. The racial unrest finally did explode and cities around the country, like Cleveland, the Watts section of Los Angeles, and Newark, burned during violent riots that were not quelled until the National Guard was called in. Despite civil rights legislation that was supposed to address discrimination, racial unrest was at an all-time high. As stated earlier, heroin use was also at an all-time high. The business of heroin smuggling continued under the control of Luciano's associates Meyer Lansky and Santo Trafficante, a Sicilian mobster who controlled the Tampa and Miami territories.

Trafficante had established control of many of the drug shipments entering the country as a result of his business dealings with Lansky and corrupt government officials in pre-revolution Cuba. Trafficante's connections with Cuban refugees, involved in the drug trade as couriers, would prove to be important in the coming years. The estimated number of heroin addicts climbed steadily during the 1960s, from 60,000 in the late 1950s to nearly 500,000 by 1970. Young Americans were turning on, tuning in, and dropping out in record numbers. The youth counterculture that was spawned during this time of great social and political unrest was turning more and more to psychotropic substances like marijuana and LSD. The draconian sentencing laws that lumped marijuana in with heroin and other narcotics worked as a social irritant and wedge that separated the emerging youth culture from the "establishment," the older generation. Young people pointed to what they saw as the insanity of these laws and how they were sometimes applied for political purposes; they cried out for the legalization of marijuana.

The Nixon Administration Response to Drugs

It was in this political and social climate that Richard Nixon, vice president under Dwight Eisenhower, campaigned for the presidency during 1967–68. It was Nixon's second attempt, having run unsuccessfully in 1960 against John Kennedy. Nixon used the issue of crime and the need for law and order in our streets as a mantra during his campaign. He blamed property crime on rampant drug addiction; the campus unrest he blamed on communist agitators; and he played to the predominantly white electorate's fears by pointing to racial tensions. He promised to bring an end to the Vietnam War, coining the phrase "peace with honor." Nixon strategically linked the campus protesters with race rioters, and the link was drugs. In the inner cities the drug of choice was heroin; on campus it was marijuana. He ascribed to the theory that a drug is a drug no matter how benign it appeared to be and vowed that marijuana would never be decriminalized or legalized if he was elected. He claimed that rising marijuana and heroin use was a divisive force that would destroy the values the majority of society held dear.

Nixon also took the first steps away from the concepts that were the guiding principles of the Great Society. He believed we should stop searching for the root causes of America's ills and begin to deal with the problems by placing the blame on the shoulders of individuals and not society. He wrote in an article published by *Reader's Digest* in 1967: "The country should stop looking for root causes of crime and put its money instead into increasing the number of police. Immediate and decisive force must be the first response."[13] Nixon put forth the idea that the problem was not the character of America, but that those who used drugs were devoid of good character. This shift toward placing the blame on those who used drugs and committed crime underlies drug-war philosophy to this day.

By 1969, when Nixon was elected, the leaders of the decade, Martin Luther King, John Kennedy, and Bobby Kennedy, had been killed. Malcolm X would soon be assassinated in New York, the Black Panthers were infiltrated and sabotaged by the FBI, and the lines had been clearly drawn between the counterculture and the so-called silent majority. Once elected, however, Nixon found himself saddled with an unpopular war that could not be won and election promises to restore law and order. By focusing on the drug problem Nixon was able to at least temporarily divert the country's attention away from the war. So it was that in 1969, Nixon fired the first salvo in the modern-day war on drugs: Operation Intercept.

Operation Intercept went into effect at 2:30 P.M. (Pacific time) on September 21, 1969. The mission was to close down the 2,500-mile-long Mexican-American border to prevent drugs from entering the country. Land, sea, and air surveillance efforts were undertaken as all cars, boats, and aircraft were searched for drugs. During the operation's three-week span, federal agents reportedly searched 418,161 people, 105,563 cars, and more than 100 aircraft landing at twenty-seven airports.

The automobile searches caused traffic backups at the border that stretched for miles. Businesses along the border were severely affected and many honest tourists were inconvenienced. The operation resulted in some drug seizures during the early days, but as soon as word got out, drug traffickers simply stopped trying to cross the border. U.S. government officials met during the first week of October with Mexican officials and agreed to ease up on the searches and to replace Intercept with Operation Cooperation, whereby the Mexican government agreed to intensify its own efforts to reduce drug trafficking.[14] This was an example of Nixon's rhetoric about "law and order" and "decisive action" to diminish the supply of drugs entering the country. It was also the first example of how attempts to diminish supply would always prove futile. In response to the shortage of marijuana, which was either seized or delayed due to Operation Intercept, an increase in heroin smuggling was noticed in southern California and as far north as San Francisco during this time. Whereas marijuana is pungent and bulky, heroin is odorless and compact in weight, making it easier to smuggle. Seizures of marijuana were easier to make but resulted in increased heroin traffic and use. Dr. David Smith, founder of the Haight Ashbury Free Clinics in the mid-sixties, noted an increase in the number of young people showing up at his clinic for treatment of heroin abuse. As he told *Newsweek:* "The government line is that the use of marijuana leads to more dangerous drugs. The fact is that the *lack* of marijuana leads to more dangerous drugs."[15]

In one of the best books written about the war on drugs, *Smoke and Mirrors*, Dan Baum outlines this period of increased heroin use and describes Smith as being furious over the government's misdirection. Baum wonderfully characterizes the players and the politics behind the drug war, and his book should be consulted by anyone seeking a more detailed understanding of this time period.

It might seem odd that marijuana, generally regarded as a "soft" drug, nowhere near as dangerous as opiates, barbiturates, or other illicit pharmaceuticals, should be tied to the most addictive substance then known, heroin. But the two were related, inversely, as seen during Operation Intercept. When marijuana flow was curbed, heroin and other drug use increased.

This was exactly what happened in Vietnam. By 1968, Americans had seen TV reports showing GIs smoking marijuana in the battlefields of Vietnam. CBS news had broadcast a report on the problem of drug use among the troops, and the public perception was that all U.S. soldiers were getting stoned while serving in Vietnam. Because many indeed were, the military took measures to search its soldiers, arresting those caught with marijuana. As a result of this crackdown, marijuana became harder to obtain. But it also caused young soldiers who had stayed away from heroin, even though it was readily available, to switch to the more easily concealable drug. To compound matters, the heroin available in Vietnam originated in the Golden Triangle area and was extremely pure. It was also odorless, cheap, and easy to use. Because of its purity many were able to get high by smoking it in cigarettes, drinking it in beverages, or inhaling it intranasally. Baum points out that the need to use some sort of drug in a situation like that in Vietnam only makes sense: for a young man in a jungle thousands of miles from home, with an unseen enemy trying to kill him, the temptation to find a mood-altering, tension-relieving substance would be great. It could be argued that it's part of the survival instinct. So once again, the government's supply-reduction efforts of one drug resulted in increased use of another more deadly substance.

In *The Politics of Heroin,* Alfred McCoy acknowledges that this theory of increased heroin use in Vietnam may hold some truth, but he points out that the spread of heroin use would not have been possible without the cooperation of South Vietnamese officials. He believes corrupt officials protected those

who sold heroin to American soldiers, and that they did it simply for the money; he estimates that $88 million per year was
enough incentive for these officials to distribute heroin to
bored GIs looking to escape their harsh reality.[16] By 1971 the
heroin problem in Vietnam had become so widespread (an estimated 20,000 to 30,000 users) that another drug crackdown
was initiated. This time the government used urine testing to
ferret out drug users.

On July 28, 1971, a drug testing program put into effect in
Vietnam checked virtually all personnel being tested specifically for heroin use.[17] Soldiers were tested as they were
processed to return to the states and those found "dirty" remained in-country until they were detoxified. The effect of
this crackdown was to make heroin harder to obtain. As a result, the basic economic tenet of supply and demand took effect and prices rose while purity decreased. So, no longer able
to dilute very cheap, nearly pure heroin in liquid or ingest it
via smoking or sniffing, soldiers tended to conserve the now
more expensive drug and use it in a more effective manner—
injection. The military's effort to rid its ranks of heroin use resulted in more soldiers becoming even more severely addicted
to the drug due to intravenous use. The lesson we could have
learned from Vietnam concerns the importance of environment
as a contributing factor to heroin addiction: very few of the
soldiers who tested positive for the drug overseas continued to
use it after returning to America.[18] This type of cause-and-effect
merry-go-round between enforcement efforts and drug use
would be seen again and again in the years to come. The process
is similar to squeezing a water balloon: when one end is
squeezed, the water engorges the balloon at the other end;
when the other end is squeezed, the water moves back again;
and if the water moves back and forth enough, the balloon can
explode.

On the home front, the Nixon administration was busy
trying to deliver on its campaign promises to reduce crime

and diminish drug abuse. In 1970 Congress passed several pieces of legislation that came to be of importance in future efforts to curtail drug abuse and prosecute drug offenders. The Comprehensive Drug Abuse Prevention and Control Act (Public Law 91-513), the Omnibus Crime Control Act (Public Law 91-644), the District of Columbia Court Reorganization and Criminal Procedure Act (Public Law 91-358), and the Organized Crime Control Act (Public Law 91-452) all were signed into law that year.[19]

All of these new laws would prove to be valuable in future law enforcement efforts. The only one that really helped heroin addicts, though, was the Drug Abuse Prevention and Control Act, which eliminated mandatory sentences for first-time offenders and reduced simple possession of a controlled substance from a felony to a misdemeanor punishable by up to one year in jail and a fine of up to $5,000. It also increased the maximum penalties for "professional criminal trafficking" in drugs to a $100,000 fine and a mandatory ten-year sentence for first-time offenders. The new law made money available through the Department of Health, Education, and Welfare for more treatment, prevention, and drug abuse rehabilitation, and it guaranteed confidentiality to individuals who sought treatment. Funding went to many narcotics rehabilitation clinics that were treating heroin addicts with methadone maintenance. One of the major effects of the new law was that many more heroin addicts could receive such treatment. Methadone had been shown to decrease addicts' criminal behaviors in several studies and was viewed as a viable way to deal with the crime that addicts were believed to be responsible for.

The government's belief in methadone during this time can be seen by the number of addicts who were quickly enrolled in this form of treatment. By 1973, there were an estimated 400 clinics across the country treating more than 80,000 heroin addicts. On the downside, because methadone was seen to be effective in curbing criminality, it was cited as proof that heroin use causes crime, a concept that while certainly true to an extent has been widely overestimated. In 1971, for example, Nixon declared that heroin addicts were responsible for $2 billion of property crime annually. The fact was that all property crimes that year, including hijackings and organized crime ventures, amounted to $1.3 billion for the year.[20] By placing the blame on addicts' drug use, the focus was turned to the individual and away from root social causes, which in turn justified reduced social spending and increased police spending to diminish drug supply. Unfortunately, the status of methadone maintenance has not experienced much growth since the early 1970s. Today, nearly thirty years later, there are only an estimated 115,000 heroin addicts being treated with methadone, leaving anywhere from 500,000 to 1,000,000 untreated.

Other laws passed in 1970 gave future law enforcers valuable tools to fight the drug war. The District of Columbia Criminal Procedure Act authorized controversial "no-knock" search warrants, which allowed police to simply break down doors unannounced. Police had complained for years about having to announce themselves when executing a search warrant, while inside, the suspected drug offenders were busy flushing evidence down the toilet. The law also provided for "preventive detention" before trial. In other words, a drug offender arrested for a felony that carried a mandatory ten-year sentence was deemed to be a dangerous criminal who was likely to flee before trial. The onus was placed on the defendant to prove his or her worthiness to be released on bail until trial. Perhaps the most powerful law from that era, one whose potent crime-fighting capabilities were not immediately understood, was the Organized Crime Control Act. The law was designed to prosecute members of the Mafia via the RICO (Racketeering Influenced Corrupt Organizations) statute, whereby anyone proved to be profiting from an organized criminal enterprise was subject to criminal seizure of any assets derived from that enterprise. It would take law enforcement officials nearly ten years before they learned how to use these measures against drug traffickers. These seizure laws eventually would prove to be among the most effective tools supplied to law enforcement in the war on drugs.

Meanwhile, by the early 1970s, major changes were underway in the global heroin trade. Turkey, under pressure from the Nixon administration, which supported giving $35 million in aid to the Turkish government, put a ban on opium cultivation, drying up the source of most of the world's opium supply. Turkey was believed to produce 80 percent of the world's opium at the time.[21] With French police putting pressure on the processing laboratories in Marseilles, where heroin was refined, this created a situation where the organized criminal enterprises were forced to find new sources of opium and new refining laboratories. In the 1960s, Santo Trafficante had profitably managed his heroin smuggling business by using the connections he established with Cuban criminals before the revolution. As the 1960s progressed, many Cubans fled from life under Fidel Castro's regime, settling primarily in Miami. Trafficante's control of gambling expanded to include Bolita, a favorite game of Cuban immigrants and an illegal version of what many states now legally run as the Pick 3. Trafficante's use of Cubans in his heroin and cocaine business initially caused confusion about who was running the smuggling and distribution rings. But the Cubans were in fact acting only as couriers and later as intermediaries when the drug trade shifted to Central and South America in the 1980s.

The problems with opium supplies and processing that would develop in the early 1970s had become apparent to Trafficante as early as 1968, as he observed the internal wars being fought in the Italian Mafia. Criminal factions were waging war against one another and bringing down the weight of the police on themselves as a result. The conflicts helped to disrupt the flow of Mediterranean heroin, so Trafficante, astute businessman that he was, traveled to the Far East in 1968 to scout new production venues. He visited Hong Kong, Saigon, and Singapore and established relationships with the more reliable heroin providers. The heroin that began to hit the streets of American cities as a result of his travels came to be known as "China white" and was noted for its high purity. Many older heroin addicts who have managed to survive their addictions fondly recall this period.[22]

In 1968 Lyndon Johnson had combined the Bureau of Narcotics in the Treasury Department with the Bureau of Drug Abuse Control in the Department of Health, Education, and Welfare; he designated the new agency the Bureau of Narcotics and Dangerous Drugs (BNDD) and put it under the control of the Justice Department. During the Nixon administration, several reorganizations of law enforcement agencies occurred.

In 1972 Nixon appointed the head of U.S. Customs, Myles Ambrose, as his special consultant for drug abuse and law enforcement. Ambrose's office was not designed to be a separate agency but was staffed by law enforcement personnel from Customs and BNDD as well as by state and local cops on loan for provisionary eighteen-month periods.[23] The special unit, the Office of Drug Abuse and Law Enforcement (ODALE), was designed to use the RICO statute and no-knock warrants, as well as preventive detention, in an all-out, gangbuster approach to drug enforcement. Agents would break down doors and roust suspected drug dealers, detaining them until they cooperated. This was somewhat of a departure from how federal law enforcement agencies had historically operated. Prior to this they concentrated on high-level smugglers, sometimes working a case for over a year. Ambrose changed all this and took the government into the business of street-level enforcement. ODALE received attention from the media, but not always the kind the agency was looking for. Agents were known to occasionally make mistakes and break into innocent people's homes, ransacking, terrifying, and unapologetically leaving homes in shambles. Often it was just a case of having the wrong address or bad information.

In 1972 Nixon also established, with the approval of Congress, the Special Action Office for Drug Abuse Prevention, under the direct supervision of the president (Public Law 92-255).[24] This office eventually would become the Office of National Drug Control Policy. Its initial purposes were to coordinate federal drug abuse programs, except law enforcement; finance and devise strategy for prevention efforts; and provide research funds. The first director was a psychiatrist and academic researcher, Jerome Jaffe, who had been administering a methadone program in Chicago. His position eventually would be known as that of "drug czar."

Nixon took many steps toward dealing with America's drug problem during his first term. In 1973 Congress approved Nixon's request to form the Drug Enforcement Administration, or DEA, controlled by the Justice Department. That year, Nixon also set up the National Institute on Drug Abuse, or NIDA, under the leadership of Dr. Robert DuPont. NIDA still conducts research and finances studies in the field of substance abuse and alcoholism, particularly in the area of pharmacological approaches to treating substance abuse.

Unfortunately, Nixon's preoccupation with the Watergate scandal hampered progress during his second term, and by 1974 he began a pattern that would continue through the Reagan years—slashing funding for treatment while increasing spending on law enforcement. Whether or not Watergate affected his spending policies for treatment and prevention is open to speculation, but Nixon's record before the scandal was commendable. Between 1970 and 1974 he increased the annual budget for demand reduction from $59 million to $462 million.[25] However, by the time Nixon resigned the presidency, America's youth were using more drugs than ever; heroin and particularly marijuana use would reach all-time highs by 1978.

The Defeat of Harm-Reduction Strategies

Nixon's successor, Gerald Ford, is perhaps best remembered as the man who pardoned Nixon. But in fairness to Ford, he was not in office long enough to accomplish anything of significance in the area of drug abuse treatment. He did not share Nixon's fervor in the effort to rid the country of drugs. A research study concerning marijuana that had been buried by Nixon during his first term was published in September 1975. The White Paper on Drug Abuse, prepared by the Domestic Council Drug Abuse Task Force, stated that total elimination of drug use was unlikely and that government should concentrate on those drugs that are most harmful. It said this without mentioning marijuana, but one could read between the lines. Ford's 1976 Federal Drug Strategy was a complete departure from strategy of the Nixon years, when moral poverty was blamed for drug abuse; rather, Ford's strategy pointed to environmental root causes again. Ford's strategy was published just before Jimmy Carter assumed the presidency and set the stage for what was to come, including efforts to decriminalize marijuana.

Carter's presidency is criticized by many Republicans as an example of poor strategies used by the Democrats in trying to contain drug abuse. Carter appointed a psychiatrist, Peter Bourne, as his first drug czar. Bourne was an Englishman who had come to America at age seventeen to study at Emory University. He earned his medical degree, joined the Army, and served in Vietnam, where he studied combat stress in soldiers. Upon his return to the states, he completed a psychiatric residency at Stanford University and earned a degree in anthropology. After his studies at Stanford, he helped found the Haight Ashbury Free Clinics. In 1970, when Carter was elected governor of Georgia, he hired Bourne to run the state's drug abuse programs. So when Carter became president, it was Bourne who got the job of drug czar, or head of what was then the Special Action Office for Drug Abuse Prevention.[26]

The Carter administration would be the last to publicly acknowledge that it was impossible to totally eliminate all drug use. Marijuana use had been steadily rising among the young, the White Paper on Drug Abuse had been published in 1975, and many voices cried out for the decriminalization of marijuana. Ten states had already decriminalized possession of small quantities of marijuana. The concept of establishing civil fines for possession offenses was gaining popularity because of organizations like NORML, the National Organization for the Reform of Marijuana Laws, which was led by Keith Stroup, a Georgetown law graduate. Even certain members of the establishment, like Senator Birch Bayh of Indiana, were lobbying for changes in the federal marijuana laws. So when Carter and Bourne were devising strategy in the early days of the administration, it was natural that the issue of marijuana should be one they addressed.

Carter went on public record August 2, 1977, in a message to Congress advocating changes in the federal marijuana laws. He stated: "Penalties against possession of a drug should not be more damaging to an individual than the use of the drug itself; and where they are, they should be changed. Nowhere is this more clear than in the laws against possession of marijuana in private for personal use. . . . Therefore, I support legislation amending Federal law to eliminate all Federal criminal penalties for the possession of up to one ounce of marijuana."[27]

At the time Carter addressed the issue of marijuana, many in the medical field, particularly Peter Bourne, felt that because heroin and other narcotics were vastly more damaging than marijuana, drug prevention efforts should be directed at those more harmful drugs. Unfortunately, this type of rational thinking would end with Bourne's departure from office. There were still those who felt marijuana was a "gateway" drug that led to the use of much stronger drugs. Grassroots antidrug efforts, such as the one led by Marsha Manatt in Georgia, were under way. Manatt mobilized parents of the country's youth against drug use. Members of her organization, the Nosy Parents Association, campaigned against the softening of drug laws, pointing to the growing number of younger teens smoking pot. Once again, as in the 1960s, marijuana had become a divisive force in the country and diverted attention and strategizing away from the harder drugs like heroin.[28]

Carter's chances for accomplishing anything meaningful in the area of drug abuse prevention and treatment were dashed by a series of miscues by Bourne beginning at the end of 1977. That year Bourne attended NORML's annual Christmas party. Why he did so is open to conjecture, but at the time he was known to frequently meet with Keith Stroup, and perhaps he failed to see the political ramifications of his attending the party, where there were, of course, people smoking marijuana. The rumor was that Bourne was in a room with Stroup where others were sniffing cocaine. One can only speculate as to Bourne's motives at the time, but he obviously failed to see the public relations significance of the country's drug czar attending a pot party. His error in judgment would come back to hurt him. Amazingly, nothing about the party appeared in the press—for a while.

The friendly relationship between Stroup and Bourne would soon deteriorate. In the spring of 1978, the Mexican government was in the midst of spraying its opium fields with the herbicide 2-4-D, also known as paraquat. They had begun doing so at the strong urging of and with financial support from the United States. The spraying was carried out in the hope of diminishing the Mexican heroin supply, which had begun to make its way into America. After the Turkish opium ban in the early 1970s, Southeast Asian heroin became available thanks in part to Trafficante's smuggling rings, but black tar Mexican heroin had also begun to replace the supply once provided by Turkey. To the Mexican government, however, marijuana was a greater problem for its citizens, so it also sprayed as many marijuana fields as it could. The news soon leaked out that paraquat-laced marijuana was endangering the health of millions of primarily white, middle-class young Americans. Stroup and the supporters of NORML were furious. Here was the first administration that was friendly to their cause poisoning the lungs of marijuana smokers. They demanded that the spraying stop. Under pressure, and out of fear that the spraying would harm young Americans, the U.S. government ordered the paraquat spraying to stop—at the expense of continued opium cultivation. This episode marks yet another point in history where marijuana issues intersected with those concerning heroin.

The relationship between Stroup and Bourne was never the same. Stroup remained bitter and would eventually help orchestrate Bourne's demise. Strategically, for the NORML movement, the battle over paraquat spraying may have been won, but the war was lost; the marijuana legalization movement was about to lose the only friend in government it would ever have.

Mexican brown heroin
and Southeast Asian heroin
Photo courtesy of the Drug Enforcement
Administration, U.S. Department of Justice

During the summer of 1978, a young female assistant to Bourne asked him to prescribe something to help her sleep. She had been going through a rough time emotionally because of personal problems, she complained. He obliged her by writing her a prescription for quaaludes, a hypnotic sedative, making it out to a fictitious name. This was a common practice in Washington's insider circles, where documentation of mental or emotional problems was generally avoided. The assistant, perhaps looking to further protect her anonymity, sent a friend to pick up the prescription. When she could not produce identification at the pharmacy, the friend was arrested for trying to pick up a phony prescription with Bourne's signature. The press ran with the story, and it caused great embarrassment to the Carter administration. Shortly after this incident, an assistant to Jack Anderson, the syndicated columnist, pressured Stroup to confirm, off the record, Bourne's presence at the Christmas pot-smoking/coke-sniffing party. Stroup repaid Bourne for the paraquat spraying, acknowledging that Bourne was in fact at the party; Stroup did not say whether Bourne used any drugs, but it didn't matter. Bourne's presence at the party was enough to seal his fate. On the morning of July 20, 1978, on *Good Morning America,* Anderson accused Bourne of using cocaine at NORML's Christmas party. Bourne denied using any drugs, of course, but a public and political outcry forced him to resign that day.[29]

It was the end of any hope for a rational approach to demand reduction and the end of tolerance for any sort of drug use. Once again, politicians retreated into preaching zero tolerance of any and all drug use for fear of being seen as soft on drugs. Carter abandoned the harm-reduction effort entirely. A number of problems had arisen that seriously damaged his chances for winning reelection, and he could not politically afford to champion such an easily exploited hot-button issue. To make matters worse for him, the 1978 figures on teen drug use showed an increase in the number of young marijuana smokers. His detractors pointed to tolerance of marijuana as the reason for the increase. The Bourne fiasco was not all Carter had to deal with. Other images and allegations included his brother Billy's alcoholism, his son Chip's rumored marijuana use, and accusations that White House Chief of Staff Hamilton Jordan had sniffed cocaine at Studio 54, a trendy New York nightclub. Most of these were never proved, but politically, the damage had been done. The end of the Carter years would be the end of official discussion of tolerance for any form of drug use and the beginning of a new era—the Reagan years.

Reagan's Declaration of War on Drugs

Ronald Reagan is remembered as one of the most popular presidents in recent history. Often referred to as the "Great Communicator," he exuded personal confidence in his speech making, promising the country a return to the days when the United States was the preeminent world power. The American hostage crisis in Iran had been a terrible national embarrassment that included a failed military rescue attempt during which eight U.S. servicemen were killed and five others injured when a cargo plane collided with a helicopter over the desert in the Middle East. The hostages' release just two days before Reagan assumed the presidency allowed him to step into the White House as the gallant hero he had played so often throughout his acting career. Millions of Americans grew up watching westerns in which the good guy, who always wore white, was shot by the bad guy dressed in black. The good guy always managed to survive the shooting, stoically remarking, "It's only a shoulder wound." Just two months after Reagan's inauguration, on March 30, 1981, life imitated Hollywood as the world watched a live broadcast of the president being shot by a lone gunman. John W. Hinckley, his assailant, would later be found not guilty by reason of insanity. Reagan survived the shooting, bolstered his image as a tough guy, and won the hearts of many. Popularity is hard to measure because it has to do with sentiment, but perhaps surviving the assassination attempt reinforced his image as the "good guy," while Hinckley's avoiding prison clearly marked him as the "bad guy"—all of which contributed greatly to Reagan's popularity.

The Reagan-Bush administration had been elected on promises it made to right the economy, which was burdened with high inflation and high unemployment, and to reduce the national deficit. The administration vowed to dismantle the bureaucracy of the government, cut taxes, and disentangle regulations that made it difficult for businesses to do business. It promised to get the government out of people's lives, to stop being a burden to the taxpayer. Buzzwords such as "supply-side economics" and "trickle-down effect" were part of the new "Reaganomics," as Reagan's economic policies were known. Just as the 1960s had ushered in an era of hope with the election of Kennedy, the 1980s were viewed as a new start by many Americans, particularly the wealthy. Reagan proposed tax cuts for big business and the wealthiest of our nation, theorizing that the result would be more jobs created by the increased investing of profits earned by the rich. This was the basis of the trickle-down effects. Let the rich get richer, and more jobs and a better way of life will trickle down to those lower on the socio-economic ladder. The economy would turn around, interest rates would drop, and the rising national debt could be reduced. For those involved in the fight against the scourge of drugs, Reagan also offered hope. The frustrated followers of Marsha Manatt, part of the growing antidrug movement, looked hopefully for results, because Reagan had promised to "get tough on drugs."

They say hindsight is always twenty-twenty but Reaganomics and the Reagan-Bush years did not reduce the national debt; the Clinton administration inherited the largest federal deficit in the history of the United States, nearly three times the highest deficit recorded during the Carter years. Tax cuts and incentives for the wealthy helped the wealthiest 5 percent grow disproportionately wealthier, while those on the lower rungs of the economic ladder struggled harder to hang on. Studies by the Congressional Budget Office and the Economic Policy Institute have found that the gap between the rich and the poor has steadily widened since the late 1970s. Seemingly unstoppable, it is a trend that has continued since Reagan and Bush left office. A recent study by the Center on Budget and Policy Priorities, a Washington-based research group, also showed that the gap between the wealthiest 20 percent in the country and the poorest 20 percent continued to widen over the last ten years.[30] Significantly, this study found that the gap was widest in New York, despite Wall Street booms during the 1980s and 1990s. The creation of new jobs did not keep up with job loss during the 1980s, as more than 300,000 manufacturing jobs were lost or done away with. Businesses borrowed record sums of money during this time in a frenzy of buying and selling other businesses, a phenomenon that allowed a small number of individuals to amass large paper fortunes. Manufacturing companies began to expand overseas and were encouraged to move plants to Mexico by the Reagan and Bush administration and, more recently, the Clinton administration. In characteristic fashion, drug users in the workforce were blamed for the malaise of business in America. In August 1983 *Newsweek* ran a story about the crisis American business faced in the form of drugs in the workplace. That same month corporate profits hit a record high.[31]

This was typical of the doublespeak that prevailed throughout much of the 1980s under the Reagan and Bush administrations. The administration that promised to leave business alone bailed out the savings and loan industry to the tune of $200 billion, despite indications of wrongdoing on a massive scale. The administration that promised to dismantle the government bureaucracy, interfere less in people's lives, and provide greater individual freedoms led the charge to reinterpret the

Constitution to allow previously illegal searches—searches initiated without probable cause—of not just luggage or the clothes a person was wearing, but the very contents of his or her stomach. International travelers now can be detained and requested to submit to an X-ray examination of their internal organs, not because they acted suspiciously, or because the authorities may have received a tip about them, but because they fit a drug courier profile. If they refuse to be examined, they can be detained until such time as they defecate into a bucket under the watchful eye of a government representative. The profiles that many law enforcement officials have come to rely on almost always target minority-group members and have led many state and local law enforcement agencies to subject minorities to routine traffic stops. Many who have suffered from this form of discrimination sarcastically refer to the experience as being guilty of "driving while black."

Supporters of such law-enforcement approaches argue that these are perilous times in which we live, and that extraordinary measures are needed to stem the tide of drug use. "This is war," they say. In 1985, Supreme Court Chief Justice William Rehnquist, while upholding the constitutionality of detaining an international traveler and forcing him to defecate, said that "the freedom to control one's own bodily functions is a justifiable sacrifice to the veritable national crisis in law enforcement caused by smuggling of illegal narcotics."[32]

President Reagan is thought by many to have been the first to declare war on drugs. To make such a conclusion, however, would be to discount substantial previous efforts to curb drug importation and distribution, particularly during the Nixon years. Yet Reagan is given credit largely because of his flair for the dramatic and his speech-making abilities. On June 24, 1982, he gave a speech in the Rose Garden in which he officially declared a "war on drugs."

On October 14, 1982, he reiterated the call to arms against drugs, saying that America had been operating for too long under the misguided perception that root social conditions such as poverty were to blame for crime and drug use. He placed the blame for society's ills squarely on the shoulders of individuals who break the law, preaching that "right and wrong do matter, that individuals are responsible for their actions, that evil is frequently a conscious choice, and that retribution must be swift and sure."[33] This attitude permitted the administration to proceed on a course of dramatically cutting social spending. If drug use is the individual's fault and not society's, then the government's only responsibility in the matter of the drug problem is to provide "swift and sure" retribution.

During the eighties, forces were building nationally and abroad that required deep, insightful decision making devoid of political agendas. At the very moment in history when AIDS was starting to claim lives in the gay community and the crack epidemic was poised to strike, the U. S. government chose to ignore the warning signs and instead pursued a politically expedient philosophy aimed at eliminating marijuana use among the young, while it ignored the heroin problem altogether. The Reagan era's first drug czar, Carleton Turner, was a chemist who had been in charge of the government's research pot farm in Mississippi, and as such knew everything there was to know about marijuana. But when it came to directing the agency that was responsible for drug control strategy, he had some peculiar ideas. He felt that the drug prevention and enforcement focus should be on marijuana, and that heroin was not worth the expenditure of resources because hardly anybody used it. Turner compared the number of heroin addicts with the number of young people smoking pot and concluded that, as a population, heroin addicts just didn't matter. Some critics suggested that this dismissal of heroin addicts resulted from the belief that they didn't vote and were concentrated mostly in the inner cities. Whatever the logic behind the strategy, discounting anywhere from 500,000 to 1,000,000 heroin addicts is peculiar thinking for a drug czar, thinking that would cost thousands of lives as AIDS ran rampant among intravenous drug users—with no strategies even under consideration at the federal level for how to slow it.

Reagan had been elected in large part by voters in the suburbs and rural areas of the country, which could explain why he cut urban funding so deeply. At the moment that crack was ready to explode on the scene, when it began to ravage the inner cities, Reagan was signing off on $20 billion worth of cuts in social programs that provided health care, education, day care, and drug treatment programs to the major cities. At the same time he was supporting the Nicaraguan contras, who were fighting to overthrow the communist Sandinistas—the same contras who were smuggling cocaine and protecting drug smugglers in return for cash, which they used to supplement CIA support and finance their revolution effort.[34] By 1985 Reagan had slashed 80 percent of the urban funding budget. So, when crack hit the streets of south central Los Angeles, the administration's view was that it was not underlying causes such as unemployment and discriminatory hiring practices that led people to use heroin and cocaine, it was simply a matter of bad people making bad choices.

Swift and sure retribution against drug transgressors was the goal of the Reagan and Bush administrations, and the way they set out to achieve that goal was through tougher crime bills. William French Smith, Reagan's attorney general, and Ed Meese, his chief adviser, led the way in the pursuit of harsher measures. They felt that the exclusionary rule as it applied to the Fourth Amendment to the Constitution (any evidence obtained as a result of an illegal search is "fruit from the forbidden tree" and as such is inadmissible in court) needed to go. There were too many times a drug dealer was let go, even though he was found to be carrying drugs, simply because the arresting officers had no probable cause to search him. The Fourth Amendment reads:

The right of the people to be secure in their persons, houses, papers and effects, against unreasonable searches and seizures, shall not be violated, and no Warrants shall issue, but upon probable cause, supported by Oath or affirmation, and particularly describing the place to be searched, and the persons or things to be seized.

The issue of probable cause and illegal searches had been upheld since 1966. No one had thought to challenge the exclusion of evidence obtained without a proper warrant since then, but Smith and Meese felt that law enforcers would be better able to do their jobs if they did not have to worry about the exclusionary rule or the Miranda warnings, which also dated back to the 1960s. (Miranda guaranteed the rights of people under arrest to have an attorney present during questioning and advised them that anything they said could be used against them if they chose not to have an attorney present.) The country's political attitudes had shifted to the right, however, and the members of the Supreme Court reflected this shift. A reinterpretation of the exclusionary rule would have been unthinkable in the two prior decades. But the prevailing political philosophy of the 1980s was one that pitted "us against them," the "good guys versus the bad guys"—the cops versus drug dealers. In January 1984 the Supreme Court ruled on the case of Alberto Leon, who had been arrested in California on a charge of selling quaaludes. Three lower courts had found the search warrant used to obtain the evidence illegal, yet the highest court of the land overturned their decisions, citing the need for good faith in allowing police officers to perform their duties. In essence, a police officer could now obtain a warrant under false pretenses, and if the information he gave was wrong and drugs were found during the search, he could simply say he acted on good faith, sending the "bad guy" to jail.[35]

While police and prosecutors were celebrating the Supreme Court decision, organized crime forces were still hard at work smuggling and distributing heroin and cocaine. The estimated number of heroin users between 1979 and 1985 remained relatively stable, showing little decline. The Trafficante family in Florida, the Gambinos in New York, and numerous other Mafia families across the country were heavily invested, if not directly involved, in the drug trade.

Trafficante was still using Cuban couriers who had helped both establish links to the Cali and Medellín cocaine cartels in Colombia and distribute heroin brought in from Southeast Asia. The Reagan administration was able to hire an additional 1,000 new federal agents for the DEA, the FBI, and Customs as a result of the Omnibus Crime Bill of 1982, but organized crime would also have the benefit of fresh, young, tough recruits. In 1980, Fidel Castro allowed 125,000 Cubans to leave the island from the port of Mariel. A certain percentage of these exiles were criminals or those suffering from mental illness who had been released from Cuban prisons and mental hospitals. The majority of the Cubans who arrived on the boats from Mariel were decent people, but there was a criminal element slipped in by the crafty Cuban dictator, who has relished thumbing his nose at America for nearly forty years. Immigration authorities who processed the new arrivals in Miami and Key West became aware of the problem and detained many in military bases and prisons in Puerto Rico, Pennsylvania, Arkansas, and Wisconsin. But some did manage to slip through the screening process and became involved in the burgeoning cocaine business that was changing the economy and character of Miami. Trafficante's ring certainly benefited from the help of desperate people like these. They were people for whom the prospect of an American jail term was no deterrent; after all, they had spent considerable time in Cuban prisons. They spoke no English, were unskilled, and had survived under some of the harshest conditions imaginable. The money to be made in the drug trade was too hard to resist. Many have found their way into state prisons across the country for a variety of crimes, and as of July 1997, the federal prison system held almost 3,000 Cuban inmates, many arrested on drug charges and most of them *Marielitos,* as they came to be known.

During this period, government seizures amounted at best to minor disruptions in the steady flow of hard drugs, while the enforcement emphasis was placed on marijuana through efforts like CAMP, the Campaign Against Marijuana Production, an attempt to stamp out home-growers of marijuana. These efforts were funded by money that could have been spent on needle exchanges, methadone maintenance, and community outreach programs to curb heroin use.

The concept that those who became addicted to heroin did so because they were bad decision makers, and that such decisions had only to do with character and nothing to do with the environment in which they lived, is the same kind of isolationist thinking that allowed the AIDS epidemic to claim thousands of lives in the early 1980s. The implied reasoning was that, after all, AIDS was only affecting male homosexuals, and that this population, according to this logic, simply didn't matter. This kind of thinking can be characterized as homophobic at best and genocidal at worst, but its unintended result was that, despite dire warnings from the medical community, the administration did not foresee the implications to society if a homosexual infected with the virus also happened to be an intravenous heroin user.

By 1984, heterosexual heroin users had started showing up in the statistics of AIDS deaths. The government responded by further toughening the drug laws. Among these new laws was one of the most powerful tools law enforcement has ever had against suspected drug dealers: the right to seize any and all assets of a person accused of drug trafficking.[36] The law was introduced by Senators Joe Biden and Gordon Humphrey and signed by Ronald Reagan; it approved the right of the government to seize assets not just after criminal indictment, but upon probable cause, the same amount of evidence needed to obtain a search warrant. By 1984, assets seized from those accused of profiting from the drug trade were being sold and shared by law enforcement agencies. Such assets have come to be a source of income for many local and state police agencies. The sharing of seized assets by the federal government with the states is something that would have boggled the imagination twenty years ago, but it is common practice today. The new law denies drug defendants the right to retain money with which to pay an attorney on the grounds that the cash seized was illegally obtained. Few will complain about such a constitutionally suspect practice if the accused is truly guilty. But what if the accused is not guilty?

By 1986, President Reagan had signed Executive Order 12564, known as the Drug-Free Workplace Act. Most federal employees now had to undergo drug testing. In practice today, the significance of this law is that many employers require job candidates to take a preemployment urine test. Preemployment screening is both discriminatory and of marginal value because it is extremely easy to beat a urine test for heroin and cocaine, which clear the body in a matter of days, but marijuana use can be detected for as long as a month. Therefore, a job applicant could be an otherwise upstanding citizen, yet if he or she smokes a joint two weeks before applying for a job, the applicant could be locked out of the workforce. Preemployment urine testing is consistent with the enforcement emphasis on marijuana at the expense of other drugs and other models of use reduction. It also reemphasizes the us-against-them mentality. Are you with "us," the people who believe in the "traditional values" that America has held dear for so long, the values that say it's perfectly acceptable to drink alcohol, for example; or are you with "them," the counterculture individuals who believe marijuana use is as acceptable as drinking?

The Drug War in the 1990s

Not much has changed in the approach to drug strategy since President Bush left office in January 1993. Hope for more tolerant or rational strategy may have been dashed when President Clinton fumbled the ball on the marijuana issue, at the expense of the heroin problem. When he admitted that he had smoked marijuana but claimed he had not inhaled it, Clinton drew his line in the sand. He could not then advocate more moderate approaches in the handling of the drug problem for fear of being seen as soft on drugs. Clinton and his drug czar, retired Army General Barry McCaffrey, have taken a hard-line stance on marijuana, fighting propositions for its medical use in California and Arizona. Alarming statistics show marijuana use on the rise among American youth, but the numbers are still nowhere near the levels they reached in 1978. However, continued focus on this drug once again coincides with a resurgence in heroin use.

Despite ever-increasing drug-control budgets, nothing seems to have changed. In 1981, the annual federal budget for the drug war was more than $1.5 million. During the Reagan and Bush years it climbed steadily each year to almost $12 billion by 1992. The proposed budget for 1997 was slightly more than $15 billion, a 9.3 percent increase from 1996. These figures do not include expenditures on the local and state levels, which push the total money spent on the drug war even higher.

The drug strategy for 1996 listed five major goals:[37]

1. Motivate America's youth to reject illegal drugs and substance abuse.
2. Increase the safety of America's citizens by substantially reducing drug-related crime and violence.
3. Reduce health, welfare, and crime costs resulting from illegal drug use.

4. Shield America's air, land, and sea frontiers from the drug threat.

5. Break foreign and domestic drug supply sources.

These are valiant goals, but the lion's share of the budget still goes to enforcement, with less than $3 billion annually allocated to treatment. For thirty years we have failed to accept that arresting a street-level dealer merely creates a job opening for the next person lured by the money involved.

Additionally, we have not been successful in stemming drug use even when those at the top are arrested, because new smuggling rings always seem to crop up. Witness the recent resurgence of high-purity heroin available on the streets today. When pressure was placed on the cocaine smugglers, they switched to heroin, because they could make greater profits smuggling lesser quantities. This is nothing new: it is the same reasoning Lucky Luciano used in 1931, when he switched from bootleg liquor to heroin.

The Heroin Resurgence in the 1990s

American Mafia money and Colombian cocaine cartel profits have created a temporary heroin resurgence.

The Cali cartel, under the leadership of Helmer "Pacho" Herrera and Jose Santacruz Londono, established a cocaine distribution network that served as the conduit for much of the nearly pure heroin that found its way into many major U.S. cities beginning in the early 1990s. In the New York area, where much of the new South American heroin winds up, the cartel employed mostly Latinos to retail the drug. During the 1980s, Dominicans supplied by the Cali cartel had almost monopolized the cocaine distribution in the city. When Colombia began opium cultivation and heroin refining, the cartel already had its distribution networks in place; the dealers were mostly young men in their twenties or early thirties, sometimes members of violent street gangs like the Nasty Boys or CNC gangs, or the notorious 112th No Fear gang. In November 1996 New York City police arrested thirty-five members of the No Fear gang. Police estimate the gang was grossing as much as $3 million a year in heroin and cocaine sales. The gang members arrested face life terms in prison for their drug activities and related violent crimes, such as the murder of a drunken neighborhood man who was making too much noise on a street corner where gang members were openly peddling their drugs. The gang members decided he had to go; it was bad for business to have a drunk getting loud and attracting the police. Apparently, they felt the easiest method of solving the problem was to kill him.

The economics of the heroin trade is the reason new recruits are so easy to find. A kilogram of heroin costs about $85,000 and can yield anywhere from 30,000 to 35,000, $10 bags of street heroin. This can result in a net profit of over $250,000 on just one kilo. A kilogram of cocaine can sell for anywhere from $10,000 to $15,000. Even at $100 per gram,

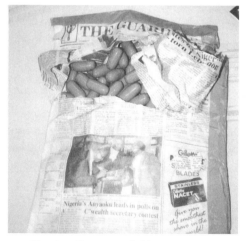

Heroin pellets smuggled in a newspaper
Photo courtesy of the Drug Enforcement Administration,
U.S. Department of Justice

which is more than twice its current retail price on the streets of Washington Heights, New York City, the net profit is about $85,000. This explains why many of the Dominican cocaine dealers were easily convinced to carry heroin as well as cocaine, or to switch entirely to heroin distribution.[38]

Heroin smuggled by the Cali cartel and distributed by Dominican drug dealers has been intercepted in such places as Rhode Island, Massachusetts, Connecticut, Philadelphia, Baltimore, Cleveland, the Carolinas, and as far west as Milwaukee, Wisconsin. The DEA has been successful in bringing down some of the higher-up members of the Cali cartel through the agency's international efforts, but this has simply set the stage for the next group of players to emerge. The DEA predicts the next heroin push will probably come once again from Mexico, where there are three major cartels that have been doing business for years.

The Mexican Heroin Cartels

The Tijuana cartel headed by the Arellano family, the Gulf cartel run by Juan Garcia Abrego, and the Chihuahua cartel headed by Amado Carillo Fuentes pose a special challenge to law enforcement. The Mexican cartels ultimately may be harder to smash than their Colombian counterparts for two reasons: the Mexican government has a long history of being corrupted by narco-dollars, and for sixty-six years it has been run by the Institutional Revolutionary Party, or PRI. Perhaps the biggest challenge lies in the 2,500-mile-long land border the United States shares with Mexico. It is virtually impossible to patrol every mile of border unless the United States builds a wall similar to the Great Wall in China.

Whether because of these challenges or despite them, America continues to spend more on interdiction, eradication, and street-level enforcement. The most damaging of these is arguably street-level enforcement, which perpetuates the siege mentality, the us-versus-them mind-set. Many instances of police misconduct due to overzealousness have been reported. One example is the case of New York City Police Sergeant Kevin Nannery, who was arrested after investigations into corruption at the 30th Precinct station house in Manhattan. He pleaded guilty in November 1994 to conspiring to violate civil rights and to income tax evasion for not reporting $10,000 he had stolen from drug dealers. Nannery took a plea bargain, agreeing to testify against his superiors, Captain Lewis Manetta, and precinct commander Peter Buccino. Nannery testified that his superiors had condoned and encouraged a practice known as "booming"—smashing down doors with a sledgehammer—alleging that Manetta even handed him a sledgehammer, leading him to believe that this was how his superiors wanted things done. The 30th Precinct, which serves Harlem, was the subject of investigations that led to police officers being charged with drug trafficking, illegal searches and seizures, taking cash from drug dealers, and lying in court to uphold illegal arrests.[39]

Wanted posters in English and Spanish for Ramon Arellano-Felix of the Mexican Tijuana Cartel

Reuters/HO/Archive Photos

Aggressive and illegal police enforcement has begun to prove costly to the cities where the unleashing of police power, strongly advocated by William French Smith and Ed Meese during the Reagan-Bush years, has come home to roost. In Philadelphia, the American Civil Liberties Union (ACLU) filed a class-action lawsuit against the city for a case involving a young black man, Darryl Shuler. In 1989 Shuler was arrested by Philadelphia police officers at his home. The officers said they had a search warrant for drugs and ransacked his home, which was actually his father's, confiscated $17,000 belonging to Shuler's father, and claimed to have found a bag of cocaine. Several months later, the officers who had arrested Shuler were indicted by a federal court on charges of corruption, illegal searches, planting evidence, and lying under oath. Six officers, five of whom were white, pleaded guilty to the charges, which involved cases they had worked on in which nearly all of the defendants were African American or Latino.[40]

The charges against Shuler were dropped in 1991, and the convictions in fifty-six other cases involving these police officers have been overturned. Investigations into more than 1,600 arrests these officers made between 1987 and 1994 were under way at this writing. So far, thirty lawsuits have been filed as a result of illegal arrests. The mayor and police officials contend that these cops are rogues—isolated rare cases—and that the 6,300-member department does not use discriminatory or overly aggressive enforcement measures.

Stefan Presser, legal director of the Philadelphia chapter of the ACLU, disagrees. He claims that city government officials have been "deliberately indifferent to the pattern of abuse and unconstitutional conduct that has become an integral part of policing in Philadelphia." Presser supports his allegation by pointing out a 1985 police action that attempted to stamp out street-level drug dealing at seventy street corners in predominantly minority neighborhoods. Massive sweeps were conducted, with 1,500 people detained or arrested in a week, at which point the ACLU obtained an injunction to stop the police action. The ACLU, representing the 1,500 detainees, almost all of whom were black or Latino, sued the city and won $500,000.

Presser alleges that white police officers treat minorities differently and unequally, a charge that has been heard time and again recently. Most observers agree that racial tension in America continues to build as a result of cases such as that of Johnny Gammage, a black man from upstate New York who was traveling through the Pittsburgh area in late 1995. Three of the officers involved in Gammage's death during a routine traffic stop have been tried twice for murder in state courts, with both trials ending in mistrials. The last trial empaneled a jury of eleven whites and one black man. All of the police officers are white. After nine days of testimony, the white jurors were ready to acquit after just twenty minutes of deliberation. The lone black juror held out, and eventually a mistrial was declared. Civil rights activists believe that the Gammage case is a direct result of overly aggressive police tactics used during drug-search traffic stops made only because the suspect fits a profile; they hope the federal government will prosecute the officers involved. Gammage was neither armed nor carrying drugs, yet he was asphyxiated during the attempt to arrest and handcuff him.

Another victim of the Philadelphia police officers convicted in 1995 was Betty Patterson, a grandmother who was arrested for and convicted of selling crack.[41] She spent three years in prison as a result of the officers' malfeasance. After an investigation it was determined that the officers had planted evidence in her arrest. Her conviction was overturned and she was released from prison. Patterson sued the city and was awarded $1 million for her suffering. The ACLU's Presser states, "We thought that policing the way it has been done here [in Philadelphia] ended in 1955." But policing problems have not been confined to any one U.S. city. In one night, on

April 9, 1988, Los Angeles police rounded up more than 1,400 young black and Latino men during "Operation Hammer."[42] The men were arrested on charges ranging from parking tickets and possession of small amounts of drugs to illegal weapons and violation of curfews that existed only in poor neighborhoods.

Mass criminalization of a segment of our society has been the result of the thirty-year war on drugs, but little else has really changed. A report released by the Department of Health and Human Services reveals that marijuana use by teenagers declined slightly in 1996 for the first time in five years. The report also states that "overall use of illegal drugs showed no change." Nonetheless, "administration officials were heartened by the survey's report of an unexpected decline in overall drug use for youths between the ages of 12 and 17." Drug czar Barry McCaffrey was "enormously encouraged" by the report but maintains that we still have a long way to go. Interestingly, the same report shows an estimated increase of 141,000 new heroin users in 1995, most under age twenty-six.[43]

The drug-use statistics the government relies on are produced annually by the National Household Survey. They show minor fluctuations between 1979 and 1996 in the number of heroin users who answer the survey. It seems odd that we do not have a more accurate method of measuring our problem with drugs, particularly heroin. The numbers that have caused the most excitement over the past thirty years have to do with young people smoking pot. That is what makes the headlines. Only when ten white kids die of heroin overdoses, as occurred recently in Texas, does the country become alarmed. The belief is that marijuana is the gateway drug, so it's that drug that matters. As for heroin addicts, as Reagan's drug czar, Carleton Turner, intimated more than fifteen years ago, there aren't that many of them anyway.

CHAPTER

12

Heroin and the
Criminal Justice System in America

Tragically, it is true that until the second half of this century, America's criminal justice institutions, like many other American institutions, were guilty of discrimination based on race. Fortunately, however, the justice system, like the rest of American society, has come a long way.

WILLIAM BENNETT, Drug Czar, 1989–90

June 30, 1970. The U.S. federal prison census shows 20,686 men and women sentenced and incarcerated. Of those inmates, 3,384 were convicted drug offenders, representing 16.3 percent of the total inmate population.

May 1, 1997. The weekly population report released by the Federal Bureau of Prisons lists 87,471 sentenced individuals, with another 23,126 awaiting sentencing, for a total population of 110,597. Of those sentenced, 52,611 were convicted drug offenders, representing 60.1 percent of the total population.[1]

The number of inmates convicted on drug charges and held in state prisons has skyrocketed in similar fashion. The total number of inmates in America has more than tripled since the escalation of the drug war under the Reagan administration. In August 1996 there were 1,127,132 inmates in state prisons, which, combined with the estimated 500,000 in local jails and those in federal institutions, brings the total American prison population to more than 1.7 million.[2] This does not include the more than 600,000 people on parole, 3,000,000 on probation, or more than 60,000 in juvenile facilities.[3]

Clearly, if the effectiveness of the war on drugs can be measured by attrition and sheer numbers, it has been enormously successful. We have locked up more Americans than at any time in our history. And yet, heroin production and consumption have soared. Heroin purity levels have steadily risen while prices have declined. Estimates of hard-core users range from 600,000 to 1,000,000.[4] So, has the war on drugs succeeded? Is locking up drug offenders the answer to America's drug problem?

While addressing the need for alternatives to incarceration, General Barry McCaffrey, director of the Office of National Drug Control Policy, responded to such questions by stating, "What we're convinced doesn't work is to just arrest people, lock them up and throw them back on the street the way you got them."[5]

Drug War or Race War?

The United States has the highest incarceration rate in the world, with 426 of every 100,000 Americans behind bars. The next two countries on the list, South Africa and the former Soviet Union, imprison 333 and 268 per 100,000, respectively. Black Americans are four times more likely to be in jail than black South Africans.[6]

The states with the highest numbers of prisoners are California (135,646), Texas (127,766), New York (68,484), Florida (63,879), Ohio (44,677), Michigan (41,112), Illinois (37,658), and Georgia (34,266).[7] The highest per capita rate, however, belongs to Washington, D.C., where 1,650 of every 100,000 residents are locked up.[8] (North Dakota has the fewest number of state prisoners with only 85 of every 100,000 incarcerated.) The problem in the District of Columbia is symptomatic of a larger national problem. Washington, D.C., is predominantly black. The national average of incarcerations per 100,000 is 426. D.C.'s rate of 1,650 is more than four times the national average, illustrating how African Americans are disproportionately represented in the number of citizens convicted and sentenced to prison.

During the 1980s the number of African American males between ages twenty and twenty-nine in the criminal justice system climbed steadily, reaching to 609,690 by 1989; the figure represented 23 percent of that age group's population. By 1995, 827,440 black males between twenty and twenty-nine were in the system, representing nearly one-third of this population. Even more alarming is the fact that the percentage of African American women in the criminal justice system nearly doubled between 1990 and 1995, although there are still six times as many black men in jail as there are black women in jail.[9]

Figures from the Bureau of Justice Statistics have been interpreted to show that the imprisonment rate for African Americans is 1,534 per 100,000. Caucasians are imprisoned at a rate of 197 per 100,000.[10] This can be viewed in one of two ways: (1) disproportionate numbers of African Americans are criminals; (2) blacks are victims of a biased legal system or a culture in which the deck is decidedly stacked against them or both. Both theories seem to have some validity. Figures show that more than 60 percent of those arrested for robbery are black, though blacks account for only 12 percent of the U.S. population.[11] However, criminologists James Lynch, of American University, and William Sabol, of the Urban Institute, point out that law enforcement patterns target inner-city neighborhoods. They report that discrimination in housing has created geographic segregation, denying many blacks a chance to move away from pockets of poverty where unemployment and limited job opportunities exist. As a result, some working-class blacks turn to the drug trade because of their limited options.[12]

A Rand study of young African Americans arrested for drug offenses found that two-thirds were employed at the time of their arrest, but at low-paying jobs; they used drug dealing as a means of compensating for their economic status. "The implication is that the absence of opportunities for better paying jobs in racially segregated urban areas acts as an added pressure to sell drugs," the study stated.[13]

Given all this, it is hardly surprising that statistical evidence shows people of color disproportionately represented in the prison population. Figures from the Bureau of Prisons show that by 1991, 21 percent of all state prison inmates were there on drug offenses. Eight percent were sentenced for drug possession and 13 percent for drug trafficking. Women were more likely to be incarcerated for a drug offense than men (33 percent versus 21 percent). African Americans were more than twice as likely to be serving time for a drug offense than whites (25 percent versus 12 percent). In addition, 33 percent of Hispanic inmates were imprisoned on drug charges.[14] A walk through a cell block in almost any state prison would corroborate this, as a sea of colored faces stares back from the wrong side of the bars, providing ammunition for those who believe that the war on drugs is really a race war.

As discussed earlier, inner cities have been the primary targets for domestic enforcement efforts. Here, heroin and cocaine fuel an underground economy and yield high profits. The police, under political pressure to reduce crime, substantiate their funding by producing arrests. They measure their effectiveness in two ways: number of reported crimes and number of arrests. Their effectiveness is often magnified with arrests for minor violations. For example, in New York City since 1994 the number of arrests for possession of marijuana has increased by more than 400 percent while the number of arrests for the sale of the drug has stayed the same. Arrests for the sale of heroin also have remained at the same level. This is in keeping with the enforcement of quality-of-life crimes on which the current administration has embarked. It appears the police are being more effective, when in fact there is still just as much hard-drug activity taking place as there was before 1994. It has just become less visible. It is simply easier to arrest a person for buying a small quantity of marijuana on the street than it is to jail a dealer, just as it is easier to concentrate police efforts in a segregated inner-city area. African Americans claim they are being targeted by police and the courts, and they cite the inequity of sentencing guidelines for possession and sale of cocaine as an example of how the system is stacked against them.

In 1986, during the height of the crack cocaine epidemic, mandatory sentencing guidelines were passed by Congress. Possession of 5 grams of crack carried a mandatory five-year sentence under the new law, whereas an offender would have to be arrested with 500 grams of powder cocaine to merit the same five-year sentence, a 100-to-1 ratio. To make 5 grams of crack costs about $150 to $250. It weighs about the same as two copper pennies. Five hundred grams of cocaine weighs slightly more than a pound and costs approximately $10,000 to $15,000. The rationale behind the law was that the crack epidemic was devastating the inner cities, and cocaine in crack form was thought to be much more addictive than powder cocaine. The intent of the law may not have been racist, but in the underground economy of cocaine, where crack can sell for between $3 and $10 per vial and powder cocaine can sell for anywhere from $30 to $150 per gram, the inevitable result was that blacks in poor urban areas would be affected disproportionately by the law. Again, the intent of the legislators may not have been racist, but the effect of the law certainly is. Although the fairness of this law is still being debated as of this writing, the practical consequence of it is that nearly 89 percent of crack cocaine defendants are African American. Hispanics account for 7 percent and whites make up 4 percent. For powder cocaine, 27 percent of those arrested are black, 32 percent are white, and 39 percent are Hispanic.[15]

Associate special agent in charge William Mochler of the DEA in New York City says that cocaine retailers have increasingly expanded into selling heroin as well. Bureau of Justice statistics report that 40 percent of all state inmates who had used drugs in the month preceding their arrests injected heroin, 28 percent other opiates, and 28 percent cocaine.[16]

It appears that police making heroin arrests are increasingly targeting black men as well. Anecdotal evidence points to cocaine and heroin going hand in hand in the inner cities, driving the underground economy, and providing fodder for the prison industry as it struggles under the strain of overcrowded conditions while calling for more prisons.[17]

According to a Bureau of Justice report, "If recent incarceration rates remain unchanged, an estimated 1 of every 20 persons can be expected to serve time during their lifetime. The lifetime chances of a person going to prison are higher for men (9%) than for women (1%) and higher for blacks (16%) and Hispanics (9%) than for whites (2%). At current levels of incarceration, newborn black males in this country have a greater than 1 in 4 chance of going to prison during their lifetimes, while Hispanic males have a 1 in 6 chance, and white males have a 1 in 23 chance of serving time."[18]

New York City, home to almost half of America's heroin addicts, has always had an underground economy revolving around drugs, prostitution, and the sex trade. When Rudolph Giuliani was elected mayor in 1993, he vowed to clean up the streets and embarked on a crusade against quality-of-life crimes. Legions of police officers took to the streets with a new strategic approach to law enforcement. Before 1993, drug and vice enforcement was handled by specialized task forces. Former police commissioner William Bratton changed all that and returned many responsibilities to the precincts, making it possible for beat cops to arrest prostitutes, panhandlers, "squeegee artists" (men who cleaned windshields at stoplights), street drug dealers, and a variety of other small-time offenders for crimes ranging from loitering to carrying open containers of alcohol and public urination. The strategy is similar to fishing with a net: you will catch a lot of small fish, but occasionally a big fish will also be snared. The result has been a dramatic drop in crime and an increase in the city jail population. Most of the offenders arrested for simple possession of heroin wind up serving their time at Rikers Island, the largest jail facility in the country, with an average daily population of anywhere from 15,000 to 19,000 inmates. Another result of the new strategy has been a shift in the demeanor of the police on the street.

A sweep, or enforcement effort, bears close resemblance to a state of siege. In 1996, I witnessed a sweep of a one-block area on the Lower East Side of Manhattan. Police vans positioned themselves on opposite ends of the block, with approximately ten to twenty uniformed and plainclothes police officers checking each car that drove through for motor vehicle violations or expired inspection and registration stickers. Cars with malfunctioning headlights or taillights and cars with out-of-state plates and suspicious-looking passengers were detained while motor vehicle records were checked for any outstanding warrants. Pedestrians carrying brown bags with open beer cans were arrested and also checked for outstanding warrants. Loiterers were asked to produce identification, and if unable to do so, were taken in and processed through the system. Groups of men standing around or playing cards, as is the custom in many Caribbean cultures, were positioned against building facades and frisked for weapons or drugs. If no drugs were discovered and one could produce identification, the individual was asked to move along. I tried to film an arrest in progress and was emphatically instructed to cease doing so; I was told to move along or risk being arrested for obstruction of governmental administration. Granted, the block under siege was a known open market for drug selling, and legitimate arrests for the sale and possession of drugs were made, but the effect is chilling on a law-abiding citizen who might happen to be walking through on his way home or, as in my case, conducting legitimate research and documentary film work.

Without doubt, this type of enforcement activity decreases drug dealing, takes wanted criminals off the street, and helps to build the morale of a police force that for years has felt handcuffed, so to speak, in its efforts against street-level crime. But at what cost? Law-abiding citizens, primarily people of color, often have their constitutional rights trampled simply because their socioeconomic status relegates them to segregated areas where high crime rates exist. As Norman Siegel, executive director of the New York Civil Liberties Union, said in a recent *New York Times* article, "You want effective law enforcement but you don't want it at the expense of civil liberties. In a democratic society, no citizen should be required to show identification to walk down a public street."[19]

Heroin behind Bars

Once incarcerated, drug offenders do not necessarily have to stop using drugs; there exists a lucrative drug trade behind bars. In 1990 seven of every eight U.S. prison facilities conducted urine tests on inmates to detect drug use.[20] The results attested to the existence of a thriving prison drug trade. In the state prisons an average of one in seventy-five inmates tested positive for heroin use. On the federal level, 1 in 250 tested "dirty" for heroin. If we extrapolate the numbers, this means that an estimated 16,000 inmates in state prisons and 440 in the federal system tested positive for heroin use.

The lower number in the federal prisons could be due to a much lower census and tighter controls and security. Visitors at federal institutions are often questioned and subjected to searches of any bags or gifts they might be carrying; occasionally, they are required to undergo pat-down or body-cavity searches. In 1990 more federal prison visitors (27.5 percent) underwent body-cavity searches than did state prison visitors (22.4 percent).[21] It should be noted, however, that during a body-cavity search the visitor is merely asked to expose his or her cavities; he or she is not touched or probed by hand, so it is still possible to hide a cache of drugs deep inside the body, to be retrieved later while in the privacy of the visitors' restroom.

Significantly, heroin was not the most prevalent drug in recent urine testing of state inmates: one in sixteen tested positive for marijuana, one in twenty-eight for cocaine, and one in fifty for methamphetamine.[22] This can be interpreted in a few ways. Heroin is more cost prohibitive, harder to withdraw from, and therefore perhaps less appealing as a drug of choice in prison. Anecdotally, however, prison inmates declare that heroin is more prevalent than the positive urine tests show and claim that it is in fact the most sought after drug in prisons. This makes sense if you analyze the heroin high and consider the prison setting—they are a perfect match. The sedate euphoria works well in an atmosphere where inmates have nothing but time on their hands and a world of hurt to endure.

Visitors are not the only ones subjected to scrutiny. Prison staff members are questioned in 45 percent of federal facilities and in 23 percent of state prisons when they come under suspicion. Once under suspicion, 19 percent of federal prison workers and 14 percent of state prison workers are patted down.[23]

Once heroin is smuggled into prison, whether by staff members or by visitors, the value of the drug increases dramatically, as does the value of any commodity. Estimates range from three to four or five times the going price on the street. Information of this nature is hard to obtain from official sources, but interviews conducted in the New York and New Jersey areas with former inmates reveal that a bag of heroin selling for $10 on the street can go for as much as $40 behind bars.[24] Thus, an inmate with good connections on the outside can make substantial money while he or she is incarcerated. Conversely, an inmate who becomes addicted to heroin needs friends and family members on the outside to supply the cash necessary to sustain the habit, or else be willing to do whatever it takes to obtain the drug. Doing what it takes sometimes means performing acts of sexual slavery that only a physical and mental obsession with heroin can justify.

Balloons and condoms are two of the items most commonly used to smuggle heroin into prison. They can be passed from the mouth of the visitor during a kiss, swallowed by the inmate, and later retrieved upon defecation or regurgitation. Needles, however, are harder to smuggle and are at a premium, creating an atmosphere in which sharing used syringes is common, which increases the chances of HIV transmission.

Because access to cash is limited at most facilities, a barter system exists among inmates, and prisoners will sometimes do

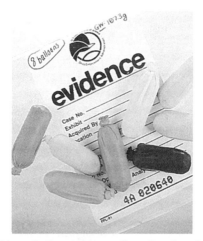

Heroin-filled latex balloons to be swallowed so that the drug can be smuggled onto airplanes inside the courier's body and retrieved later following elimination. If the balloon should break while inside the body, it means almost instant death for the courier.

Photo courtesy of the Drug Enforcement Administration,
U.S. Department of Justice

anything to get their drugs. Cigarettes, clothes, gifts, food, items stolen from workshops—all are used to pay off drug debts. Inmates are often forced into prostitution, providing sex to feed their heroin habits. Most do not use condoms, which also raises the risk of HIV infection.

Heroin and the HIV Epidemic in Prisons

Few studies have been done to see whether HIV is transmitted in prisons, but researchers believe that it is. A study conducted in Illinois in 1988 supports this theory. Among 1,309 inmates, 47 were found to be HIV positive; one year later there were 80 inmates who tested positive.[25] Logic and common sense should lead to the conclusion that if inmates are sharing needles and having unprotected sex, HIV will flourish.

In a study conducted in six South Carolina prisons, more than 40 percent of the inmates surveyed reported knowledge of needle sharing. Sixty percent reported sexual activity among inmates in the past year. Eight percent reported injecting drugs, and 40 percent of these shared needles.[26]

The war on drugs has created a prison and jail population of which the majority are drug offenders, violent criminals who committed crimes while under the influence of drugs, or offenders who committed crimes in order to obtain drugs. It stands to reason that we would find a higher prevalence of HIV and AIDS in the prison population than in the general population, but trying to understand just how serious the situation is becomes problematic, again because of politics and public attitudes. In a *New York Times* article, Ronald Bogard, a former general counsel for the city of New York who is now a national spokesman on AIDS in prisons, said, "There is little effort to determine the extent of the problem. Not only do we not know, we don't really care because of the people involved and the money that is involved."[27]

During the 1990s the numbers of HIV and confirmed AIDS

cases in our prisons have steadily risen. Anecdotal evidence suggests that the numbers may be underreported due to the absence of a nationwide mandatory testing policy, but the documentation and research we do have show that in 1991 there were 17,551 HIV-positive inmates in state and federal prisons. By year-end 1995, there were 24,226 HIV-positive inmates, a 38 percent increase and almost the same rate of growth (36 percent) as the entire prison population experienced during that period. These numbers represent 2.3 percent of male inmates and 4 percent of female inmates incarcerated as of 1995.[28]

New York and Florida held a little less than half of all the country's HIV-positive inmates in their facilities, as of 1995. According to Bureau of Justice Statistics, New York housed 9,500 HIV-positive inmates, Florida held 2,193, Texas had 1,890, and California had 1,042. New Jersey, Georgia, and the federal system reported numbers in the low to mid-800s, whereas Connecticut and Maryland had 755 and 724, respectively. Numbers for states with less than 700 HIV-positive cases were not available.[29]

Of all HIV-positive inmates, 21 percent, or 5,099 inmates, were confirmed AIDS cases. In 1995, there were 3,133 reported deaths in state prisons across the United States, with AIDS being the second leading cause of death. Nearly one-third, or 1,010, of those prison deaths were due to AIDS. The leading cause was illness or natural causes (1,569). The remaining deaths were attributed to suicide (160), accident (48), execution (56), homicide (86), and other unspecified or undetermined causes (204). New York state, which had the highest number of AIDS deaths, reported that 65 percent of its inmates who died while in custody died of AIDS.[30]

The number of confirmed AIDS cases in state and federal prisons is more than six times higher than in the general population. Approximately .51 percent of all prisoners have AIDS, whereas only .08 percent of the general public has been diagnosed with the disease. About one in ten deaths in the general population is AIDS related, whereas in prison, almost one of every three deaths is attributed to AIDS.[31]

For women, statistics indicate an alarming increase in both numbers incarcerated and reported HIV cases. As stated earlier, the number of women in prison doubled during the first half of this decade. But between 1991 and 1995, the number of incarcerated males reported to be HIV positive increased by only 28 percent, while the number of HIV-positive female inmates increased by 88 percent during that period. Looking at these statistics, we can fairly say that more females are being sent to prison and a greater percentage of those women are HIV positive. Although it should be reiterated that the vast majority of convicts are male, nearly twice the percentage of women (4 percent versus 2.3 percent) are HIV positive. As with the males, the majority of female inmates are people of color, imprisoned for drugs or drug-related crimes.

At Rikers Island in New York City, where a majority of the inmates at any given time are held on drug-related charges, 26 percent of the female inmates are reportedly HIV positive, whereas 12 percent of the males are HIV positive. The jail estimates that 3,000 inmates a year require AIDS-related services and care. According to a report in *The New York Times*, Rikers housed 9,500 HIV-positive inmates during 1996. With this large concentration of needle users and sex-trade workers comes a high price tag where medical care is concerned. Before 1996, the cost of treating an AIDS patient at the jail was approximately $2,000 per year. Now, with the advent of protease inhibitors as the most effective AIDS treatment option on the market today, the cost of providing medication to AIDS prisoners has skyrocketed to almost $13,000 per inmate per year. New York City was set to begin providing protease inhibitors to AIDS inmates in July 1997. City officials expect to spend $5.4 million in 1998 on the medication, $1 million less than they now spend for all other inmate medicines.[32] The numbers are staggering. If we were to provide every known HIV-positive inmate currently in custody (24,226) with protease inhibitors, at an annual cost of $13,000 per inmate, the total public taxpayer expense would be over $300 million per year. At a time when public sentiment seems opposed to inmates having such so-called frivolous benefits like weight-lifting equipment and libraries, and when grant money to provide inmates with college educations has been cut, it seems unlikely that an additional $300 million annual prison expenditure would fare well if put to a vote in Congress—at least not as part of legislation that had nothing to do with new prison construction, one of the largest growth industries in America today.

With or without additional funding, HIV treatment and prevention efforts behind bars face some special challenges. Three major dilemmas confront prison administrators: (1) Should mandatory testing for HIV be required in all prison settings? (2) Should all inmates who test positive for HIV be segregated from the general prison population? and (3) Should condoms, bleach, and clean needles be made available to inmates? These are questions that need to be addressed before effective strategies can be devised and implemented.

Does an inmate have the right to refuse testing for HIV? Is it fair to segregate those who test positive for the virus from the general prison population? Some see segregation as a form of discrimination; after all, society outside of prison doesn't segregate individuals who have AIDS, so why should it occur in prison? By segregating HIV-positive inmates, inmates left in the general population may wrongly assume they can freely engage in high-risk behaviors such as needle sharing or unprotected sex. And how feasible is it that we would consider sterile needle exchange programs for prisons when the idea is still viewed skeptically as a viable harm-reduction strategy outside of prison walls?

The prison system has been slow to regard HIV/AIDS as a public health issue. This is not surprising in light of society's persistence in viewing addiction itself as a criminal justice rather than public health issue. That is, public policy has generally reflected a belief that it is more expedient to lock up addicts and dealers than to provide drug treatment outside the prison setting. Therefore, to be a heroin addict in America today is to be a criminal, and every time an addict buys heroin he or she breaks the law and risks going to jail. If the addict needs to steal to support his or her habit, he or she again breaks the law and risks jail. Because it is from this starting point that we as a society view the heroin addict, abdicating social responsibility for the problem of addiction to the criminal justice system rather than treating it as a public health issue, it is only a small leap of logic to consider the HIV risk in prisons as merely another facet of the right and proper punishment society metes out for criminal acts.

In an article in *The Lancet,* Timothy Harding and Joachim Nelles indict this type of thinking, arguing that the criminal justice system bears the responsibility for humanely treating individuals with HIV/AIDS who wind up behind bars. They state, "The overall failure to apply a pragmatic and effective response to the HIV/AIDS epidemic in prisons is due to pre-existing inadequacies in prison health care, the lack of independence of prison medical services, and the adoption of policies that serve the needs of institutions rather than those of inmates."[33]

Research on harm reduction shows that condom distribution and needle exchanges are two very effective ways to prevent the transmission of HIV; yet at this writing only two states, Mississippi and Vermont, make condoms available to inmates. Only the cities of New York, Philadelphia, San Francisco, and Washington, D.C., distribute condoms to their jail inmates.[34] Virtually no jails or prisons make bleach available, although because bleach is a cleaning agent easily found in any prison laundry, one could say there is a de facto policy of providing it. Dr. Ann S. DeGroot reports that one jail in Houston, Texas, distributes bleach with instructions on how to clean needles. DeGroot is an M.D. who specializes in treating female inmates with AIDS and is a vocal supporter of reform in the treatment provided to HIV/AIDS inmates.[35]

Education and risk-reduction counseling are the most widely used forms of treatment for HIV/AIDS inmates, perhaps because they are the least controversial of choices. However, this approach, at least absent complementary strategies, has not been successful with this at-risk population.

Unfortunately, ignoring the public health implications of HIV in prisons has potentially dire consequences for society. In 1991, for example, there were an estimated 4,000 HIV-positive inmates released on parole.[36] If we extrapolate statistics and use anecdotal evidence, we can conclude that the majority of those released will relapse and go on to have sex with partners who are unaware of their condition or who are unwilling, as in the case of rape, and that the general population will be very much at risk. So what is the answer? The United States could emulate Fidel Castro's policy in Cuba, where HIV/AIDS patients are quarantined in sanitariums, or perhaps we could follow a more humane course, as some prisons in Switzerland have chosen to do.

An act of conscience by Dr. Franz Probst while working in a Swiss prison eventually led to a successful twelve-month experiment by the Swiss Federal Bureau of Health. Probst, an M.D. working part-time at the Oberschongrun prison in the Swiss canton of Solothurn, was faced with an ethical dilemma: fifteen of the seventy inmates he treated were intravenous drug users who shared needles regularly. Many of them suffered from severe abscesses as a result of using unsterile needles. He decided to disregard prison policy and began distributing needles to these patients. When his superiors discovered this, rather than dismissing Probst, they listened to his argument for needle distribution and obtained approval from the government to continue the practice.

The change in policy at Oberschongrun led to an experiment at a women's prison in the canton of Bern, Switzerland, where 110 inmates were monitored over a twelve-month period. A syringe dispenser was installed where the women could trade used needles for sterile ones on a one-to-one basis. Condoms were also distributed to those who were allowed furloughs for home visits. Inmates were interviewed four times during the twelve months of the experiment, and the prison staff members who monitored them were interviewed three times during that year. The interviews focused primarily on levels of inmate drug use and risk behaviors related to drug intake and sexual contacts.

At the start of the experiment 6 percent of the women were HIV positive, 50 percent had hepatitis B, and 30 percent had hepatitis C. Fifty percent reported sharing needles regularly before the experiment. During the course of the year, 5,335 syringes were exchanged. At the end of the year, no injection abscesses were observed, and needle sharing had virtually ceased. Significantly, the proportion of inmates using heroin regularly remained stable, with no increase in drug use as a result of access to needles, and there were no seroconversions (changes in status from HIV negative to HIV positive) observed during imprisonment.[37]

Detractors of this form of harm reduction in America often ask, "Why should we make it easier for addicts in prison to obtain needles to shoot heroin? Didn't we put them in prison for that very behavior?" And when heroin addiction is viewed strictly as a criminal justice problem, these are perfectly logical questions to ask. When we see addiction as a public health issue, however, both inside and outside of prisons, it becomes clear that it is in our best interests to make available not only clean needles, but also treatment that addresses issues such as prostitution, drug addiction, poverty, poor education and job training, limited life options, and trauma.[38]

How do we explain the seeming unwillingness of American policy makers to see a disease epidemic in the penal system as a health issue? Part of it undoubtedly results from entrenched societal homophobia combined with deep ambivalence, despite the unequivocal position of the medical establishment, regarding addiction as a disease. Certainly, the large sum of taxpayer money that would be required to provide adequate medical intervention for HIV/AIDS inmates in prisons plays a role. But we are also reminded of what Ronald Bogard said about society's disdain for the affected population. By 1992, African Americans and Hispanics accounted for 51 percent of all AIDS cases in the United States, though they constituted only 21 percent of the general population. Of all AIDS cases reported in prisons, 44 percent were black, 42 percent were Hispanic, and only 14 percent were white.[39] Is race a factor in our general disregard for this population?

The most recent statistics from the Centers for Disease Control show the first drop in the number of new AIDS cases in the general population reported since the epidemic began in the early 1980s. In 1996, an estimated 56,730 people were diagnosed with AIDS, down from 60,620 new cases in 1995, a 6 percent decrease. However, new AIDS cases diagnosed in 1996 among heterosexual black men rose 19 percent; new cases among heterosexual black women rose 12 percent. The CDC went on to say that the drop in overall cases was due to the advent of protease inhibitors and especially to HIV patients who started taking the new medication early.[40]

Given that needle sharing is one of the main causes of HIV transmission inside and outside of prisons, drug treatment for offenders becomes an important complementary strategy for HIV risk reduction. It seems logical that prison and jail drug treatment would be a national priority given the number of drug offenders that wind up behind bars, but as recently as 1991 the General Accounting Office reported that only 1 percent of the inmates who had drug abuse problems received treatment, and that less than half of all treatment slots available were filled.[41]

A study published in 1990 showed that of 16,998 intravenous drug users, 83 percent reported having been in prison or jail, and 81 percent said they had never participated in formal drug treatment while behind bars.[42] The number of inmates receiving treatment today is greater than it was in 1990, but even optimistic estimates put the number at 20 percent to 25 percent of those who need treatment.[43] A study done in 1992 concluded that of those arrested for drug offenses, there were 280,000 opiate users and 780,000 injection drug users who could benefit from some form of intervention.[44]

It should be noted, however, that at least one study suggests that HIV-positive inmates who do receive treatment while in prison do not necessarily fare well once paroled. This study, conducted with fifty-five HIV-positive inmate parolees, showed that 67 percent relapsed upon release, even though 84 percent of them had completed some form of treatment while in prison. The reasons for relapse were listed as poor housing, limited social support, lack of continued drug treatment, and less frequent visits with case managers.[45] Other research, however, suggests that the prognosis for drug treatment in prison is not as gloomy as that study seems to indicate. Studies of drug treatment programs that in some fashion attend to the other life concerns cited above show a far more optimistic outlook for drug treatment behind bars.

Drug Treatment in Prison

Historically, prisons have not provided adequate drug treatment for inmates with substance abuse problems. In 1979 there were 160 treatment programs serving about 10,000 inmates, or 4 percent of the total inmate population. Ten years later, though the number of inmates receiving treatment nearly tripled, vast numbers of prisoners who could have benefited from treatment remained untreated. In 1997 researchers estimated that between 20 percent and 25 percent of the total prison population was being treated for drug abuse.[46] Bureau of Justice Statistics show that 78 percent of all jail inmates in 1989, 79 percent of state prisoners in 1991, 60 percent of federal prisoners in 1991, and 83 percent of youth in long-term public juvenile facilities in 1987 had used drugs at some point in their lives. Twenty-five percent of jail inmates, 33 percent of state prisoners, and 40 percent of youths in long-term state-operated facilities admitted they were under the influence of drugs at the time of their offense.[47] These numbers show that we can safely say there are many more who need treatment, and prisons and jails are the most logical places to begin the process of recovery. Prisoners in treatment are literally a captive audience. If one of the primary measurements of treatment effectiveness is retention, or length of time in treatment, then we should take advantage of the opportunity imprisonment provides.

One reason there is no comprehensive effort to provide treatment may be the perception that treatment does not work. The public, legislators, and even prison staffers have often expressed skepticism about the efficacy of drug treatment programs. In many cases, prison staffers may not be convinced that treatment works to rehabilitate or to reduce recidivism, but they are in favor of it because it reduces the number of reported prison drug incidents, enhances security, reduces drug dealing, and aids inmate management by providing inmates with something to do.

There are more than five million Americans currently "on paper," that is, involved in the criminal justice system, in either prisons or jails, on parole, or on probation. Eighty percent of these people are recidivists.[48] The attitude that "nothing works" with the incarcerated population has developed over the last several decades, and detractors of treatment highlight the aforementioned statistics to emphasize their point. Effective treatment of these individuals is still in its infancy, and perhaps over the coming years public attitude will begin to change as better results are achieved. Treatment of substance abusers behind bars has not really been given a fair chance if you look at the numbers who are still not treated.

Unfortunately, some legislators are reluctant to support treatment for fear of appearing soft on crime; they feel that their constituents do not value rehabilitative efforts as a priority. A survey done in the state of Michigan refutes this. While only 12 percent of the legislators in Michigan believed that the public was in favor of rehabilitation, in reality 66 percent of the public believed rehabilitation should be the primary goal of prisons.[49] Legislators have been more concerned with how to effectively and securely manage prison overpopulation, and pushing for the construction of more prison space has the politically advantageous effect of creating jobs as well. As a result, overcrowding in prisons has been the priority, and the need to provide adequate housing and beds comes before providing treatment slots.

Effective drug treatment from the viewpoint of the public and their legislators is defined by a reduction in recidivism. Once an inmate with a drug problem completes treatment he should not return to crime upon release from prison. From a health perspective, the measure of effective drug treatment is cessation of drug abuse, though this expectation must be viewed in the context that addiction is by definition a chronic disease and that the addict is susceptible to relapse. So the health care worker and the legislator seemingly have different definitions of effective treatment. A parolee, for example, who relapses and is arrested for possession of heroin would be classified as a recidivist when he returns to jail. To the drug counselor, however, if the addict commits no other crime but to be in possession of heroin and has demonstrated progress in other life areas during an extended period of sobriety, the "offense" is consistent with the dictates of the disease, which by nature involves relapse. The legislator's point of view reemphasizes the idea that to be a heroin addict is to be a criminal, no matter what other progress the addict may have made in other areas of his or her life. Such progress may include holding down a job and staying away from other criminal activity. It can be argued, however, that the two definitions of effective treatment are compatible and should be interwoven to accomplish the agendas of both sectors. It is possible to rehabilitate an addict who winds up in prison by addressing his or her drug problem while working on the life issues that may lead the offender back to drugs and eventually to other criminal activity.

The statistical odds are stacked against inmates who are released untreated. A study conducted in the late 1980s showed that 60 to 75 percent of untreated parolees with histories of heroin use return to drug use within three months after release and become reinvolved in criminal activity.[50] The relapse rate for treated inmates is about 20 percent lower. Some treatment efforts have produced remarkable results. The Amity program in California, for example, claims that only 16 percent of those who completed just a few months of treatment were rearrested, a success rate of 84 percent rehabilitation.[51]

Research findings offer great promise for reducing relapse and, consequently, recidivism rates upon release. The Federal Bureau of Prisons has devised a comprehensive model of treatment that many states are emulating. Based on the therapeutic community model discussed in chapter 6, it strives to address the root causes of addiction while allowing inmates a chance to work on issues such as trauma, poverty, prostitution, and character defects through the development of interpersonal relationships among a group of their peers in group therapy, special seminars, and aftercare. Continuity of care after release is essential and is offered through halfway houses and supervised care by case managers.

The federal program is a multitiered approach with one level of drug education for all inmates with a history of substance abuse; the program provides individual, group, and self-help drug abuse counseling services, comprehensive residential (segregated from the general population) drug treatment units, and transitional services for community reentry. Based on research, it has been determined that the optimal duration of treatment is nine to twelve months and that the therapeutic community model produces better results than education and counseling.[52]

There are several successful state programs that report reduced recidivism rates as a result of using the TC, or therapeutic community, treatment model. They include Stay'n Out in New York, Cornerstone in Oregon, Amity Prison TC in California, and Key-Crest in Delaware.

The Key-Crest program, under the supervision of Dr. James Inciardi, is a three-stage model currently being studied in Delaware. The first stage of treatment is a twelve-month residential prison TC model in which the inherent problems of the addict's lifestyle are confronted. During the second stage, as inmates near their parole date, they hold paying jobs in the outside community, returning to the prison TC in their off-hours, until their release. Once paroled, they are supervised by case managers and receive outpatient counseling via group and individual therapy sessions. They also return to the prison TC for reinforcement sessions, weekly groups, and one day a month of service at the work-release TC.

An eighteen-month study was conducted of the men and women who participated in the Key-Crest program. Seventy-two percent were African American, 82 percent had previous drug treatment, and the average age was 29.6 years; 81 percent were men, the average age at first arrest was seventeen, and the number of previous incarcerations averaged two.[53]

The study participants were assigned to one of three groups: Key, Crest, or Key-Crest. A control group received no treatment while in prison other than HIV education and no work-release or after-prison treatment.

Those in the Key group received TC treatment only; the Crest group received after-prison work-release treatment only;

and the Key-Crest group completed an in-prison TC program, an after-prison work-release program, and aftercare.

After eighteen months, among those in the control group who received no treatment, only 17 percent remained drug free and 64 percent had been rearrested. The Key group, with only in-prison TC treatment, showed slightly better results, with 34 percent remaining drug free and 46 percent avoiding arrest after eighteen months.

Those participating in the work-release only, or Crest, program fared slightly better yet, with 46 percent remaining drug free and 60 percent avoiding arrest after eighteen months.[54]

The best results were obtained by the individuals who successfully completed the Key-Crest program, which included in-prison TC treatment, work-release, and aftercare supervision. After six months, 94 percent were drug free and 92 percent had avoided arrest. After eighteen months 75 percent were still drug free and 72 percent had not been rearrested.

The difference between those who received no treatment and those who completed all phases of the Key-Crest program is 36 percent arrest free versus 46 percent to 72 percent arrest free. If we were to extrapolate and apply these numbers to 4,000 HIV-positive inmates released on parole, 2,800 would return to prison if not treated while incarcerated, and 3,240 would return to using drugs. If treated, 2,840 of the 4,000 would not be rearrested and only 960 would be using drugs again: 960 versus 3,240. The public health *and* criminal justice implications are immense.

Prison treatment in New York state is financed by the Omnibus Prison Bill, which was approved in 1989 by the state legislature. The bill provided for a 750-bed alcohol and drug abuse treatment facility with seven 200-bed annexes throughout the state. Treatment is provided by outside contractors such as New York Therapeutic Communities, Phoenix House, and Daytop. Inmates are selected from those who are within two years of parole and who have histories of drug and alcohol abuse.

Upon release, they are guaranteed placement in the noncorrectional treatment facilities of the participating contractors.

New York's model is patterned after the Stay'n Out program, a therapeutic community established in 1977 by a group of recovering addicts who were also ex-offenders.[55] Stay'n Out uses an in-your-face approach to force the addict to confront his or her addiction and its inherent denial.

A group of about 2,000 former inmates in New York state was studied to determine the effectiveness of the TC model versus other forms of treatment. Follow-up was performed in 1986 on inmates released between 1977 and 1984. The findings indicated that parolees who received TC treatment fared better than those who participated in counseling only. The longer they remained in the TC setting the better they did. Among men, for example, 49.2 percent of those who completed less than three months showed a favorable outcome, or completion of parole; the rate was 77.3 percent for those who completed nine to twelve months of TC treatment. However, those receiving more than twelve months of treatment did not necessarily do better; the rate of successful parole outcome dropped to 57 percent for those in this category. The conclusions are that nine to twelve months is the optimal time for TC treatment, and that TC treatment produces better results than counseling and education/prevention efforts alone.

California's treatment program for inmates with substance abuse problems is based on New York's Stay'n Out model. Called the Amity Prison TC, the program was begun in 1989 and is based at the R. J. Donovan Correctional Facility near San Diego. The facility houses approximately 4,000 men and has one 200-bed housing unit set aside for participants of the Amity TC program.

The program draws its name from Amity, Inc., an organization staffed mainly by recovering addicts who are also ex-offenders. Many of them have relocated from another Amity program in Tucson, Arizona.

In order to qualify for the Amity program inmates must be within nine to fifteen months of a parole date, have a history of substance abuse, and show no history of mental illness. Child molesters and those guilty of sexual assault while in prison are ineligible.

A study conducted of the Amity participants showed them to be hard-core felons with extensive criminal histories; they averaged 321 offenses committed in their lifetimes. Sixty percent were intravenous drug users (mostly heroin), more than 70 percent had committed a violent crime, and the average inmate had spent more than half his life in prison.[56]

The treatment lasts about twelve months and consists of three stages. The first, lasting two to three months, is used to assess the inmates' needs and problems. This is followed by a five- to six-month period during which the inmates are given more and more responsibilities within the community. They participate in group counseling sessions and provide assistance to newer members of the group. They begin to develop self-confidence through this process and can measure their progress against the newcomers. The last phase prepares the inmates for reentry into society and lasts from one to three months. After completion and graduation, they are offered a bed in a residential TC in a noncorrectional Amity facility. All participants are also encouraged to attend AA/NA meetings after release.

A 1995 study done by H. K. Wexler of the first inmates paroled from the program showed that those who completed treatment and participated in aftercare fared better than those who received no treatment.

Sixty-three percent of a control group who received no treatment were reincarcerated within twelve months of parole. Fifty percent of the Amity program dropouts were recidivists, and 42.6 percent of those who completed the program were reincarcerated. Yet only 26.2 percent of those who graduated and participated in an aftercare program were reincarcerated within one year. This emphasizes the importance of aftercare programs.[57]

Oregon began treating inmates with substance abuse problems in 1975. The state's Cornerstone program is a thirty-two-bed therapeutic community. Although modeled after the Stay'n Out program, Cornerstone uses more professionals and trained corrections officers than the New York or California programs, which are staffed primarily by recovering individuals.

A study of Cornerstone participants three years after release showed that program graduates did better than dropouts and those paroled without treatment. Seventy-one percent of the graduates had avoided reincarceration three years after release, whereas only 26 percent of dropouts avoided reincarceration. As was found in the studies of programs in New York, California, and Delaware, the amount of time in treatment played a significant role in the reduction of criminal activity upon release. The more time in treatment, the less criminal activity—up to a point, as indicated by the results in the New York study, which showed no added benefit after twelve months.

Results such as these have been documented by Dr. Douglas S. Lipton, senior research fellow and principal investigator at the National Development and Research Institute in New York, and published by the National Institute of Justice. His findings show in-custody treatment to be highly effective in preventing recidivism among very high-risk offenders: chronic heroin users with predatory criminal histories, felons who committed a yearly average of 40 to 60 robberies, 70 to 100 burglaries, and more than 4,000 drug transactions. It would seem to be in the best interests of society to allocate more dollars to the treatment of such offenders; a study done in California showed that for every dollar spent on treatment, $7 were saved in crime and health care costs.[58]

Drug Courts and Other Alternatives to Incarceration

"Drug Courts will contribute to reduction of the demand for illicit drugs by mandating treatment for drug-addicted offenders. The link between drug use and criminal activity has been well documented and drug treatment has been shown to reduce both the drug use and the criminal activity of drug involved offenders."[59]

The above, stated in a report to the assistant attorney general of the United States in 1996, reflects a growing trend in America, that of diverting drug offenders to treatment programs by courts specially designed for that purpose.

Drug courts are funded by grants established under Title V of the Violent Crime Control and Law Enforcement Act of 1994 (Public Law 103-322). "The Crime Act authorizes the Attorney General to make grants to States, State courts, local courts, units of local government, and Indian Tribal Governments for the establishment of drug courts."[60]

Since the establishment of the first drug court in Miami, Florida, in 1989, under then-Dade County Chief Prosecutor Janet Reno, more than 109 drug courts have been established around the country to divert drug offenders to court-mandated and supervised treatment, with at least another 77 courts in the planning stages. There are now forty-four states with drug courts, and after Janet Reno became the U.S. attorney general, requests for funding increased to almost $30 million for fiscal year 1995.

The 1996 report to the assistant attorney general states: "A key component of successful drug courts is effective cooperation among the courts, other criminal justice system agencies, [and] treatment and social services."[61]

Typically, a person arrested for a nonviolent drug crime such as possession can be referred to drug court, where the charges are set aside while the defendant undergoes treatment. If the defendant does not comply with treatment, he or she faces jail, providing strong motivation to complete the treatment program. Many judges like drug court because it allows them to follow the progress of every defendant. Because all defendants must make periodic appearances before the bench, the judges become closely involved in each offender's case; they can keep up to date, for example, on the results of random urine testing of each offender through computerized tracking. If the defendant completes treatment, charges may be dismissed or a sentence reduced. More often than not, the defendant has an opportunity to avoid jail time and begin a supervised recovery.

Statistics show that 44 percent of offenders convicted of drug possession are rearrested within three years. For those who receive drug court intervention, the recidivism rates range from as low as 4 percent to 28 percent across the country.

Fifty percent to 65 percent of defendants who enter treatment because of drug court intervention successfully complete their programs. The most frequently reported reasons for success among participants are supportive counseling and fear of going to jail.[62]

Defendants with long criminal histories are generally not eligible for drug court; it is used primarily for misdemeanor offenders without previous felony convictions. Yet it is the hope of government officials that this form of diversion to treatment will alleviate the swelling prison population and avoid sending nonviolent offenders to prison, where they can become hardened and more disenfranchised before their release into the community.

Drug courts are just one of the alternatives to incarceration under review across the country. In Florida, the Department of Corrections is administering a "Drug Punishment Program" for drug offenders twenty-one years of age or younger. The program targets four Florida counties and the cities of Tampa, Sarasota, and St. Petersburg.

Under the program's guidelines, offenders receive a probationary term instead of prison time, as long as they complete the three phases of an eighteen-month program. The first phase consists of six months of intensive residential treatment in a secure facility. Offenders are diagnosed, given a treatment plan with measurable behavioral criteria, and required to participate in group counseling. The second phase, a three-month period, is carried out in a nonsecure facility with services provided by a contracted community treatment provider. The final nine months consist of probation with employment or study supervised by a correctional probation officer, each of whom has a 30-to-1 caseload. If the offenders fail in any of the phases, they go to jail. This program can handle approximately two hundred participants per eighteen-month period.

Connecticut has what it calls the Fresh Start program. Based in Hartford, the program serves female offenders between the ages of sixteen and thirty who would otherwise be headed for prison on drug charges. Participants receive drug treatment and education and counseling in parenting and living skills, all aimed at reducing involvement in crime and drug use.

There are four phases to the program, which lasts from sixteen to eighteen months. The first phase involves assessment and a medical examination. The second is intensive drug treatment based on the therapeutic community model, with special emphasis on women's issues; it lasts nine to twelve months. The third phase prepares the women for community reentry with instruction in living skills, parenting, budgeting, cooking, nutrition, family planning, recreation, and smoking cessation. For the final phase, the participants are placed in subsidized apartments and encouraged to develop supportive networks through involvement in AA/NA, the health care system, and social service networks.

Recently, a made-for-TV-movie showcased another alternative to incarceration. The film, *First Time Felon,* depicted California's High Impact Incarceration program, more commonly referred to as "boot camp."

Officially, the program is called the LEAD Boot Camp and Intensive Parole Program. The acronym LEAD stands for Leadership, Esteem, Ability, and Discipline. It was originally opened in 1993 at the Fred C. Nelles School in southern California, under legislation initiated by Governor Pete Wilson's administration.

Aimed at youthful (under age twenty-five) offenders, the program consists of four months in an intense, highly structured boot camp, followed by six months of intensive parole supervision, usually under house arrest with electronic monitoring. Upon successful completion of the ten months, any remaining parole time must still be served out.

Based on court records, the makeup of participants is predominantly older minority juveniles facing first-time convictions on felony drug charges. Twenty-five percent are parole violators.

The treatment modality at the boot camp consists of group and individual counseling, physically challenging activities, military procedures established in collaboration with the California National Guard, and intensive parole supervision with emphasis on relapse-management strategies.

New York City has a similar program in operation at Rikers Island; it's run by corrections officers who dress and act like military drill instructors. These military-style programs have been highly heralded, but research has not yet been able to determine their effectiveness. As with other forms of treatment, relapse is inevitable for some, though the highly disciplined and structured environment is believed to be beneficial for many of the program participants.

Because there is no one surefire way to treat criminality and drug addiction with a 100 percent success ratio, some skeptics choose to believe that "nothing works" and that, therefore, we shouldn't bother. Amazingly, even some within the medical community share this belief.

Dr. James W. Wiggs used the results of a study done in Maryland with 162 heroin addicts to argue that treatment doesn't work. The study, conducted at the Addiction Research Center in Baltimore, measured the effectiveness of buprenorphine versus methadone in treating opiate addiction. Wiggs extrapolated the findings of the study in curious ways and wrote a letter to the *Journal of the American Medical Association*, which published the study. Wiggs's lengthy letter and the even longer response to it, both used with permission from JAMA, are reprinted here in their entirety because they illustrate the passion, prejudices, and contradictory uses of data that characterize the debate over the efficacy of drug treatment in prisons, even in the scientific community.

> I read the article by Johnson et al. with interest. At least 75% of street crime is accounted for by drug abusers. The average drug abuser steals to maintain his or her habit, and the amount stolen or damaged ranges from $100,000 to $1,000,000 per year per drug abuser. A prison bed costs society about $35,000 per year.
>
> Drug abuse was elevated by the media to the status of a social protest in the 1960s and 1970s, but serious studies in the early 1970s confirmed that it was simply hedonism: people took drugs because they liked the way drugs made them feel. The vast majority of drug abusers, therefore, are sociopaths with no allegiance to anyone and very little ability to learn from experience or to postpone gratification.
>
> With all of this in mind, 162 volunteers "seeking treatment for opioid dependence at the Addiction Research Center in Baltimore, Md." were studied. By the end of 4 months, between 60% and 80% of the patients had quit the study and were back on the street doing drugs. By the end of a mere half-year, between 70% and 94% were back on the street doing illicit drugs. Even those who stayed in treatment had urine samples with positive results for cocaine between 52% and 64% of the time. This means that

in addition to the cost to the taxpayers of providing this treatment, at least half of the drug abusers were still getting the money somewhere on the outside to use cocaine or heroin. They were spending on the average $110 every day for their opioid supply, and at the usual ratio of $10 to $1 for stolen goods, that meant that they were stealing an average of $1,000 per day to support their habits.

My point is that even if the program at the Addiction Research Center in Baltimore was free, during the best part of the 25-week program, 50% of the drug abusers enrolled were costing society $1,000 per day in supporting their outside habits. By the end of one-half year, 70% of them had completely dropped out of the program, and of those remaining in the program, 50% were still stealing on the outside to support their habits.

As a working taxpayer who pays not only for the Addiction Research Center but for the welfare system, the police, the courts, and the inflated cost of insurance to cover the crimes that these people commit before, during, and after treatment, I think it's pretty clear that the "treatment" saves us essentially no money and that a far better place to spend the dollars would be on prison beds. Each prison bed would save society between $60,000 and $940,000 per year. By contrast, the "treatment" is an expensive illusion.
James W. Wiggs, M.D.[63]

The doctors who conducted the study, Rolley E. Johnson, Jerome H. Jaffe, and Paul J. Fudala, were given the opportunity to reply. They wrote

Dr. Wiggs has used our article comparing buprenorphine with methadone as a launching pad for his view that treatment for opioid dependence is an "expensive illusion" and that the public would be better served if the money now devoted to treatment were spent instead on prison beds. Wiggs' estimate of a bed's cost ($35,000 per year) is reasonably accurate, but most of the other figures he cites to support his views are based on wild extrapolations of the costs of opioid-related crime, a misreading or misinterpretation of our article, ignorance of other work published in this area, and naiveté about the workings of the criminal justice system.

We stated explicitly in the article that, in order to focus on the effects of pharmocologic agents (and in contrast to methadone treatment programs), psychosocial components were minimized in our trial. Three other important aspects were noted that differentiated our study from standard methadone treatment programs: there were no take-home doses (a great burden to patients), there was no promise of continuing care at the termination of the study, and there were neither rewards nor adverse consequences associated with urine test results. Wiggs is incorrect to assume that almost all who dropped out were back on the street "stealing an average of $1,000 per day to support their habits." As we stated, some patients who left the study did so to enter comprehensive methadone treatment programs. Further, there is no basis for his supposition that all patients who discontinue treatment return immediately to pretreatment levels of drug use and crime.

To assess illicit opioid use, we monitored urine specimens (an objective measure) three times weekly. On admission, patients were using opioids a minimum of twice daily. The urine screening methods used in our study could detect an average dose of opioids for approximately 48 hours. Hence, a patient who reduced opioid use from 14 to two or three episodes per week (an 80% reduction) might still have had urine sample test results that were positive for opioids 100% of the time.

Most studies of treatment programs that have assessed illicit drug use have found a sharp reduction in the frequency of patient-reported use after entry into treatment, with further decreases over the subsequent 12 months. Wiggs' assumption that high levels of opioid use and other antisocial or criminal activity continued for every patient whose test results were positive for opioids cannot be inferred from our data. Sharp reductions typically seen in better treatment programs are associated with decreased crime, increased legitimate employment, and a decreased risk of spreading the human immunodeficiency virus.

Methadone maintenance treatment of opioid dependence has been studied more thoroughly than any other therapeutic approach. The literature has been reviewed by independent scholars, the Institute of Medicine of the National Academy of Sciences, the Office of Technology Assessment of the U.S. Congress, and the General Accounting Office. All have concluded that methadone treatment, given in appropriate doses and with adequate psychological counseling, results in a sharp and substantial decrease in illicit opioid use and is cost-effective.

Wiggs asserts that incarceration at $35,000 per year is more cost-effective than such treatment. Even assuming that all drug users could be arrested and convicted and that prisons were not overcrowded (both dubious assumptions), the average drug-dependent felon who is sentenced to prison remains incarcerated for only about 19 to 22 months; and barring any behavioral modification, two out of three will return to drug use within a few months and will be re-arrested within three years after release.

Pharmacotherapy, as well as other nonpharmacologic treatments for drug dependence, can make substantial contributions to the effort of decreasing crime and the spread of infectious disease. It is always useful to consider alternative approaches to such goals, but the process is not advanced by the use of numbers or arguments that will not stand up to scrutiny.

A review of the study referred to in these letters can be found in chapter 9, which is devoted to pharmacological approaches to treating heroin addiction.

In his 1975 book *Thinking about Crime*, John Q. Wilson wrote, "Belief in rehabilitation requires not merely optimistic but heroic assumptions about the nature of man." Prison beds cost between $50,000 to $70,000 to build, and anywhere from $20,000 to $35,000 per year when filled. The per pupil expenditure of some of the best equipped schools in the United States is $15,000 per year. Schools in the inner cities are tremendously overcrowded and underserved. As social critic Jonathan Kozol points out in his book *Savage Inequalities*, "America's failure to

provide all children with access to quality education guaran-
tees an ever-growing supply of potential inmates."[64]

What will America be like when our sons and daughters in-
herit the consequences of our current drug, criminal justice,
and education policies?

CHAPTER

13

Heroin, Popular Culture, and the Media

As a young alcoholic, I grew up thinking heroin addicts were the coolest, the most outlaw.

They lived a lifestyle I was too scared and middle-class to live.

JIM S., recovering alcoholic

In the 1990s, the lifestyle and look of heroin users, once relegated in the public perception to only the most distant margins of the social fabric, has been romanticized in mainstream and alternative news media and in popular culture as glamorous, sexy, fundamentally hip, and desirable. In film, television, music, and popular literature, this look, currently know as "heroin chic," enjoys enormous popularity, much to the consternation of parents, educators, and government officials. President Clinton recently criticized the fashion industry for promoting heroin chic in its advertising.

Are the advertising and entertainment industries responsible for the surge in the numbers of middle-class heroin users? The allure of heroin—and whatever role the media have played in promoting that allure—is difficult to define and measure. Yet one thing is certain: in recent years, heroin has made its presence felt in middle- and upper-middle-class communities throughout America.

"It's the chic drug of choice now," a New Jersey state drug agency official reported to the Newark *Star-Ledger* newspaper.[1] Newark, New Jersey, is one of the many cities across the country that has been flooded with high-purity heroin and a steady flow of buyers who usually drive in from surrounding suburban communities.

Sandor Swidler, a drug and alcohol counselor at Saint Barnabas Behavioral Health Network in Livingston, New Jersey, says he's seen the number of middle- and upper-class heroin users quintuple in the past seven years. "Probably the biggest increase has been among adolescents. There are a tremendous number of students using it," he says.

Other reports from around the state of New Jersey bear witness to this. In March 1997, an Associated Press story described how an eighteen-year-old Toms River High School student was arrested on aggravated manslaughter charges following a hit-and-run accident that killed an eight-year-old Newark boy. Police said the youth was in the city to buy heroin.[2] Toms River is about an hour's drive south of Newark on the Garden State Parkway. Like a magnet, the allure of heroin pulled this white middle-class student up the parkway on a trip that forever changed his life—and ended that of an inner-city boy.

Across the country, such dramas are being played out on the streets of the inner cities, as middle- and upper-class suburban residents search for the image, the thrill, the high that heroin offers. Sometimes, the thrill is in the buying of the drug. "Here I was, this white, middle-class kid going to the inner city and coming out with drugs and money to spare. I felt cool," says an eighteen-year-old addict who enjoyed the adventure of buying heroin in Philadelphia and Newark.[3]

What was once considered a drug and lifestyle associated solely with avant-garde artists and inner-city people of color has become entrenched in the homes of mainstream America. Linda Chapman, program director of addiction at Elizabeth General Medical Center in New Jersey, says her "rehab clients have included pilots, lawyers, and a lot of teachers."[4]

During the 1980s, cocaine was fashionable in middle-,

upper-middle-, and upper-class social and business circles. Heroin, it seems, is fulfilling that role today. How did this happen? One key factor to the current popularity of heroin is that the higher purity level found on today's market makes it possible to get high from sniffing the drug, thereby avoiding the use of needles. Needles, and the accompanying stigma of needle use, are still only for the most hard-core users. The majority of today's heroin users are ingesting the drug by sniffing or smoking. The absence of needles makes heroin use more socially acceptable and, with the stigma diminished, many are willing to experiment with a drug that has a history of being "cool." Heroin use then allows a suburbanite to identify with the dangers of the underclass, to feel like an outlaw, someone willing to play with fire—and to do so in the relative safety of his or her suburban environment.

Heroin and the Popular Music Industry

At the core of modern heroin chic is a history and tradition that goes back to the jazz era. The lifestyles of the "coolest" jazz musicians, those of the thirties, forties, and fifties, have been well documented. The saxophone of Charlie Parker, the trumpet of Miles Davis, and the voice of Billie Holiday have all played the song of heroin.

Billie Holiday, born Eleanora Fagan in Baltimore, Maryland, in 1915, was one of the greatest jazz and blues singers of all time. After an impoverished childhood, she began her career in the late 1920s in New York City, working as a singer in clubs in Harlem. She made her breakthrough in 1933, after which she had her first recording session and went on to sing with the bands of Count Basie, Artie Shaw, Lester Young, and the pianist Teddy Wilson. Her voice began to show the effects of heroin use by the 1940s, and the following decade closed with her death in 1959 at Metropolitan Hospital in New York.

She was forty-four years old, under arrest at the time for heroin possession.[5]

Charlie Parker, acknowledged as a pioneer on the alto saxophone, also succumbed to heroin addiction. Born in 1920 in Kansas City, Kansas, he grew up listening to the great bands that traveled through Kansas City, Missouri, and moved on to New York in 1938 at the age of eighteen. By 1946 he had suffered a mental breakdown and was hopelessly addicted to heroin; in 1955 he died as a result of physical problems related to his addiction. The coroner who examined the body reported that Parker appeared to be fifty-five to sixty years old at the time of his death, twenty years older than the thirty-five years he had actually lived.[6]

It seems that in the world of jazz during the thirties, forties, and fifties, there were few who escaped the allure of heroin. To be a jazz player during the fifties was to embody the concept of "cool"; there was even a style of music called "cool jazz," heralded by the playing styles of Miles Davis and Chet Baker.

Miles Davis, one of the foremost trumpet players the world has seen, was addicted to heroin but managed to overcome his dependence by the 1960s. Davis, born in 1926 in Alton, Illinois, went on to record classic jazz albums until his death in 1991 at the age of sixty-five. He was known for introducing cool jazz—as opposed to the "hot," uptempo bebop—with his collaborator Gil Evans.[7] The style, images, and tragic lives of these and other jazz icons continue to exert a powerful romantic appeal for rebellious youths in search of an identity. For just a few dollars, a middle-class suburbanite can sniff a bag of heroin, put on a set of headphones, and visit a world of smoky clubs and sexy horns and the slow, easy times of a bygone era; he or she can escape the humdrum existence of family life, job, or college studies and for a short while be transported into another, more exciting, riskier, and more creative way of life.

Manhattan therapist Dr. Roy Spungin, who has studied heroin addicts and their lifestyles extensively, says, "People have a strong urge to push limits, to feel better about their average existence. They need to feel the thrill of danger. To successfully dabble with a dangerous drug in a scary part of town sometimes fulfills a need they have to feel larger than their small, defined lives. Heroin provides this inexpensively."[8]

The two media that have done the most to popularize the image of the musician/heroin addict as a rebel hero are film and television. Over the past thirty years we have seen numerous documentaries chronicling the lives of musicians who have died from heroin. The stories of Janis Joplin, Jimi Hendrix, Sid Vicious, Kurt Cobain, and Jerry Garcia all have been told in rich biographical detail. And while many prominent artists have died as a result of heroin use, there are many who have been addicted and have survived; the list includes names such as Ray Charles, Keith Richards, Gregg Allman, Pete Townshend, Dee Dee Ramone, James Taylor, Marianne Faithfull, Eric Clapton, and Axl Rose. Yet in today's popular music world, heroin is still claiming victims despite the tragic experiences of previous generations of rock, pop, blues, and jazz players.

A recent phenomenon in the music scene was the emergence of "grunge," a subgenre of "alternative" music. Born in Seattle, Washington, grunge mixed punk and heavy-metal styles and fast became mainstream rock and roll. Seeking the grunge "look," scores of young men and women dressed in dirty clothes, unkempt and unwashed. They rocked to the music of bands like Cobain's Nirvana. Grunge culture featured qualities similar to the counterculture of the sixties; both were predicated on hostility to established bourgeois culture. Grunge culture, like the counterculture of the sixties, was spawned in the suburbs. The former, however, lacked the political idealism of the sixties version. Another major difference between the two was that the youth of the sixties came mostly from middle-class, two-parent families, whereas the defining family image for grunge kids was the broken home—a consistent theme in grunge music.

The life of Kurt Cobain is a case study in the angst of the white middle-class American boy who becomes addicted to heroin. Cobain, whose parents divorced when he was eight years old, grew up in a troubled home. His mother lived with a man who was abusive, a womanizer, and a heavy drinker. "I'm a product of spoiled America," Cobain said. "Think how much worse my family life could be if I grew up in a depression or something. There are so many worse things than a divorce. I've just been brooding and bellyaching about something I couldn't have, which is a family, a solid family, for too long."[9] Ironically, fame, fortune, and the opportunity to have his own family unit with his wife, Courtney Love, and daughter, Frances Bean, were not enough for Cobain. Depressed and disillusioned, he killed himself with a shotgun blast to the head in 1994. Heroin was found to be in his bloodstream at the time of his demise.

Cobain's death elevated him to martyr status among his followers, his final act seen by some as a statement of the futility of it all. Ironically (but not, perhaps, surprisingly), what was interpreted as his fatal symbolic gesture of desperation and alienation (almost certainly an overstatement of the breadth of Cobain's intentions at the time of his suicide) has fueled the very consumerism he decried: Nirvana record sales skyrocketed following his death.

Another heroin fatality in the Seattle music scene was that of Andrew Wood, leader of the now-defunct band Mother Love Bone. Wood died of a heroin overdose in 1990. His haunting song about his addiction, "Chloe Dancer/Crown of Thorns," appears on the soundtrack of the movie *Singles*, filmmaker Cameron Crowe's look at the Seattle singles scene.

The music industry's response to the rise in heroin addiction among musicians has been to set up an outreach program called MusiCares Substance Abuse Initiative. Mike Greene, head of the National Academy of Recording Arts and Sciences, called together four hundred members of the industry for closed-door sessions to discuss the issue in 1996. "The idea is for executives, managers, and agents to stop looking the other way when an artist clearly has a drug problem. It's a moral question. . . ."[10]

The problem with this approach, according to Ron Stone, a manager at Gold Mountain Records, is that "the reality is, none of the record companies are going to let go of a platinum artist because they're on drugs. And if they would take a position saying 'We don't want to do business with you,' then there's 20 other record companies that would do it in a second."[11]

Young people emulate their idols, and the music and film businesses are about creating idols. "You got a million needles tattooing kids," says Exene Cervenka, poet and singer in L. A. punk band X. "You got a million needles piercing their ears, piercing their noses, piercing their lips. You got a million needles shooting drugs into their veins. And to them it's all the same thing. I don't think kids can differentiate between behaviors."[12] The sad truth is that kids *do* move to Seattle and live the heroin life just because Kurt Cobain did it.

Heroin in Hollywood

The popular music industry is not alone in producing its share of performers with heroin problems. Hollywood has historically been a place where excess and decadence have been tolerated. Over the years, heroin and addiction have provided the subject matter for more than a few noteworthy films. In the 1955 Otto Preminger film *Man with the Golden Arm*, based on a novel by Nelson Algren, Frank Sinatra portrayed Frankie Machine, a man addicted to heroin and struggling through a cold-turkey withdrawal.

In 1971, Al Pacino starred in *The Panic in Needle Park*, which tried to present both the sleaziness and the romance of the life of a street junkie. Pacino went on to star in *The*

Godfather in which Marlon Brando portrayed the wise and moral Mafia don who refused to take the family into the heroin business and nearly paid for it with his life.

Three recent films that have depicted heroin use are *Pulp Fiction*, *Trainspotting*, and *The Basketball Diaries*.

In *Pulp Fiction*, directed by Quentin Tarantino, John Travolta vividly portrays a hip, dispassionate, heroin-addicted professional murderer. Travolta's character is the outlaw-as-hero, a man surviving (even thriving) by his charm, wits, and élan on the fringes of society. In one of the film's more graphic scenes, the crime boss's wife, played by Uma Thurman, accidentally overdoses on heroin. Travolta's character resuscitates her by jamming the large needle of a syringe filled with adrenaline directly into her heart. In another scene, however, the ritual of heroin injection is graphically glamorized. America has a history of popularizing its gangsters and criminals on the silver screen, and *Pulp Fiction* continues that tradition.

Trainspotting, a British film by Danny Boyle, is based on a novel by Irvine Welsh that depicted the lives of heroin addicts in economically depressed Scotland in the 1980s. During that time, Edinburgh, Scotland, became the heroin and AIDS capital of Europe. The book was a cult hit in Britain and inspired the movie, which quickly became the second most popular film in Britain during 1996, behind *Four Weddings and a Funeral*. *Trainspotting* cost $2.5 million to produce. By the summer of 1996 it had grossed over $20 million in Britain alone.

The film follows a group of addicts in their pursuit of heroin and tries to provide an inside view of heroin addiction in all its squalor. Boyle said that while working on the film, he realized that, for those inside the drug world "it becomes about survival, about getting what you want, whether it be a fix or a girl or whatever."[13] The film's uncompromising yet almost surreal treatment of heroin addiction has drawn both praise and condemnation. The British newspaper the *Daily Mail* criticized the film's "irresponsible, lofty refusal to judge or condemn heroin addiction."[14] The filmmaker disagrees, saying that "it doesn't condone drug taking, it just accepts bounds of reality. I think it's a responsible film because it shows what goes wrong if you take heroin."[15]

The film's distributor in America is Miramax, which is owned by Disney, meaning the company that brought us *Snow White* also profits from the movie-going public's curiosity with heroin addicts. Disney says it is not worried that the film will promote drug use: "If you are going to give heroin a look, this will be the movie to persuade you to look away."[16]

The film *The Basketball Diaries* also attempts to show the hell of heroin addiction. Directed by Scott Kalvert, the film is based on an autobiographical novel by Jim Carroll. It depicts the teen years of a New York City boy whose aspirations for a basketball career are sidetracked by heroin. Starring Leonardo DiCaprio and Juliette Lewis, *The Basketball Diaries* takes the viewer on a roller-coaster ride through the streets of Manhattan's Lower East Side. The story tracks the slide of a healthy young man into the degrading world of the street junkie. The protagonist eventually lands in jail at Rikers Island and goes on to recover and reclaim himself upon his release. The young hero chronicles his story in a notebook he titles "Basketball Diaries." Even though the film does depict addiction in a nonglamorous way, it has reportedly had the reverse effect on many viewers. One young New York City addict stated, "I wanted to go out and get high right after I saw the movie the first time."[17] The film portrays heroin addiction almost as a rite of passage for any self-respecting, hip, city kid.

Hollywood's problem with heroin is not confined to the screen, however. Many film actors struggle with their own personal demons. One of the more widely publicized stories is that of Robert Downey Jr. Hailed as one of the great acting talents of his generation, Downey has been on a steady heroin slide for a number of years. He starred in the movies *Less than Zero, The Pick-up Artist, Air America, Soapdish, Natural Born Killers,*

Short Cuts, *Home for the Holidays*, and *Restoration*. His career peaked after making the 1992 film *Chaplin*, for which he received an Academy Award nomination.[18]

Not since River Phoenix died from a combination of heroin, alcohol, and other drugs has an actor's drug use received such public scrutiny as has Downey's. A series of embarrassing arrests has characterized his slow descent. He has been arrested while driving naked in a Porsche, reportedly throwing imaginary rats out the window. He has been arrested for possession of an unloaded .357 Magnum, heroin, and cocaine, and for trespassing when he mistakenly crawled into a neighbor's bed, where he was found asleep in his boxer shorts by the young daughter of the house. The police were called, paramedics arrived, and Downey was injected with narcan, which reversed the effects of the heroin in his system. His explanation of the incident: the limo driver had dropped him at the wrong address.

Downey began his acting career at the age of five, in a film made by his father, independent filmmaker Robert Downey Sr., best known for his 1969 film *Putney-Swope*. The junior Downey grew up in Greenwich Village and says that his parents had a very liberal hands-off attitude toward his upbringing. His parents thought it would be hypocritical to discourage smoking marijuana, so they condoned it. In retrospect, Robert Downey Sr. says that was a mistake: "We thought it was cute to let them smoke it, and all that was an idiot move on our parts to share that with our children."[19]

While Downey was on probation following his series of arrests, director Mike Figgis took a chance and cast him in the film *One Night Stand*. Figgis had to fight the film's insurers (it has become standard practice in Hollywood for films to be insured against an actor's inability to perform as a result of a drug problem), but he reported that the actor was punctual and never missed a day of shooting on the project. The film was completed more or less on schedule. However, in December

1997, at about the time the film was being released, Downey had his probation revoked for continued drug use and was sentenced to six months in the Los Angeles County Jail.

Jerry Stahl, a TV writer whose recent book *Permanent Midnight* documents his own ten-year battle with heroin addiction, explains why cases like Downey's occur: "People in Hollywood are so self-obsessed that they don't notice what you're doing as long as you're doing your job."[20]

The official response by the industry is to refer to treatment any performer or professional who presents with a substance abuse problem. The financial reality can sometimes get in the way, however, when the actor still produces. After all, if a picture has to shut down or change stars, it can cost millions. Sometimes the tendency is to shrug shoulders and look the other way until it is too late, as in the case of comedian John Belushi, who died from a lethal speedball injection (a heroin and cocaine cocktail) administered by a female companion.

Heroin in Advertising

American culture is heavily influenced by the power of advertising, and advertising today presents very contradictory images of heroin use to the American public. The perspectives of groups like the Partnership for a Drug-Free America, which focuses on portraying drug dependence in a harsh light, and companies like Calvin Klein, which has been criticized for ad campaigns that feature wan, waiflike models who look like heroin addicts ("heroin chic"), couldn't be more disparate.

In October 1996, National Families in Action, a group based in Atlanta, Georgia, called for a boycott of Calvin Klein products as a result of a series of ads the company ran in fashion magazines and TV spots to promote its new fragrance, cK be. The ads' models looked like heroin addicts, according to the group. "Addiction is neither chic nor glamorous," says Sue

Rusche, co-founder and executive director of the organization. "We trusted Calvin Klein products and encouraged our children to buy them. But Calvin Klein has betrayed that trust in a misguided and dangerous effort to glamorize heroin addiction to appeal to adolescents. The company has the right to market its products however it chooses. But we have the right to choose not to buy them. Until Calvin Klein stops glamorizing

The Partnership for a Drug-Free America uses ads such as this one and the one on the opposite page to counter the portrayal in popular culture of heroin use as "chic" and desirable.

Partnership for a Drug-Free America

heroin addiction, we refuse to buy Calvin Klein products. We are asking America's families to join us."[21]

Calvin Klein's response was that the company was not promoting addiction, but merely reflecting the look of today's youth.[22]

The Partnership for a Drug-Free America is on the other side of the battle, with its own campaign of antiheroin TV spots. In one of its more effective ads, the group shows a model finishing a photo shoot. The viewer feels compelled to watch as this beautiful woman begins to take off her makeup and false eye lashes—then pulls out her false teeth and tells the viewer

HEROIN IS A RELIGIOUS EXPERIENCE.

"Often you pray
to God to let you die."

Rebecca, ex-model

PARTNERSHIP FOR A DRUG-FREE AMERICA

how she lost everything to heroin addiction. The model is deglamorized and so, consequently, is heroin. The campaign, aimed at eighteen- to twenty-five-year-olds, seeks to counter the image of heroin as a chic substance of abuse. The partnership is attempting to "un-sell" the drug. Richard Bonette, the group's president and chief executive, says that "you have a whole new group of young people who don't know the terror, the horror, the tragedy of heroin. They look at it as a clean way to get a high without needles or the threat of AIDS."[23]

The danger of antidrug ads is that they walk a fine line between effectively deterring young people and turning them off altogether to the message. John Armistead, managing partner and chief creative officer at Highway One, one of the agencies that produced the Partnership for a Drug-Free America spots, says that "the intention was not to say you're going to die, but to give a sense that heroin's a dead end. Everyone agrees that the same old warnings—'Gee, drugs are bad, they're going to kill you'—will not scare anyone off. We're talking to people who have progressed from grass to cocaine to pills to whatever, but have not taken that last step. Those people are already jaded about drug messages. But if you can get to someone who is flirting with using heroin, and maybe raise a red flag, make that someone pause, then the advertising is successful."[24]

In the end, however, if the battle for the hearts and souls of America's youth is finally only about image, the deck is stacked against the Partnership for a Drug-Free America and its allies. The hero makers of the film, TV, music, and advertising industries will prove a formidable foe for the antidrug crusaders; those industries not only have far greater resources at their disposal, they are not burdened by the mission of telling the truth.

And if the number of young heroin users in the United States is any indication, the popular media message is clearly making the greater impact. This should not, however, come as a great surprise. After all, what do most young Americans like to do in their leisure time? They listen to music, go to movies— and strive to emulate their heroes.

CHAPTER

14

Heroin Addicts: Beyond Redemption?

Maybe they're deluding you. Maybe they're deluding
themselves. Maybe they want to believe in their hearts
what they have programmed their mouths to say: that
this time, this time, maybe they're going to make it.

GEORGE JAMES, in *The New York Times*

Throughout the better part of this century experts have proclaimed to have the answers to the heroin problem in America.
Law enforcement proponents believe they can win a drug war
through interdiction and incarceration, but even they have admitted that we can't arrest our way out of the problem.[1] There
simply aren't enough prisons, and although new prison construction has become one of the fastest growing industries in
America, it is incredulous to think that incarcerating heroin
users is the answer.

Treatment experts have suggested that perhaps we could
provide mandatory treatment to prisoners, but thus far we
have not been able to effectively deliver treatment even in prisons, where many heroin users end up. It is estimated that as
few as 15 percent of those who could benefit from treatment in
prison receive it.[2] Prevention and education experts believe
that keeping the upcoming generations of youth informed
holds the key to avoiding future problems.

The current approach to the heroin problem could perhaps
best be described as a piecemeal compromise that primarily

focuses on interdiction and enforcement, with varying degrees of commitment to prevention, education, and treatment mixed in. But it is an uneasy compromise at best. Many feel that too much emphasis is placed on enforcement and that not enough is placed on treatment. For example, in New York state, there are an estimated 600,000 heavy drug users (all drugs), with only 39,000 treatment slots available.[3] Currently, the bulk of the drug war's budget goes to interdiction and enforcement. Why? Politics may be the reason. Big drug busts make for good TV news and headlines. They give the impression that the war is being won. But if the strategy is to reduce the supply of heroin on the street, thereby driving the price higher and making it harder to obtain, why is there more cheap, pure heroin available now than ever before?

On the other hand, if treatment is the answer, why are so few actually treated? And of the ones who do receive treatment, why do so few succeed? As for education, if we were to blitz the airwaves with antidrug messages, would our children respond and grow up drug free?

It is easy to see how a can-do society like America would arrive at such a three-pronged attack strategy against the heroin problem. After all, why not use everything we have in our arsenal? Yes, we can lock up drug dealers in maximum-security prisons and at least temporarily hamper their ability to deal drugs. Yes, treatment *can* work, though it requires an earnest effort on the part of the addict. Yes, the prevention message is vital and does reach many young people, though one wonders why, when they turn thirteen, many who were previously scared to use drugs suddenly begin using. Part of the problem is that this three-pronged strategy, though seemingly comprehensive, is ultimately a simplistic solution to a very complex problem.

Historically, America has chosen to demonize heroin and those who use it. An article in *Popular Science Monthly,* published in June 1930, reported that one of every sixty people in

America was a drug addict. The author, John E. Lodge, interviewed one of the leading medical experts of the time, William I. Sirovich, a medical doctor and a member of Congress. Sirovich estimated that there were two million "dope fiends" in America. He blamed the prohibition era, stating that without liquor, these weak individuals turned to narcotic drugs to help them cope. He pointed out, accurately, that addicts could be found among the rich, poor, and middle class, among the socially respectable and those in the underworld. Their common trait, said Sirovich, was that "they all are psychopathic constitutionally inferior types. They are mostly men and women who are afraid to face the unpleasant realities of life; in other words moral cowards." Needless to say this is a powerful indictment. Can there be any hope for such people? He went on to say, "The mental condition that causes thousands of people to turn to drugs is lack of courage or initiative. They take dope for sustenic purposes; that is to say, as a stimulant to bolster up their nerve."[4]

It's easy to see why addicts were generally written off as beyond redemption in the 1930s. Any hope for social reclamation such "moral cowards" ever had would almost certainly be annihilated by society's attitudes toward them, especially if they admitted they had a problem. Sirovich's description of what an addict faced in order to return to the mainstream of society is daunting indeed: "To return, they also have to cross four bridges—the bridge of sighs, the bridge of humiliation, the bridge of degradation, the bridge of infamy." It's a tough road for a "constitutionally inferior type" to walk; there are some serious tolls on each of those bridges.

But you say this is a new century; that was 1930. We've come a long way in our perceptions about who is addicted, and our attitudes toward them have changed. Or have they? For example: Two individuals have a history of abusing heroin. One has sought treatment several times and has now been drug free for five years. The other has never admitted a problem, never been treated, and never stopped using. Assuming that neither has a criminal record, the addict who has never been treated and still uses heroin daily is eligible to receive a permit to carry a handgun. The addict with a documented history of treatment would be denied such a permit under the current gun laws in most states, even though he or she is now a functioning member of society. Who is more likely to use that gun to rob in order to obtain drugs? The difference between the two is the stigma of being branded an addict. To be an addict is to be seen as untrustworthy in our collective thinking. Why would we deny the gun permit to someone who had a problem, but put his life back together again, and be willing to arm an individual who is unstable? Because one of them admitted he had a problem, and "once an addict, always an addict. You never know when he or she is going to fall off the wagon."

Our perception of addiction as an incurable disease has not changed much, either. In 1930 Sirovich stated: "Thus medical science is almost powerless to redeem these unfortunates. The only way to combat this grievous evil is eternal vigilance on the part of the Government and, better still, the cessation of manufacture of all narcotics not required for medical or other scientific purposes." Today we say treatment *can* work, but the fact is it works for relatively few, and these few are viewed skeptically, not embraced as redeemed members of our society. Mark Parrino, president of the American Methadone Treatment Association, points to an analogue in Pygmy culture. In that society, drunkards and drug users are driven out of the tribe in the middle of the night, jabbed with pointed sticks, and forbidden from returning. They are beyond redemption. Do we not do this with our heroin addicts? Do we not banish them to the fringes of society? To our prisons?

Our perceptions of who is an addict, and who winds up in prison because of addiction, are tainted by decades of assumptions and judgments, like those of Sirovich, and by our cultural legacy of racism. Two studies, one by the FBI and the other by the National Institute for Drug Abuse, describe the typical cocaine user as a white male high school graduate living in a small city or suburb. Both studies came to the same conclusion: that African Americans make up only 12 percent of the nation's drug users. Yet law enforcement focuses the vast majority of its resources and efforts on minorities. Ninety-two percent of those arrested for drug offenses are either African American or Latino.[5] In New York state, where they account for only 7 percent of the arrests on drug charges, whites occupy 47 percent of the state-funded treatment slots. University of Chicago law professor Norval Morris says, "The whole law and order movement that we've heard so much about is, in operation, anti-black and underclass. Not in plan, not in design, not in intent, but in operation."[6]

Where do we go from here? Dr. Herbert Kleber, former deputy to U.S. drug czar William Bennett during the Bush administration, predicts that by the year 2000 we will have 1,000,000 heroin addicts. Some say we have more than that already, with estimates ranging from 600,000 to 2.8 million. It is hard to get an accurate estimate, but all seem to agree that heroin use is rising. How can this be? As we've seen, we're expending enormous energy and vast resources to solve the drug problem in America. How can it be getting worse?

Perhaps it is time for America to really focus on the underlying societal problems that lead one to seek the escape heroin provides. It is true that men and women have been using psychotropic substances for at least as long as humankind has recorded its history, and it is perhaps arrogant to think we can ever eliminate heroin entirely from our streets. But it is possible to change our focus and begin to address the problem in new ways. It is possible to treat addicts with some dignity, to stop criminalizing our minorities, and to work toward an understanding that fear of our differences is what keeps addicts and nonaddicts apart, and maybe even what keeps us all from becoming whole.

All the facts and statistics about heroin only tell a small part of the story. The real story is a human one. If you want to get an idea of who uses heroin and why, you won't find the answer in the National Household Survey—you've got to go to the street.

On the street is where you'll meet people like Robert M. whom I came to know when I spent the better part of a year on the streets of New York, hanging around, watching the tide of heroin traffic, and getting to know the patterns of addicts. Robert is a short, slightly built man in his early forties. His light brown complexion has begun to give way to a pallor that bears witness to the years he has devoted to heroin. His street uniform of hooded sweatshirt, jeans, and army fatigue jacket conceal a man who once helped his mother raise four younger brothers and sisters when his father, still a young man himself, was stabbed to death on a Friday night for his week's earnings. Robert assumed the role of protector and provider, quitting high school and taking whatever work he could find. When the pressure became too much for a teenager to bear, he turned to the comfort of heroin, until eventually that became but another pressure. Robert managed to help his family survive a life of food stamps, social workers, and public assistance before heroin got the better of him, but by then, his youngest brother had graduated high school. Robert is proud of having seen his siblings through to adulthood, but says it came none too soon, since by that time he could no longer help support anything but his own habit. His obsession with heroin and lack of education make him unemployable, forcing him to hustle anything and anybody he can to get by. For more than twenty-five years, Robert has battled his addiction; in and out of methadone programs, jails, and detoxes, he has not managed to maintain any kind of long-term recovery—but he *has* survived.

Robert was my guide to a secret world. After months of building a trust, we began to learn each other's ways. Some days he'd be sick, and I'd help. He helped me, too, protected me in a potentially dangerous environment, made me feel safe. In short, Robert was another human being: no more, no less.

When my research was completed, I told Robert I would not be hanging around anymore, that it was time for me to go. He looked away, and when he turned to face me again, I could see that his eyes were wet. He lifted his shoulders, sighed, and said, "Well, I guess all good things end sometime." He laughed, zipped up his green army jacket, and went back into character as if embarrassed by his moment of sentiment.

"But hey, you could still come around sometime, you know, say hello to a friend."

"I'll do that, Robert," I promised.

He reached into the pocket of his jeans, pulled out some money, and separated a $10 bill from a few singles.

"Yo man, here I want you to have this." He offered me the bill.

"No Robert, I can't, really, but I appreciate the gesture," I told him.

"What, come on man, you gonna insult me now? I want you to have it, a token, from me to you. Here, go on buy yourself something. I want you to have it."

What could I do? I saw that to refuse would be ungrateful, a symbol of judgment and reproach, so I let him hand it to me.

"Thanks, Robert. I'll see you. You take care of yourself," I said.

"I always do, I always do."

We shook hands and walked away. He yelled back at me, "Yo, you gonna mention me in the book?"

I turned the corner, folded the $10 bill, and put it in my wallet, tucked behind the pictures of my kids.

NOTES

Notes to Chapter One

1. John Garraty and Peter Gay, *The Columbia History of the World* (New York: Harper and Row, 1972), 55.
2. Ibid., 57.
3. Robert O'Brien et al., *The Encyclopedia of Drug Abuse, 1992 Facts on File* (New York: Facts on File), xiv.
4. *Encyclopedia Britannica,* Britannica CD (1997), s.v. "opium."
5. Matt. 27:34. Authorized (King James) Version.
6. *Webster's New Universal Unabridged Dictionary,* Deluxe 2nd ed. (1983), s.v. "gall."
7. *Encyclopedia Britannica,* s.v. "opium."
8. Alfred W. McCoy, *The Politics of Heroin: CIA Complicity in the Global Drug Trade* (New York: Lawrence Hill, 1991), 3.
9. *Microsoft Encarta* (1994), s.v. "Polo, Marco."
10. Ibid., s.v. "East India Company."
11. McCoy, *Politics of Heroin,* 4.
12. Ibid., 86.
13. Ibid.
14. John Newsinger, "Britain's Opium Wars," *Monthly Review* 49 (1 October 1997): 40.
15. *Microsoft Encarta* (1994), s.v. "opium wars."
16. McCoy, *Politics of Heroin,* 80.
17. Ibid., 88.
18. Barry R. McCaffrey, "Reducing Drug Use and Its Consequences" (presentation to the annual conference of the National Association of Drug Court Professionals, Washington, D.C., 10 May 1996), 6.
19. McCoy, *Politics of Heroin,* 5.
20. David F. Musto, *The American Disease: Origins of Narcotic Control,* expanded ed. (New York: Oxford University Press, 1982), 2.
21. O'Brien, *Encyclopedia of Drug Abuse,* xv.
22. Ibid., xiv.

Notes to Chapter Two

1. Ben Attias, "History of Opium," [Online], p. 2. California State University. Available: http://www.csun.edu [Accessed 15 October 1996].

2. Ibid., 1.

3. David F. Musto, *The American Disease: Origins of Narcotic Control* (New York: Oxford University Press, 1987), 7.

4. Ibid., 3.

5. Attias, "History of Opium," 2.

6. Alfred W. McCoy, *The Politics of Heroin: CIA Complicity in the Global Drug Trade* (New York: Lawrence Hill, 1991), 5.

7. Musto, *American Disease*, 12.

8. McCoy, *Politics of Heroin*, 9.

9. Attias, "History of Opium," 1.

10. Musto, *American Disease*, 132.

11. McCoy, *Politics of Heroin*, 16.

12. Ibid., 18.

13. "A Review of Government and Politics in the Postwar Years," *Congress and the Nation 1945–64* (Washington, D.C.: Congressional Quarterly, Inc., 1965), 1186.

14. U.S. Department of Justice, *Crime in the United States, FBI Annual Crime Index Report* (Washington, D.C.: U.S. Government Printing Office, 1996).

15. McCoy, *Politics of Heroin*, 16.

16. Ibid., 18–19.

17. "A Review of Government and Politics in the Postwar Years," 1,187.

18. Ibid., 1,191.

19. McCoy, *Politics of Heroin*, 19.

20. Ibid., 17.

21. Ibid., 17.

22. "A Review of Government and Politics in the Postwar Years," 712.

23. Ibid., 580.

24. McCoy, *Politics of Heroin*, 19.

25. John Leland, "The Fear of Heroin Is Shooting Up," *Newsweek* (26 August 1996): 55.

26. "Colombian Military Gets $40 Million in Aid," [Online]. Reuters News Service. Available: www.infoseek.com (keyword: heroin) [Accessed 4 October 1996].

27. Reuters News Service, 8 October 1996.

28. Ibid., 9 October 1996.

29. Ibid., 1 October 1996.

30. Ibid., 17 October 1996.

31. Ibid., 20 October 1996.

32. Ibid., 25 September 1996.

33. Ibid., 15 October 1996.

34. Elizabeth Snead, *USA Today*, July 17, 1996.

35. Robert Silbering (special prosecutor for New York City), interview by the author, New York, N.Y., August 1996.

36. Snead, *USA Today*.

37. Reuters News Service, 7 October 1996.

Notes to Chapter Three

1. Alfred W. McCoy, *The Politics of Heroin: CIA Complicity in the Global Drug Trade* (New York: Lawrence Hill, 1991), 21–22.

2. William Mochler (associate special agent in charge), interview by the author, New York, N.Y., December 1996–January 1997.

3. Mochler, interview.

4. Rita Charon, interview by the author, New York, N.Y., December 1996.

5. Street addicts (on the process of injecting heroin), interviews by the author, September 1996.

6. H. Thomas Milhorn Jr., *Chemical Dependence: Diagnosis, Treatment, and Prevention* (New York: Springer-Verlag, 1990), 168–71.

7. Rita Charon, interview by the author, New York, N.Y., September 1996.

8. Milhorn, *Chemical Dependence,* 170.

9. Charon, interview, September 1996.

10. [Online]. The Discovery of Endorphins. Available: www.users.interport.net/%7eclueless/discover.html [Accessed 21 December 1996].

11. Ibid.

12. Ibid.

13. Charon, interview, September 1996.

14. Milhorn, *Chemical Dependence,* 172.

15. Ibid., 171.

16. Charon, interview, September 1996.

Notes to Chapter Four

1. The information about the psychology and culture of heroin users presented in this chapter was gathered from several sources in interviews conducted by the author during 1996 and 1997: Roy Spungin, D.S.W., New York, N.Y.; David Smith, M.D., Haight Ashbury Free Clinics, San Francisco, Calif.; Richard Seymour (managing editor, *Journal of Psychoactive Drugs*) interview by the author, San Francisco, Calif.; Bruce Bracco, I.C.A.D.C., Hampton Hospital, Rancocas, N.J.

Additional information was obtained from heroin addicts in interviews conducted by the author in New York, N.Y., during 1996 and 1997.

Notes to Chapter Six

1. Caroline Jean Acker, "The Early Years of the PHS Narcotic Hospital at Lexington, Kentucky," *Public Health Reports* 112, no. 3 (May–June 1997): 245.

2. Ibid., 246.

3. Herman Joseph and Phil Appel, "Historical Perspectives and Public Health Issues," State Methadone Treatment Guidelines, Treatment Improvement Protocol Series (Rockville, Md.: U.S. Department of

Health and Human Services Center for Substance Abuse Treatment, 1993), 13.

4. Charles Dederich (obituary), *Time* 149, no. 11 (1997): 19.

5. "Treatment of Opiate Addiction with Methadone," *State Methadone Treatment Guidelines,* Treatment Improvement Protocol Series (Rockville, Md.: U.S. Department of Health and Human Services Center for Substance Abuse Treatment, 1993), 2.

6. Mark Clifford, "Selling Synanon," *Forbes* 137 (June 1986): 208.

7. Ibid., 208.

8. Ibid., 209.

9. *Alcoholics Anonymous,* 3d ed. (New York: Alcoholics Anonymous World Services, 1976), 59.

10. *Narcotics Anonymous,* 4th ed. (New York: Narcotics Anonymous World Services, 1987), 17.

11. *Alcoholics Anonymous,* 13.

12. *Twelve Steps and Twelve Traditions* (New York: Alcoholics Anonymous World Services, 1981), 5–8.

13. The story of the founding of the Hazelden Foundation presented here is condensed from Damian McElrath, *Hazelden: A Spiritual Odyssey* (Center City, Minn.: Hazelden, 1987); see also Jerry Spicer, *Minnesota Model: The Evolution of the Multidisciplinary Approach to Addiction Recovery* (Center City, Minn.: Hazelden, 1993).

14. Richard Seymour, phone interview by the author, November 1997.

15. Ibid.

16. Ibid.

17. Herbert Kleber, M.D. (presentation to the Partnership for a Drug-Free America, New York, N.Y., May 1996).

18. "Cost of Methadone Maintenance," National Institute on Drug Abuse, 1994.

19. Kleber (presentation to the Partnership for a Drug-Free America).

NOTES TO CHAPTER SEVEN

1. Joseph A. Piszcor and William Weddington, "The Treatment of Opioid Dependence," *Manual of Therapeutics for Addictions,* ed. Norman S. Miller, Mark S. Gold, and David E. Smith (New York: Wiley-Liss, 1997), 111.

2. National Household Survey 1997 (U.S. Department of Health— Office of Applied Studies).

3. Mark Parrino, interview by the author, New York, N.Y., January 1997.

4. Herman Joseph and Phil Appel, "Historical Perspectives and Public Health Issues," *State Methadone Treatment Guidelines,* Treatment Improvement Protocol Series (Rockville, Md.: U.S. Department of Health and Human Services Center for Substance Abuse Treatment, 1993), 11.

5. Ibid., 13.

6. Ibid., 13.
7. This was also due in part to bootlegging, prostitution, and the involvement of organized crime in the heroin market.
8. Joseph and Appel, "Historical Perspectives," 12.
9. Ibid., 14.
10. Ibid., 14–15.
11. Ibid., 15.
12. Ibid., 16
13. Ibid., 16.
14. R. G. Newman, *Methadone Treatment in Narcotic Addiction* (New York: Academic Press, 1977).
15. J. Ball and A. Ross, *The Effectiveness of Methadone Maintenance Treatment: Patients, Programs, Services, and Outcome* (New York: Springer-Verlaf, 1991).
16. D. M. Novick et al., "Absence of antibody to human immunodeficiency virus in long-term socially rehabilitated methadone maintenance patients," *Archives of Internal Medicine* (January 1990): 97–99.
17. Parrino, interview. See also Marsha Rosenbaum, Alyson Washburn, Kelly Knight, Margaret Kelley, and Jeannette Irwin, "Treatment as Harm Reduction, Defunding as Harm Maximization: The Case of Methadone Maintenance," *Journal of Psychoactive Drugs* 28, no. 3 (July–September 1996): 242.
18. Parrino, interview.
19. Ball and Ross, *Effectiveness of Methadone Maintenance.*
20. Rosenbaum et al., "Treatment as Harm Reduction," 242.
21. Ibid.
22. Ibid., 243.
23. Ibid., 243.
24. Parrino, interview.

Notes to Chapter Nine

1. Glenn Frankel, "U. S. War on Drugs Yields Few Victories," *Washington Post,* June 8, 1997, section 1, A01.
2. J. W. Fernandez, *Bwiti: An Ethnography of the Religious Imagination in Africa* (Princeton: Princeton University Press, 1982).
3. Alexis Jetter, "The Psychedelic Cure," *New York Times,* April 10, 1994, magazine section, 50.
4. Howard S. Lotsof, interview by the author, Staten Island, N.Y., June 1997.
5. Lotsof, interview.
6. Jetter, "The Psychedic Cure," 52.
7. E. D. Dzoljic, C. D. Kaplan, and M. R. Dzoljic, "Effects of Ibogaine on Naloxone-Precipitated Withdrawal Syndrome in Chronic Morphine Dependent Rats," *Archive of International Pharmacodynamics* 294 (1988): 64–70.
8. S. D. Glick et al., "Effects and Aftereffects of Ibogaine on Morphine

Self-Administration in Rats," *European Journal of Pharmacology* 195 (1991): 341–45.

9. I. M. Maisonneuve, R. W. Keller Jr., and S. D. Glick, "Interactions Between Ibogaine, a Potential Anti-Addictive Agent, and Morphine: An in Vivo Microdialysis Study," *European Journal of Pharmacology* 199 (1991): 35–42.

10. P. Popik, R. T. Layer, and P. Skolnick, "The Putative Anti-Addictive Drug Ibogaine Is a Competitive Inhibitor of (3H)MK-801 Binding to the NMDA Receptor Complex," *Psychopharmacology* 114 (1994): 672–74.

11. D. C. Deecher et al., "Mechanisms of Action of Ibogaine and Harmaline Congeners Based on Radioligand Binding Studies," *Brain Research* 571 (1992): 242–47.

12. D. C. Mash et al., "Identification of a Primary Metabolite of Ibogaine That Targets Serotonin Transporters and Elevates Serotonin," *Life Science* 57, no. 3 (1995): 45–50.

13. L. B. Hough, S. M. Pearl, and S. D. Glick, "Tissue Distribution of Ibogaine after Intraperitoneal and Subcutaneous Administration," *Life Science* 58, no. 7 (1996): 119–22.

14. H. S. Lotsof, "Ibogaine in the Treatment of Chemical Dependence Disorders: Clinical Perspectives (A Preliminary Review)," *MAPS* 5, no. 3 (1995), 16–27.

15. C. D. Kaplan et al., "Reaching a State of Wellness: Multistage Explorations in Social Neuroscience," *Social Neuroscience Bulletin* 6, no. 1 (1993): 6–7.

16. J. H. Woods et al., "1989 Annual Report, Evaluation of New Compounds for Opioid Activity," *NIDA Research Monographs* 95 (1990): 655–56.

17. Lotsof, interview.

18. Ibid.

19. Ibid.

20. Reckitt and Colman Pharmaceuticals, Inc., Richmond, Va. Available: http://www.recollpharm.com/buprenex/prescribinginformation/ [Accessed 12 June 1997].

21. Information obtained from Buprenex package insert.

22. R. E. Johnson, J. H. Jaffe, and P. J. Fudala, "A Controlled Trial of Buprenorphine Treatment for Opioid Dependence," *Journal of the American Medical Association* 267, no. 20 (1992): 2,750–55.

23. Ibid., 2,752.

24. Ibid., 2,755.

25. Ibid.

26. John A. Bowersox, "Buprenorphine May Soon Be Heroin Treatment Option," *NIDA Notes,* Jan./Feb. 1995, 2. Available: http://www.nida.nih.gov/nidanotes/nnvol10n1/bupren.html [Accessed 5 June 1997].

27. Ibid., 1.

28. J. Magnan et al., "The Binding Spectrum of Narcotic Analgesic Drugs with Different Agonist and Antagonist Properties," *Arch Pharmacology* 319 (1982): 197–205.

29. Press release issued by National Institute on Alcohol Abuse and Alcoholism, Washington, D. C., January 17, 1995.

30. Ibid.

31. Bruce Bower, "Opiate Blocker Boosts Alcoholism Treatment," *Science News* 142, no. 21 (1992): 341.

32. "A New Assault on Addiction," *Newsweek* (January 30, 1995): 51.

33. Office of National Drug Control Policy Statistics, 1996.

34. "New Drug Approval Approach Boosts Fight against Heroin Addiction," *FDA Consumer* 28, no. 9 (1994): 11.

35. Ibid.

36. Ibid., 12.

37. "Medication for Treating Heroin Dependence Proven Safe and Effective." Available: http://www.pslgroup.com/dg/2dobe.html [Accessed 27 June 1997].

Notes to Chapter Ten

1. L. Gostin et al., "Centers for Disease Control and Prevention, HIV/AIDS Surveillance Report, 1995," *Journal of the American Medical Association* 277, no. 1 (1997): 53.

2. Craig T. March, conversation with the author, Carteret, N.J., March 1988.

3. Centers for Disease Control and Prevention, *Centers for Disease Control and Prevention, HIV/AIDS Surveillance Report, 1995* (Atlanta: U.S. Department of Health and Human Services, Public Health Service, 1996).

4. Peter Lurie and E. Drucker, "An Opportunity Lost: HIV Infections Associated with Lack of a National Needle-Exchange Program," *Lancet* 349, no. 9052 (1997): 604–5.

5. Lawrence O. Gostin, Zita Lazzarini, T. Stephen Jones, and Kathleen Flaherty, "Prevention of HIV/AIDS and Other Blood-Borne Diseases among Injection Drug Users," *Journal of the American Medical Association* 277, no. 1 (1997): 53, quoting Centers for Disease Control, "AIDS associated with injecting drug use—United States, 1995," *Morbidity, Mortality Weekly Report (MMWR)* 45, no. 45 (1996): 392–98.

6. Centers for Disease Control and Prevention, "HIV Prevalence Estimates and AIDS Case Projections for the United States: Report Based Upon a Workshop," *Mobidity, Mortality Weekly Report (MMWR)* 39, no. 16 (1990): 8.

7. S. D. Holmberg, "The estimated prevalence and incidence of HIV in 96 large U.S. metropolitan areas," *American Journal of Public Health* 86 (1996): 642–54.

8. Gostin et al., "Prevention of HIV/AIDS," 53.

9. House Committee on the Judiciary, Subcommittee on Crime, *Mail Order Drug Paraphernalia Control Act, 1986: Hearings on H.R. 1625*, 99th Congress, 2nd session 1986; testimony of Joyce Nalepka, 16.

10. J. Normand, D. Vlahof, and L. E. Moses, *Preventing HIV Transmission: The Role of Sterile Needles and Bleach* (Washington, D.C.: National Academy Press, 1995).

11. Katherine Q. Seelye, "AMA Calls for Needle Exchanges," *New York Times,* June 27, 1997, A15.

12. Ibid.

13. "A Small Advance for Clean Needles," *U.S. News & World Report* 122, no. 8 (1997): 43.

14. Ibid.

15. The Ryan White Fund provides money for prevention efforts and treatment of at-risk populations.

16. David W. Dunlap, "Clinton Is Criticized by His Own AIDS Panel," *New York Times,* July 10, 1996, A16.

17. Jennifer Preston, "Whitman AIDS Panel Urges Needle Exchange Programs," *New York Times,* April 4, 1996, B6.

18. Ibid.

19. Ibid.

20. "Lie of the Needle: Clinton Shoots Down Needle Exchange," *New Republic* 216, no. 13 (1997): 11.

21. Julie Light, "Needle Exchange on Trial," *Progressive* 59, no. 3 (1995): 13.

22. Ibid.

23. "Special Consultation Syringe Law Addresses Epidemics, Airs Controversy," *Journal of the American Medical Association* 275, no. 21 (1996): 1,621.

24. "Drug and Sex Programs Called Effective in Fight against AIDS," *New York Times,* February 14, 1997, national section, 14.

25. Ibid.

26. Douglas Martin, "Dispensing Needles, Not Judgment: Workers Connect with Drugs' Captives," *New York Times,* November 7, 1996, B21, B24.

27. "Special Consultation on Syringe Laws," *JAMA* 275, no. 21 (1996): 1,621.

28. Ibid., 1,621.

29. C. Hartgers, J. A. R. VanDen Hoek, E. J. C. Ameigden, and R. A. Coutinho, "Needle Sharing and Participation in the Amsterdam Syringe Exchange Program," *Public Health Reports* 107, no. 6 (1992): 675.

30. A report on the current status of the epidemic, control measures, and policy implications [Online] Southeast Asian Information Network, 1995). Available: http://www.sords.org/burma/aids.html [Accessed 9 July 1997].

NOTES TO CHAPTER ELEVEN

1. Joe Rigert, "Drug Sentences Often Stacked Against Women," *(Minneapolis) Star Tribune,* December 14, 1997, 1A.

2. "Congress and the Nation 1945–1964: A Review of Government and Politics in the Postwar Years," *Congressional Quarterly* (1965): 1,186.

3. Ibid., 1,186.

4. David F. Musto, *The American Disease: Origins of Narcotic Control* (New York: Oxford University Press, 1987), 6–7.

5. "Congress and the Nation," 1,189–90.

6. Ibid., 1,191.

7. Ibid., 1,192.

8. Ibid., 1,193.

9. Gorton Carruth, *Encyclopedia of American Facts and Dates* (New York: Harper and Row, 1987), 609.

10. Alfred W. McCoy, *The Politics of Heroin: CIA Complicity in the Global Drug Trade* (New York: Lawrence Hill, 1991), 28.

11. Ibid., 29.

12. Ibid., 38.

13. Dan Baum, *Smoke and Mirrors: The War on Drugs and the Politics of Failure* (Boston: Little Brown, 1996), 7.

14. "Congress and the Nation," 261.

15. "Year of the Famine," *Newsweek* (22 September 1969).

16. McCoy, *The Politics of Heroin*, 224 ($88 million is estimated by multiplying the average of $12 per day by 20,000 users).

17. Carruth, *American Facts and Dates*, 712.

18. Musto, *American Disease*, 258–59.

19. "Congress and the Nation," 263–64.

20. Baum, *Smoke and Mirrors*, 58.

21. Musto, *American Disease*, 256–57.

22. McCoy, *The Politics of Heroin*, 75–76.

23. "Congress and the Nation," 578.

24. Musto, *American Disease*, 258.

25. Ibid.

26. Baum, *Smoke and Mirrors*, 92–93.

27. Ibid., 94–95.

28. Musto, *American Disease*, 271.

29. Musto, *American Disease*, 269.

30. Richard Perez-Pena, "Study Shows New York Has Greatest Income Gap," *New York Times*, December 17, 1997, A1, B6.

31. Baum, *Smoke and Mirrors*, 188–89.

32. Ibid., 216.

33. Ibid., 171.

34. Ibid., 214.

35. Ibid., 202, 203.

36. Ibid., 204.

37. Office of National Drug Control Policy [Online]. Available: http://www.whitehouse.drugspolicy.gov/policy/98NDCS/goals.html

38. All information and statistics concerning price, distribution rings, and criminal activity was obtained during interviews with New York DEA Associate Special Agent in Charge William Mochler and Special Agent Robin Waugh, Public Information Officer, during December 1996 and January 1997.

39. George James, "Officer Admits Illegal Apartment Entries," *New York Times*, January 10, 1996, B6.

40. Michael Janofsky, "Philadelphia Police Scandal Results in a Plan for a Suit Claiming Racism," *New York Times,* December 12, 1995.
41. Ibid.
42. Baum, *Smoke and Mirrors,* 250.
43. Substance Abuse and Mental Health Services Administration of Applied Studies, preliminary results from the 1996 National Household Survey on Drug Abuse (Rockville, Md., July 1997).

Notes to Chapter Twelve

1. Federal Bureau of Prisons, Weekly Population Report, July 10, 1997 [Online]. Available: http://www.bop.gov/weekly.html [Accessed 16 July 1997].
2. *U.S. News & World Report* 121, no 8 (26 August 1996): 8; quoting U.S. Justice Department figures.
3. Alexander Cockburn, "Clinton's Prison Fetish," *New Statesman & Society* 7, no. 318 (1994): 10 (figures based on U.S. Justice Department reports).
4. Pulse Check Report, June 1997, Washington, D. C.: Office of National Drug Control Policy.
5. Mireya Navarro, "Experimental Courts Are Using New Strategies to Blunt the Lure of Drugs," *New York Times,* October 17, 1996, A25.
6. Figures from Mark Mauer and Tracy Huling, *The Sentencing Project Report* (Washington, D.C.: The Sentencing Project, 1995).
7. *U. S. News and World Report* 121, no. 8 (26 August 1996): 8.
8. Ibid.
9. Ted Gest, "A Shocking Look at Blacks and Crime," *U.S. News & World Report* 119, no. 15 (16 October 1995): 53, comparing statistics provided by *The Sentencing Project Report* (Washington, D. C.: The Sentencing Project, 1995).
10. Cockburn, "Clinton's Prison Fetish," 10.
11. Gest, "A Shocking Look," 53.
12. Ibid.
13. "Young Black Men and Drug Policy," *America* 173, no. 17 (1995): 3, quoting *The Sentencing Project Report* (Washington, D.C.: The Sentencing Project, 1995).
14. Bureau of Prisons Key Indicators Strategic Support System, January 25, 1994, Bureau of Prisons.
15. Gest, "A Shocking Look," 53.
16. "Survey of State Prisons," *Bureau of Justice Statistics* (Washington, D.C.: U.S. Government Printing Office, 1991).
17. DEA agents, interviews conducted by the author, New York, N.Y., January 1997.
18. "Special Report: Lifetime Likelihood of Going to State or Federal Prison," *Bureau of Justice Statistics* (Washington, D.C.: U.S. Government Printing Office, 1997).

19. Kit R. Roane, article about the blockade on 163rd St., New York, N.Y., *New York Times,* September 21, 1997.

20. U.S. Census Data, 1990 [Online]. Available: http://www.census.gov

21. Drug Enforcement and Treatment in Prisons, 1990, Bureau of Prisons.

22. Bureau of Justice Statistics, prepared by ONDCP, Anita Timrots, "Drug and Crime Facts 1994" (June 1995): 24.

23. Ibid.

24. Corrections officers, interviews conducted by the author at Union County Jail, Elizabeth, N.J., June 1997; also, former inmates of Rikers Island jail, New York, N.Y., and Fishkill Prison, upstate New York, interviews conducted by the author, August 1997.

25. K. G. Castro, R. Schansky, and V. Scardino, "Evidence of HIV Transmission in Correctional Facilities" (abstract presented at the Thirty-first Interscience Conference on Antimicrobial Agents and Chemotherapy, Chicago, Ill., September 1991).

26. Polonsky, Kerr, Harris, Gaiter, Fichtner, and Kennedy, "HIV Prevention in Prisons and Jails: Obstacles and Opportunities," Public Health Reports 109, no. 5 (September–October 1994): 615.

27. Matthew Purdy, "As AIDS Increases behind Bars, Costs Dim Promise of New Drug," *New York Times,* May 16, 1997, 128.

28. Laura Maruschak, "HIV in Prisons and Jails," *Bureau of Justice Statistics* NCJ-164260 (Washington, D.C.: U.S. Government Printing Office, August 1997): 1.

29. Ibid., 2.

30. Ibid., 5.

31. Centers for Disease Control, *HIV/AIDS Surveillance Report* for 1994 and 1995; see also *Monthly Statistics Report* 42, 43, and 45. All materials published by Centers for Disease Control in Atlanta, Ga.

32. Purdy, "As AIDS Increases," 128.

33. Timothy Harding and Joachim Nelles, "Preventing HIV Transmission in Prison," *Lancet* (1995): 1,507.

34. Polonsky et al., "HIV Prevention in Prisons and Jails," 615.

35. Purdy, "As AIDS Increases," 128.

36. J. B. Glaser and R. B. Greifinger, "Correctional Health Care: A Public Health Opportunity," *Annual of Internal Medicine* 118 (January 1993): 139–45.

37. Harding and Nelles, "Preventing HIV Transmission in Prison," 1,507.

38. Polonsky et al., "HIV Prevention in Prisons and Jails," 617.

39. Ibid., 618.

40. Associated Press, *New York Daily News,* September 15, 1997.

41. Polonsky et al., "HIV Prevention in Prisons and Jails," 615.

42. "Risk Behavior for HIV Transmission among IDUs Not in Drug Treatment—U.S. 1987–1989," *Morbidity and Mortality Weekly Report* 39 (April 1990): 273–76.

43. Polonsky et al., "HIV Prevention in Prisons and Jails," 620.

44. Douglas Lipton, "The Effectiveness of Treatment for Drug Abusers under Criminal Justice Supervision" (November 1995): 6. Published by the National Criminal Justice Reference Service, Rockville, Md.

45. J. Meyer et al., "Drug Relapse among Recently Paroled HIV+ Individuals" (paper presented at the Ninth International Conference on AIDS, Berlin, Germany, June 1993).

46. Lipton, "The Effectiveness of Treatment for Drug Abusers," 4.

47. Office of Justice Programs, "A Report to the Assistant Attorney General," *Bureau of Justice Statistics* (Washington, D.C.: U.S. Government Printing Office, January 1996).

48. Office of Justice Programs, "Probation and Parole Population Reaches Almost 3.8 Million," *Bureau of Justice Statistics* (Washington, D.C.: U.S. Government Printing Office, 30 June 1996).

49. F. Cullen and P. Gendreau, "The Effectiveness of Correctional Rehabilitation," quoted in Douglas Lipton, "The Effectiveness of Treatment for Drug Abusers," 12.

50. H. K. Wexler, D. S. Lipton, and B. D. Johnson, *A Criminal Justice System Strategy for Treating Cocaine-Heroin Abusing Offenders in Custody* (Washington, D.C.: National Institute of Justice, 1988).

51. Dan Weikel, *Los Angeles Times,* April 25, 1997.

52. U.S. Department of Justice, *Report to the Assistant Attorney General, January 1996.* Published by Office of Justice Programs, Drugs and Crime Working Group.

53. Lipton, "The Effectiveness of Treatment for Drug Abusers," 44.

54. Ibid., 45.

55. Ibid., 22.

56. Ibid., 39.

57. Ibid., 40.

58. State of California. Office of Substance Abuse Caldata (September 1992–March 1994).

59. U.S. Department of Justice, *Report to the Assistant Attorney General* (1996), 7.

60. Ibid., 6.

61. Ibid., 7.

62. Navarro, "Experimental Courts Are Using New Strategies," A25.

63. James Wiggs, *Journal of the American Medical Association* 268, no. 17 (1992): 2,376. Letter to editor.

64. Nancy Needham, "The Prison Explosion," *NEA Today* 10, no. 8 (1992).

Notes to Chapter Thirteen

1. Associated Press, "Inner City Scourge Migrates to the Suburbs." [Boston Globe Online]. Available: http://www.globe.com/dailyne [Accessed 30 May 1997].

2. Ibid.

3. Ibid.

4. Ibid.

5. *Microsoft Encarta* (1994), s.v. "Holiday, Billie."
6. Ibid., s.v. "Parker, Charlie."
7. Ibid., s.v. "Davis, Miles."
8. Roy Spungin, interview conducted by the author, New York, N.Y., May 1997.
9. "Our Hero, Heroin," *National Review* 48, no. 20 (1996): 75.
10. Karen Schoemer, "Rockers, Models and the New Allure of Heroin," *Newsweek* (1996): 53.
11. Ibid.
12. Ibid.
13. Michael Dwyer, "A Shocker on Heroin Addiction," *New York Times*, July 14, 1996, arts section, 9.
14. Ibid.
15. Ibid., 21.
16. Ibid., 21.
17. Street addict, interview conducted by the author, New York, N.Y., February 1997.
18. "Flirting with Disaster," *Entertainment Weekly* no. 339 (9 August 1996): 18.
19. Ibid.
20. Ibid.
21. Press release issued by National Families in Action, Atlanta, Ga., October 22, 1996.
22. *New York Times*, October 24, 1996.
23. Stuart Elliot, *New York Times*, June 17, 1996.
24. Ibid.

NOTES TO CHAPTER FOURTEEN

1. George James, "Beyond Redemption?" *New York Times,* September 13, 1997, section 13, 1.
2. Barry McCaffrey (presentation made to the Partnership for a Drug-Free America, New York City, June 1996).
3. Douglas Lipton, "The Effectiveness of Treatment for Drug Abusers under Criminal Justice Supervision" (November 1995): 4. Published by the National Criminal Justice Reference Service, Rockville, Md.
4. John E. Lodge, "Why 2,000,000 Americans Are Dope Fiends," *Popular Science Monthly* (June 1930): 42–43.
5. Christy B. Day, "Behind Bars: A Look at the Uneven Application of Law Enforcement," *Washington Informer* (27 April 1994).
6. Ibid.

INDEX

AA. *See* Alcoholics Anonymous
Abrego, Juan Garcia, 240
acetic anhydride, 23, 48
Adams, Samuel Hopkins, 25–26
addiction, 103
  as all-inclusive, 112
  Harrison Act on, 28–29, 137
  intolerance toward, 138–39, 258–59
  as metabolic disease, 144
  psychology of, 74–77
  as psychoneurotic deficit, 108
  as public health issue, 261–62
  relapse and, 132, 265
  See also drug addicts; drug use
advertising industry, 291–94
  chemical companies and, 24
  "heroin chic" and, 281
Afghanistan, 37, 40, 46, 47
African Americans, 137
  AIDS infection of, 189, 196, 262
  civil rights movement of, 210–11
  discrimination of, 201, 247, 299
  crack cocaine and, 249
  as drug dealers, 247–48
  as heroin addicts, 203
  law enforcement officers and, 242–44, 249
  in prison populations, 246, 247, 250
AIDS/HIV virus, 188, 189

maintenance programs and, 181
  minorities and, 189, 196, 262
  needle use and, 39, 52, 145, 187, 231–32, 235
  increase in, 188–89
  in prison populations, 255–63
  apathy about, 255
  deaths from, 256–57
  protease inhibitors and, 257–58, 262
  See also needle exchange programs
alcohol
  ibogaine and, 70
  legalization of, 29
  naltrexone and, 178–80
Alcoholics Anonymous (AA), 104, 112–19
  concept of God in, 118
  recovery in, 79, 94, 128–29, 131, 270, 274
  Twelve Steps of, 117–18
Alcoholics Anonymous (book), 114, 116–18
Algren, Nelson, 287
Allison (case study), 153–55
Ambrose, Myles, 220
American Civil Liberties Union, 242
American Disease, The (Musto), 23, 26, 134, 199
American Medical Association, 26, 191
Amity Prison TC program, 266, 269–71
Anderson, Jack, 226

Anslinger, Harry, 30–31, 33
aphrodisiacs, 9, 172–73
Arellano family, 240, 241
Armistead, John, 294
Arm's Acres, 94
Arrow War, 13–14
aspirin, 25

Basketball Diaries, The (film), 289
Bastiaans, Jan, 168, 169
Baum, Dan, 214, 215
Baum, L. Frank, 3, 4–5
Bayh, Birch, 223
Belushi, John, 291
Bennett, William, 245, 299
Beth Israel, 98
Biblical references, 3, 7, 9
Biden, Joe, 235–36
Big Book, 116–19, 128
Bigelow, George, 176, 182
"black drop," 16
Black Panthers, 211, 213
black tar, 43, 89, 224
blacks. *See* African Americans
Bogard, Ronald, 255, 262
Boggs, Hale, 34, 200–1, 202
Boggs-Daniel Bill, 34, 202, 203, 210
Bonette, Richard, 294
boot camps, 274–75
Bourne, Peter, 222–27
Boyd v. United States, 137
Boyle, Danny, 288, 289
brain functions, 57–59, 60
Bratton, William, 250–51
Brent, Charles, 25, 26

317

and the Harrison Nar-
cotics Act, 27–29, 137
See also cocaine; heroin
Narcotics, Federal Bu-
reau of, 29–30, 33, 36
Narcotics Anonymous
(NA), 104, 112–13
recovery and, 79,
118–19, 128–29, 131,
270, 274
National Families in
Action, 291–93
National Household
Survey on Drug
Abuse, 43, 244, 300
National Institute on
Drug Abuse (NIDA),
221, 299
buprenorphine stud-
ies, 173–74, 176
ibogaine and, 169, 171,
172
LAAM studies, 180–81
needle exchange pro-
grams, 195, 196
AIDS prevention
money and, 193
as effective, 191, 194,
196–97
federal ban on, 189–93
opposition to, 194, 196
in prisons, 258, 259–61
worldwide, 197–98
needle use, 19, 52–55
HIV virus and, 39, 52,
145, 187, 231–32, 235
increased use of,
188–89
laws against, 189–91,
195–97
less common now, 124,
283
sharing of, 53, 78, 145,
191
in prisons, 254, 262
Nelles, Joachim, 259
nervous system, 55–56,
57
New York Times, The, 21,
193, 252, 255, 257, 295
Newmeyer, John, ix
Newsweek magazine, 39,
214, 229
Nicaraguan contras, 232
NIDA. *See* National Institute on Drug Abuse
Nixon, Richard, 220–22
on crime and drugs,

200, 212–14, 218,
230
heroin treatment
policies of, 142,
149–50
and Operation Inter-
cept, 213–14
No Fear gang, 239
NORML (National Orga-
nization for the Reform
of Marijuana Laws),
223–26
Nosy Parents Associa-
tion, 224
*Not-God: A History of
Alcoholics Anonymous*
(Kurtz), 113
No-to-bac, 18
Nyswander, Marie E.,
139

O'Donnell, John, 110
O'Malley, Stephanie, 179
Omnibus Crime Bill, 234,
268
*Once Upon a Time in
America* (film), 22
O'Neill, Eugene, 20
Operation Intercept,
213–14
opiate receptors, 57–60,
63
ibogaine as, 170
naltrexone as, 177–78
opium, 5, 46
arms sales and, 37, 40
by-products of, 15,
16–17
drinking of, 9, 11,
16–17
Eastern trade of, 8–9,
10–12
foreign growers of, 33,
34, 37, 38
laws governing, 24,
27–29, 201
medical uses of, 8–9,
15–18, 20, 24–26
following Harrison
Narcotics Act,
27–29, 137
as patent medicine,
16–17, 18
reform movement
against, 25–27
smoking of, 11, 17, 19,
22
U.S. trade of, 22, 26–27

Opium Commission,
United States, 26
opium dens, 11, 20–21,
201
outlawed, 24
Opium Wars, 13–14
organized crime, 206
drug trade of, 200,
209, 233–34
heroin criminalization
of, 29
in the 1970s, 219
Organized Crime Control
Act, 217, 218–19
Osborne, Thomas Mott,
107
Overeaters Anonymous,
118
Oxford Groups, 114

Pakistan, 46
Panic in Needle Park, The
(film), 287
Papaver somniferum
(poppy), 6, 46
Paracelsus (Swiss
alchemist), 16
paraquat spraying,
224–25
Parker, Charlie, 284
Parrino, Mark, 146–49,
298
Partnership for a Drug-
Free America, 39,
291–94
Patterson, Betty, 243
Peck, M. Scott, 127
people of color. *See*
minorities
Permanent Midnight
(Stahl), 291
Pert, Candace, 58
pharmaceutical compa-
nies. *See* chemical com-
panies
Phoenix, River, 290
pipes, 11, 19
Polakoff, Moses, 208,
209
police. *See* law enforce-
ment
*Politics of Heroin: CIA
Complicity in the Global
Drug Trade, The* (Mc-
Coy), 36, 207, 215
Polo, Marco, 10
Popik, P., 170
poppy plant, 3–5, 6

Author and filmmaker
HUMBERTO FERNANDEZ
writes about social and
political issues. He lives
with his family in
Warwick, New York.

Photo: L. Gross

HAZELDEN PUBLISHING AND EDUCATION is a division of the Hazelden Foundation, a not-for-profit organization. Since 1949, Hazelden has been a leader in promoting the dignity and treatment of people afflicted with the disease of chemical dependency.

The mission of the foundation is to improve the quality of life for individuals, families, and communities by providing a national continuum of information, education, and recovery services that are widely accessible; to advance the field through research and training; and to improve our quality and effectiveness through continuous improvement and innovation.

Stemming from that, the mission of the publishing division is to provide quality information and support to people wherever they may be in their personal journey—from education and early intervention, through treatment and recovery, to personal and spiritual growth.

Although our treatment programs do not necessarily use everything Hazelden publishes, our bibliotherapeutic materials support our mission and the Twelve Step philosophy upon which it is based. We encourage your comments and feedback.

The headquarters of the Hazelden Foundation are in Center City, Minnesota. Additional treatment facilities are located in Chicago, Illinois; New York, New York; Plymouth, Minnesota; St. Paul, Minnesota; and West Palm Beach, Florida. At these sites, we provide a continuum of care for men and women of all ages. Our Plymouth facility is designed specifically for youth and families.

For more information on Hazelden, please call **1-800-257-7800**. Or you may access our World Wide Web site on the Internet at **http://www.hazelden.org**.